In Quest of the Mythical Mate

A Developmental Approach to Diagnosis and Treatment in Couples Therapy

In Quest of the Mythical Mate

A Developmental Approach to Diagnosis and Treatment in Couples Therapy

By

Ellyn Bader, Ph.D.

and

Peter T. Pearson, Ph.D.

BRUNNER/MAZEL *Publishers* • New York

To protect confidentiality, all names of clients and identifying details have been changed.

Library of Congress Cataloging-in-Publication Data

Bader, Ellyn.
    In quest of the mythical mate : a developmental approach to
diagnosis and treatment in couples therapy / by Ellyn Bader and Peter T.
Pearson.
        p.   cm.
  Bibliography: p.
  Includes index.
  ISBN 0-87630-516-8
  1. Marital psychotherapy. I. Pearson, Peter T.   II. Title.
  [DNLM: 1. Family Therapy. 2. Marital Therapy. WM 55 B134i]
RC488.5.B25 1988
616.89'156—dc19
DNLM/DLC
for Library of Congress   88-14556
                                              CIP

Published by
BRUNNER/MAZEL, INC.
19 Union Square
New York, New York 10003

MANUFACTURED IN THE UNITED STATES OF AMERICA

10 9 8 7 6

To my parents, who provided me with the foundation from which I have been able to create a joyful life and a loving marriage, and to my daughter, Molly, for whom I hope I will do the same. —E.B.

To Ellyn, one of those wonderful people who can "practice what they preach," and to her seemingly boundless (and sometimes puzzling) ability to love and support me for what I am and what I am not! —P.T.P.

Foreword

The way one analyzes a problem often indelibly alters subsequent perceptions. And perceptions determine outcome.

Consider the viewpoint of the man who is confronted with the task of memorizing a telephone number. "Nine–one–zero . . . one–one–one–two," he repeats to himself—but, he can't seem to remember it. He frantically seeks assistance. "I can help," his friend chuckles: "Note the sequence: Nine, ten, eleven, twelve!"

By effective labeling and *chunking*, and by relating the problem to something familiar, the task becomes easier.

This vignette has relevance to the mental health field. Psychotherapy has been plagued by overwhelming, complicated theories of personality. For example, psychodynamic speculations often provide fascinating and imaginative explanations of human pathology, but the speculations are *lenses* that both focus and limit. Perceptions gleaned through theoretical lenses often allow only limited and predetermined methods of diagnosis and treatment.

Treatment follows from diagnostic perceptions. Regrettably, the traditional purpose of diagnosis has been to describe, not to prescribe. For example, a diagnosis of 295.6 Paranoid Schizophrenia describes a pattern of behavior. It also infers the *fact* that pathology resides as a disease, exclusively within the sufferer. By implication, the treatment of choice is medication; psychotherapy is only an adjunct. Traditional descriptive diagnosis tells us about the nature of the symptom, but it does not provide overt, clear directives about psychotherapy.

It is not enough: A diagnosis should be a treatment plan. It should guide the practitioner to specific methods of alleviating suffering. And we are getting there. As the field of psychotherapy evolves, the trend is to use diagnostic and treatment concepts that promote action and to refrain from using concepts that are primarily descriptive. There is movement away from the medical model of pathology and toward an approach that "depathologizes" problems and utilizes interaction patterns existent within systems. In the modern conception, problems are seen as stymied growth strivings within developmental phases; they are not merely static illnesses. Consequently, modern approaches have emphasized patient strengths rather than viewing patients as sick or intrinsically deficient. There is also a push toward parsimony—finding the simplest way to affect constructive change and finding the simplest explanatory principles.

Ellyn Bader and Peter Pearson are psychologists who are at the forefront of modern psychotherapy, not only because of their interest in couples therapy—one of psychotherapy's most modern concerns—but because their approach embodies the movement away from an *illness* orientation. In *In Quest of the Mythical Mate: A Developmental Approach to Diagnosis and Treatment in Couples Therapy*, they provide a comprehensive model of couples therapy that offers clinicians new, effective options.

Bader and Pearson show how couples evolve through natural stages and how blocks and discrepancies in development between partners can be understood and addressed. In the process they offer an action diagnosis, so that once a therapist notes developmental arrests and discrepancies, the course for future therapy becomes clear.

There are distinct advantages to viewing some of the problems existent in couples as a matter of evolution. One of them is that the framework of developmental stages obviates the need to use labels that infer judgment or pathology: A four-year-old is not better than a three-year-old; the four-year-old simply has different tasks to master. Also, when a clinician thinks in terms of development, rather than intrinsic pathology, it is easier to be positive. Children are best influenced by building on established assets, not by analyzing deficits. Similarly, patients are best influenced by building and developing existent strengths.

Concentrating on developmental stages also helps couples not to fruitlessly blame each other. Because Bader and Pearson focus on the relationship, there is no need to think in terms of an *identified patient*.

The emphasis is on impasses, not on analyzing and rehashing symptoms and complaints. These therapists create positive interactions that help couples achieve developmental milestones. The focus is primarily on the present and the promising future, not on endlessly analyzing the past.

The theoretical formulations of Bader and Pearson have been gleaned in a manner similar to the way in which much modern psychotherapy has evolved, namely, by applying concepts and using tools from related disciplines. For example, Gregory Bateson's anthropology and philosophy was incorporated into modern family therapy. Richard Bandler and John Grinder used Noam Chomsky's transformational grammar to develop Neurolinguistic Programming. Bader and Pearson use the conceptual framework of Margaret Mahler and point out that couples progress through distinct developmental stages that are strikingly similar to the developmental stages of infancy. They also continue the trend initiated by Jay Haley, who, in *Uncommon Therapy*, put human problems in the framework of life cycle transitions.

This book is not just a matter of valuable theories; it is refreshing and specific. A process of couples therapy is outlined and the reader is provided with new methods for diagnosis, assessment, and intervention. Innovative techniques are presented, such as the Thirty-Day Plan. These techniques are easily applicable to couples and can be used by therapists of any theoretical orientation.

Bader and Pearson present a systematized method of couples therapy. In doing so they have filled a previously vacant ecological niche. There has not been enough work on treating couples, and there has been a need for a couples model that does not presuppose that family therapy is the treatment of choice.

I have used the methods outlined in this book, and they have added a dimension to my couples therapy. Bader and Pearson have discovered a better mouse trap—a new lens with a wider view and sharper focus.

Jeffrey K. Zeig, Ph.D.
Director
The Milton H. Erickson Foundation
Phoenix, Arizona

Contents

Acknowledgments

As in successfully giving birth to a baby, writing a book is generally not a solitary endeavor. We wish to express our gratitude to some of the "midwives" who helped deliver this book:

First, to Margaret Mahler and her associates, whose pioneering work in child development formed the theoretical underpinnings of our model.

To Lois Nissman, our administrative assistant, who gave us both her emotional support and her organizational help. She saw to it that we met our deadlines, while keeping The Couples Institute running like a Swiss watch.

To Maggie Phillips, Ph.D., and Lois Achimovich, M.D., who demonstrated their support for our work by providing case material for this book.

To our valued associates in the Institute, Ellen Rosenthal, M.F.C.C., Eva Tomlinson, M.S.W., Debra Weinshenker, M.A., and Gerda Young, M.F.C.C., whose cooperation and work enabled us to take the time to write.

To Bernie Mazel, who nurtured our budding desire to become authors, and to Ann Alhadeff, for her extremely perceptive editing talents.

To Pete's Monday noon mastermind group with Mark Brady and Bob Lubin, where ideas about life and living were discussed, challenged, and supported.

And especially to our clients, who share their very personal pains and joys and teach us so very much.

A SPECIAL THANK YOU TO MARGARET RYAN
FOR HER EDITORIAL GUIDANCE

We are especially thankful to Margaret Ryan for the graceful and supportive way she removed the dents and scratches from our work. Her corrections were always focused and facilitative, while her encouragement was timely and reinforcing. Writing a book is one thing; writing it with a minimum of stress with one's spouse should qualify as a vignette in Ripley's *"Believe It or Not."* We thank her for making this possible. We deeply appreciate her penetrating questions, thoughtful attention to detail, and commitment to quality.

Preface

This book is intended to give our view of one approach to that wonderfully complex, stimulating, and sometimes frustrating process called "couples therapy." The theory we have developed allows us to do more of what we do in a deliberate way and to spend less time "flying by the seat of our pants." We have found our developmental model for diagnosing and treating couples to be flexible enough to incorporate a wide variety of intervention strategies, yet purposeful enough to provide a clear sense of direction to couples in distress.

Why do we specialize in working with couples? It is in the family that we learn to love and be loved. Since the family starts with the parents, one of the finest gifts parents can give is to first love and support one another and then include their children.

The cumulative effects of rapid technological and economic changes place more and more demands on the individual, the marriage, and the family. Helping couples to help themselves is a goal we find continually challenging, exciting, and stimulating. Hopefully, our book will help you add extra enthusiasm to your own work with couples.

E.B.
P.T.P.

Introduction

What is the nature of the force we are dealing with when we work with couples in therapy? To ask such a question is to move into the mysterious terrain of *romantic love*. For centuries myths, fairy tales, plays, and epics have portrayed the potency, the numinosity, and often the tragedy of romantic love through a rich legacy of characters and events, gods and goddesses. It has been pondered and examined in the writings of both literature and philosophy, receiving noble treatments on its nature from great minds such as Plato and Shakespeare.

Plato's version of male–female origins is so graphic that it virtually anthropomorphizes the quality of romantic love into a tangible, flesh-and-blood reality. In *The Symposium*, Plato has Socrates explain how there used to be a total being, of which half was male and half was female. When Zeus was angry, in order to weaken the human creatures, he cut them in half. When the bisection was complete, it left each half with a desperate yearning for the other. They would travel the world searching for each other and when they found each other, the two halves would run together and fling their arms around each other's necks, pleading to be rolled into one. Neither would do anything without the other, and they soon began to die of hunger and inertia. Whenever one half was left alone, it wandered aimlessly clasping itself, hoping to find a spare half-man or spare half-woman.

During the Middle Ages the myth of Tristan and Isolde arose as the first story in Western literature to deal with romantic love (Johnson, 1983). It describes one of the most beautiful and tragic of epic tales and has served as the source of inspiration for many of our romantic stories, including Shakespeare's great love story of *Romeo and Juliet*. Traveling minstrels and poets would sing the story of the Knight Tristan and his fatal love for Queen Isolde:

> My lords, if you would hear a high tale of love and of death, here is that of Tristan and Queen Isolde; how to their full joy, but to their sorrow also, they loved each other, and how at last, they died of that love together upon one day; she by him and he by her. (Johnson, 1983, p. 1)

Tragedy and even insanity accompany many portrayals of romantic love throughout history. Indeed, falling in love is often viewed as madness. In the plays of Euripides, Phaedra and Medea are overtaken by insanity, which leaves them destroyed. Shakespeare says of Hamlet that he

> Fell into a sadness, then into a fast, . . .
> Then into the madness wherein now he raves. . . .
> (cited in Pope, 1980, p. 2)

There is a fascinating, cross-cultural similarity between the older view of "love sickness" and what we might label today "temporary psychosis." This "psychosis" is composed of feelings of euphoria and a compelling desire to be constantly with the lover. Often this is to the exclusion of family and friends, and is counterpointed by excessive depression and feelings of loss and incapacitation during periods of separation. There is an obsessive preoccupation with thoughts of the other, and a rapid and thorough merging of both physical and emotional boundaries. This process often takes place quite quickly and serves to bond two unrelated people together "as though one."

When romantic love is viewed through the lens of science, we get an altogether different sense of it. Mystery and tragedy fall away in the light of objective information which speaks to the *phenomenon*, rather than to the experience, of romantic love. Evidence suggests that romantic love has an evolutionary and biological significance which contributes to the survival of the species. The love reaction may be biologically preset and predetermined (Rizley, 1980). Rizley hypothesizes:

Romantic love is a psychobiological reaction based on neurochemical and hormonal processes that functions, even under difficult conditions, to increase the proximity, and hence the probability of mating, of two genetically unrelated individuals to insure the survival of the species. (1980, p. 106)

Rizley notes several general characteristics of the phenomenon of romantic love, such as its speed of occurrence (referred to as being "struck by a thunderbolt" in some cultures) and its durability or robustness. Romantic love does not depend on similarities in background, beliefs, or customs. Finally, romantic lovers exhibit stereotyped psychological and physiological reactions which are relatively constant across cultures and centuries. It is probable that many aspects of the love reaction may be instinctive and may have evolved out of "attachment behavior." (See Rajecki, Lamb, & Obmascher, 1978, or Bowlby, 1969, 1973, for summary review of attachment behavior.)

Despite the ineffable potency and all-consuming nature of romantic love, it does not seem to be sufficient for two people to sustain an intimate, long-term relationship. As much as we may want to keep the intensity and closeness of the early falling-in-love stage, it simply does not last. The "mythical mate" often becomes our worst enemy. Soap operas reinforce the idea that couples cannot live happily ever after: after trials and tortures to actually wed, they usually divorce or die from boredom.

The question "What do we do after we fall in love?" has never been addressed successfully in literature or mythology. Many tales end like Doris Day and Rock Hudson movies where the lovers ride off into the sunset and live happily ever after. No communication medium has yet explored with much depth or authenticity the gray area of how to manage a relationship on a daily basis. Even movies that seek to portray reality often depict a version of life at least a few notches off-center from what most of us experience. It is the disillusionment of not being able to re-create the fairytale romance or the Hollywood mystique, and of not perpetuating the intensity of early romantic love, that leads many couples to separate and eventually divorce.

As therapists who work with couples, we consider that finding answers to the question "What do we do after we fall in love?" has been crucial to the creation of our therapeutic techniques. As we observed a multitude of couples from a variety of cultural and professional backgrounds grapple with the "lion" of intimacy, we began to perceive a broad pattern: what occurred in a couple's relationship seemed to be the result of intense biological and psychological processes that roughly paralleled the stages of early childhood development. Problems in relationships arose when couples became "stuck" in the same or differing stage, thus inhibiting the natural thrust of growth and differentiation inherent in the interactions of two adults.

In pursuing our observations, we studied the research work of Margaret Mahler. She provided a paradigmatic model of early childhood development. Mahler describes the progressive stages in an infant's life that lead to identity and selfhood: the initial stage of autistic absorption is followed by an outreach for interpersonal, symbiotic relatedness, which is then transformed into roughly four subphases of a process of separation and individuation culminating in the psychological birth of the child.

Although an exact one-to-one correlation between the dynamics of two interacting adults and an infant and its mother would represent reductionistic thinking, the parallels between the two are striking. For both groups, the stages are often stressful and involve developing the capacity to manage closeness and distance, as well as such complex human emotions as loss, disillusionment, aggression, competition, regression, and ambivalence. Couples who master these stages attain new skills which enable them to progress from that state of "love sickness" into deeper, more committed intimacy.

We have found that the dramas we see daily in our office are much more understandable when they are placed in the context of each partner's struggle for psychological identity. It is through a deeper understanding of the goals implicit in each individual's struggles that we can intervene to help the couple create a more effective relationship. In this book, we describe the methods we have developed for understanding the evolution of the couple's relationship as a unit, and we demonstrate how to intervene to facilitate the growth and enhancement of each individual and the couple. (See Appendix F for a summary overview of our developmental model.)

In Chapter 1, we begin with an examination of the developmental model that forms the foundation of our therapeutic approach. Margaret

Mahler's theory of infant developmental stages is explored in terms of its relationship to couples phenomenology. This theme is elaborated in Chapter 2, which provides a summary overview of diagnostic techniques used in identifying a couple's developmental level. Chapter 3 then moves into an examination of the unique qualities that characterize couples therapy and the overarching principles of intervention and contract setting that we have developed.

Chapters 4 through 10 are devoted to in-depth explorations of each diagnostic category wherein the full therapeutic range from diagnosis to contract structuring to the creation of stage-specific interventions is covered.

Finally, Chapter 11 is a product of the work we have done over the past eight years training therapists in a developmental approach to couples therapy. We have found that a core group of questions are commonly asked, and this chapter reflects our desire to respond to similar questions that might come to your mind while reading our book.

Our approach is action-oriented. We take an active role in helping evoke diagnostic information and in structuring creative interventions that catalyze change. Our application of Mahler's developmental model to couples work provides a conceptual framework with which to view and understand a couple's interaction. Indeed, in our work training therapists from many divergent theoretical and clinical backgrounds, we have been delighted to discover the ease with which interventions from most schools can be used effectively in conjunction with our developmental model. Throughout the book, we have described a variety of interventions we have created as a means of facilitating a couple's movement from one developmental stage to the next. However, we would like to stress the importance of therapists' drawing upon their own inner sources of creativity and special experiential learnings and insights in the ongoing challenge of structuring effective interventions.

In Quest of the Mythical Mate

*A Developmental Approach to
Diagnosis and Treatment
in Couples Therapy*

CHAPTER 1

A Developmental Model of Relating

Edna, 28, and Steve, 30, had been living together for two years when they requested couples therapy. In appearance Edna was dressed immaculately, while Steve looked disheveled. Their fights, not surprisingly, focused on his slovenly appearance and sloppy household habits, and on her fastidious behavior and frivolous patterns of spending money. Theirs had been an intense, dramatic relationship. In the beginning they had met and fallen in love on a blind date. Now, two years later, they described a highly conflictual relationship with serious communication problems. An initial session began as follows:

Edna: Again, you left two days' worth of cruddy dishes all over the living room floor for me to trip over! And your farting is getting worse! I can't stand it any longer!

Steve: If you hadn't bought those new chairs without asking me, maybe I wouldn't create such a mess. You were just trying to get even!

During the worst of their fights at home, Steve and Edna would slam doors, throw dishes, and spit at each other. In the initial therapy sessions, given the slightest opportunity they would bicker childishly without listening to one another. On two occasions Edna became so angry that she marched out of the room, throwing a pillow rudely at Steve on her way out of the door.

What is it, after all, that compels adults such as Steve and Edna, who have all the best intentions, to regress to childlike behaviors where

1

spitting becomes a means of communication? How does a developmental model of couplehood relate to Steve and Edna? We have found
that particular aspects of childhood development will influence an
adult's capacity to create a successful relationship. Understanding
these aspects allows us to identify each partner's current stage, which
in turn identifies the overall pattern of behavior within the relationship
as a unit.

Developmental theory addresses growth as a complex process. When
early biologists studied the structure of plants and animals, they
discovered growth to be a process of transformation. Cells divide and
group themselves into new forms with new functions, and development involves progression through successive stages. These stages are
successively more complex at each level of growth. In fact, each
successive stage is based on a preceding stage and represents a transformation of the earlier stage into a more complex form. This same
process of biological organisms evolving into increasingly complex
forms also occurs in the psychological development of human beings.
Freud, Erickson, and Piaget each contributed to the process of shifting
the focus of developmental thinking from the biologically oriented
sciences into the cognitive, social, and intrapsychic areas of individual
human functioning.

Loevinger (1966) has provided a clear summary of the main features
of a developmental model:

1. There is an invariable order to the stages of development.
2. No stage can be skipped.
3. Each stage is more complex than the preceding one, representing
   a transformation of what existed previously into a new form.
4. Each stage is based on the preceding one and prepares for the
   succeeding one. (cited in Breger, 1974, p. 9)

In this book we will demonstrate how these assumptions apply to
couples and to the evolution of effective relationships. We will show
how the influences of childhood enhance or inhibit an individual's
ability to progress through the normal stages of growth and change
that characterize adult relationships.

As our developmental model of couples therapy evolved, we were
able to crystallize the assumptions on which our work is based:

1. Couples relationships go through a progression of normal developmental stages. These stages parallel the stages of early childhood development described by Margaret Mahler.

   ↓

2. Early childhood development therefore significantly affects couples relationships.

   ↓

3. Each couples stage has specific tasks to be mastered.

   ↓

4. Each stage is more complex than the preceding one and requires new skills based on the integration and transformation of what existed previously into a new form. When individuals are unable to progress through these stages in order, difficulties will emerge in their relationship.

   ↓

5. A primary source of conflict and division in a relationship occurs when one or both individuals are not able to master the developmental tasks necessary to facilitate movement to the next stage.

   ↓

6. The stages of couples development can be diagnosed.

   ↓

7. Therapeutic interventions can be tailored to the specific developmental stage.

We will now point out the way in which we utilize and work with childhood psychodynamic experiences in relation to the couple's current developmental level. Rather than beginning the therapeutic process with a thorough exploration of childhood influences, we begin with the couple's current behavior and experiences. When an impasse is reached and a partner appears unable to move through a particular conflict or develop a specific skill, then we shift our focus to the childhood history, looking for correlates and parallels between family-of-origin experiences and current-day interaction between partners. Our perspective remains "relationship-oriented" throughout this process: that is, the couple's current stage of development remains the pivotal point in reference to which we explore early developmental issues.

Edna and Steve, the couple described at the beginning of this chapter, were unable to progress beyond the first stage of their relationship without therapy. Instead, they became virtually cemented into patterns of interaction characterized by hostility and dependency. Both Edna and Steve had had difficult, deprived early childhoods. In Edna's family, physical abuse had occurred between her parents and between Edna and her mother, with her mother frequently beating her with a hairbrush. Steve's mother had abandoned the family when Steve was three, leaving him with an alcoholic father. They had both grown up anxiously anticipating the day when they could leave home and find someone who would love them unconditionally, forever.

When Steve and Edna first met, their dreams came true. They fell in love quickly and were living together after two months. It was only at the end of the first year, when the differences between them began to emerge strongly, that they encountered difficulty. Neither of them had previous experiences of stable, loving relationships and neither of them had learned that two people can be different and still love each other without either being "bad." They had no skills for conflict resolution and no role models of conflict leading to growth or a positive outcome. As a result, their anger at each other's seeming betrayal of their early unconditional love led them into increasingly primitive, childlike behavior. Without therapeutic intervention, they probably would have descended into even more severe physical abuse. Through weekly therapy, they were able to identify their differences and to develop a more effective process of resolving conflicts. Later, we will describe the specific techniques utilized in helping them grow beyond this initial stalemated stage.

MAHLER'S MODEL: THE STAGES OF CHILDHOOD DEVELOPMENT

In attempting to create a diagnostic paradigm that would reflect the dynamic and developmental nature of relationships, we sought a model of childhood development that was fluid yet comprehensive in scope. We chose Margaret Mahler's model because it describes a nonstatic process that continuously evolves over time. It is a model that can be applied easily to both the individual and the interactive characteristics of a couple's relationship.

Together with several of her colleagues, Mahler researched "average mothers and their normal babies" at Masters Children's Center in New

York City. Two studies (1959, 1963) were conducted on a total of 38 children. The researchers observed normal babies twice-weekly, conducted weekly interviews with the mothers, and visited the children's homes bimonthly until the children reached three years of age. From this research, Mahler and her colleagues described the stages leading to what they termed "psychological birth" (Mahler, Pine, & Bergman, 1975). These stages begin with a normal autistic phase, which then moves into a symbiotic phase, which in turn progresses through four subphases of separation/individuation. In the culminating stage, the child learns to form emotional attachments which endure through periods of separation and times of intense conflict.

Let us briefly examine the stages of infant development as described by Mahler, and then see how these stages relate to adult relationships.

During the *autistic stage*, from birth until the second month of life, the infant's task is to integrate himself physiologically into the world. In effect, the infant must learn how to establish a homeostatic equilibrium outside the womb. The child responds almost totally to its internal needs; and there seems to be a stimulus barrier that shields the child from external stimulation. As the infant's physiology carries out its rapid growth, sleeplike periods consume more time than periods of arousal.

As the infant's sensitivity to external stimulation increases, he moves into the *symbiotic stage*. Mahler defines her concept of symbiosis as follows:

> The term symbiosis in this context is a metaphor. Unlike the biological concept of symbiosis, it does not describe what actually happens in a mutually beneficial relationship between two separate individuals of different species. It describes that state of undifferentiation, of fusion with mother, in which the "I" is not yet differentiated from the "not-I" and in which inside and outside are only gradually coming to be sensed as different. (Mahler, Pine & Bergman, 1975, p. 44)

Blanck and Blanck (1986) describe the value of this stage:

> During symbiosis the experience of oneness constitutes a form of ✓ object relations in which the infant gains basic gratification that

lasts a lifetime. It becomes the template for all future gratification as well as for empathy and love, and it is a point of temporary reversible regression at moments of pleasure. (p. 14)

This stage lasts from about two-to-five months, at the end of which there arises a dim awareness in the infant that the mother exists as a separate gratifier of needs. Critical to the successful passage through this stage are the mother's capacity to offer nurturance and the child's innate capacity to perceive and accept mothering. The symbiotic phase constellates the basic "building blocks" of emotional attachment and relationship. Mahler writes:

> The normal symbiotic phase marks the all-important phylogenetic capacity of the human being to invest the mother with a vague dual unity that forms the primal soil from which all subsequent human relationships form. (Mahler, Pine, & Bergman, 1975, p. 48)

An unspecific smile from an infant is one sign that betokens initiation into the symbiotic stage. It indicates that perception has shifted from within the self to the external world, and that the human face has become a recognizable whole. A more focused smile directed to mother (usually at about five or six months) signifies that a mothering person can be distinguished from strangers, and shows the beginning of the baby's capacity to acknowledge the separate existence of another person. This foreshadows the child's moving into the *separation/individuation stage.*

Mahler defines separation "as the intrapsychic achievement of a sense of separateness from mother and, through that from the world at large" (Mahler, Pine, & Bergman, 1975, p. 7). She notes that "individuation consists of those achievements marking the child's assumption of its own individual characteristics" (Mahler, Pine, & Bergman, p. 4). The complex and crucial stage of separation/individuation consists of four subphases: differentiation (6–9 months), practicing (10–16 months), rapprochement (17–24 months), and consolidation of individuality. Successful navigation of these four subphases leads to "the psychological birth of the human infant."

During the height of symbiosis, at about five or six months, the *differentiation phase* of separation/individuation begins. Here the infant is more alert to his external surroundings and begins to explore both the mother and nonmother worlds by using his eyes, mouth, legs, arms, and hands. By touching fingers, toes, arms, and legs, the baby soon learns his own outer, physical boundaries and thereby experiences the first hint of differentiation from the mother. No longer interested only in Mother, the baby may still prefer to play at her feet. The child who successfully completes this stage develops a "hatched look" in which his face shines with energy and delight.

Soon thereafter the *practicing phase* begins in which the child's energy is directed outwardly. Excited by her own developing abilities to do things away from Mother, the child has "a love affair with the world" (Greenacre, 1957, cited in Mahler, Pine, & Bergman, 1975, p. 70). Early practicing begins when the child learns to crawl, while "practicing proper" occurs with walking. Then, most of all, the child is exhilarated by her escape from being held continually and will pull away from the still-existing symbiotic tie. At this stage, she will play across the room from Mother, enjoying her from a distance. Increased autonomy is the newly coveted gain in the child's life. Indeed, Mahler views the experience of autonomy as important to the child's development as is the cultivation of motor activities:

> It is *the elated investment in the exercise of autonomous functions*, especially motility, to the near exclusion of interest in mother, and not the development of motor skills per se, *that characterizes the normal practicing subphase*. (emphases added) (Mahler, Pine, & Bergman, 1975, p. 69)

The mother's response to this phase of her baby's development is absolutely crucial to a successful outcome. It is especially useful for the mother to be able to respond with *respect* to her child's need for separation and with *exhilaration* to the accomplishments. Merely tolerating the baby's budding selfhood will not provide the same strong foundation for later relationships as actively supporting, guiding, and encouraging it.

Rapprochement is often the most difficult phase for children and their mothers. It is a time of polarities—of independence and regression, of coming and going. The child reexperiences the need for the mother to be emotionally available, yet wants comforting only at specific times. This leads to confusion, power struggles, and diminished excitement about moving away from Mother. Often the mother is unsure about when to nurture the child and when to encourage independence. In order for the child's sense of self to achieve an optimal level of functioning and growth, the mother's continuing emotional support is indispensable. Without it, the toddler will expend a great deal of energy attempting to compel the mother to be more available — energy that would be better utilized in the synthesis of a diversity of ego and self functions.

During the normal rapprochement phase, there are also quick gains in the acquisition of language, reality-testing skills, and gender identification. In addition, the role of the father becomes increasingly important.

When the rapprochement phase is successfully completed, *consolidation of individuality* begins to take place. Fred Pine (1985) describes how it is the evolution through these stages that leads to attaining libidinal object constancy, which involves "the capacity to form and have available internally carried images, remembrances and sets of expectancies regarding relatedness, even in the absence of the object" (p. 102). He proposes that the establishment of libidinal object constancy goes through a developmental process from 1) developing the specific attachment to Mother, 2) being able to recognize her, 3) developing the later capacity to evoke an image of her, in her absence, and 4) developing the ability to use the image in a full, functional way so that it becomes a regulator of longing, rage, and self-esteem and gives the child the freedom to be autonomous while closeness is retained. Along with this, the child ideally solidifies a lifelong sense of individuality and an ability to form emotional connections that will endure the strains of real-life imperfections and absences.

Louise Kaplan, who worked with Mahler in her observation of infants, described this last stage very poignantly:

When constancy prevails, we are able to respect and value the separateness of others. We go on loving them even when they cannot fill us up with the perfect harmony of unconditional love. Through constancy the perfect is united with the real. Every move into separate selfhood from birth until 3 years makes its distinctive contribution to constancy and brings with it new potentials for love and hate, mastery and fear, trust and suspicion, elation and disappointment. (Kaplan, 1978, p. 35)

THE STAGES OF COUPLES' RELATIONSHIPS

It is our observation that couples evolve through stages which resemble these passages through early childhood development.

Symbiosis

The first stage of couplehood of "being madly in love" we liken to Mahler's second stage of infant growth—*symbiosis*. Here there is a merging of lives, personalities, and intense bonding between the two lovers. The purpose of this stage is attachment. To allow for the merger, similarities are magnified and differences are overlooked. One couple, for example, reported walking along Fisherman's Wharf trying to find something different between them. Finally the man said, "Wait a minute, I think I've got it! I really do like to shoot bows and arrows." His wife responded, "That's amazing! When I was at camp, archery was my favorite sport." At this point in their relationship, they were delighted by their similarities and warmed by the sameness they shared.

During the symbiotic stage, there is a great deal of passion and mutual giving and receiving. The amount of nurturance is extraordinarily high. This is a prime attraction of this stage. There are few demands or requests of the other person to change. Usually there are special efforts to accommodate and please one another. The child within each person feels responded to at so many levels that it makes it easy to give unconditionally to the other person. Since excitement and stimulation are high during this time, neither wants to risk upsetting this wonderful state of affairs by making demands or appearing to be selfish, ungiving, or insensitive. If each partner receives nurturance from the other during this stage, and the agreement to form a couple is clear, the relationship will begin with a solid foundation. This foundation then allows each partner to move beyond symbiosis into differentiation.

When this foundation is not successfully established, both partners may remain in the symbiotic stage. Usually the relationship will evolve into one of two different forms of dysfunctional symbiotic union. One type—the enmeshed—is characterized by merger, avoidance of conflict, and the minimization of differences. The other type is almost the behavioral opposite. The hostile-dependent system is dominated by anger and conflict. Too terrified to end the relationship and not mature enough to end the battles, the couple remain locked in endless rounds of mutually inflicted pain.

Differentiation

Here differences emerge, and each lover is taken "down from the pedestal" and viewed more objectively. This stage is rarely easy! As time passes, one person may start thinking about wanting more space from the other. As a couple, they begin noticing differences and feel that they don't want to spend quite so much time together. They may want more privacy and may feel guilty and ask, "What's happened? Why don't I feel the way I used to?" They begin to emerge from the symbiosis by reestablishing their own boundaries. Just like the infant who explores his body to establish external boundaries, each individual reaches back to his or her own pursuits. As the couple differentiate, they become aware of different feelings, of subtle differences in their thoughts, and of their desire to stand out as unique individuals. Often they will spend more time talking about opposite sides of issues. For some, the illusion of symbiosis is shattered quickly and the relationship ends with a dramatic suddenness. For others, differentiation is a slower and more gradual process, in which there is an increase in the mental comparison of differences and similarities before they are verbalized.

One woman in the early phase of differentiation (after three months of living with her boyfriend) came for individual therapy with the request to learn how to talk to her partner about the fact that she made more money than he did. She wondered about his professional aspirations but was cautious about raising this difference between them. For others, there is a quiet questioning or reflection: "Did I really misjudge the other person? How could I have overlooked the fact that two days a week his socks don't match? How could someone as smart as he is have voted for Reagan?" For some, these differences can be a source of continued, challenging conversations; for others, they create a larger disillusionment.

Practicing

Continuing our parallel with Mahler's model, we next see the couple entering a normal period of practicing in which each participates in activities and relationships away from the other. Here they are no longer empathically attuned to one another; indeed, they may become clearly self-centered. Each directs his or her attention to the external world. Autonomy and individuation are primary; at this point the partners are rediscovering themselves as individuals. Developing *self* becomes more important than developing the *relationship*. Here, issues of self-esteem, individual power, and worthwhileness become central. Conflicts intensify and a healthy process for resolving conflicting aims is necessary for the couple to maintain an emotional connection while developing themselves in the world.

Rapprochement

After each has developed a well-defined, competent identity, it becomes safe to look once again toward the relationship for intimacy and emotional sustenance. Now rapprochement arrives as each partner becomes more assured of his or her own individuality. Vulnerability reemerges. Partners now seek comfort and support from one another. They alternate between periods of increased intimacy and efforts to reestablish independence. Although partners in this stage may find either the intimacy or the independence at times to be threatening, their anxiety will be resolved more quickly because negotiation is not as difficult as before. Each learns to feel less afraid about being reengulfed in the earlier symbiosis. As a result of having developed a clear sense of identity, the sensitive balance between "me" and "we" will become more firmly established and greater resolution of childhood issues interfering with successful coupling will occur.

Mutual Interdependence

Encouraged to grow through external contacts in the world and strengthened by the knowledge that they are loved by each other, the couple may enter a later phase of *constancy*, in which the *perfect* is reconciled with the *real* and the stage of mutual interdependence is attained. Here, two well-integrated individuals have found satisfaction in their own lives, have developed a bond that is deep and mutually satisfying, and have built a relationship based on a foundation of growth rather than on one of need.

Case example: Jenna and Paul

The following case describes how one couple, having evolved through some of the stages, presented for therapy at the practicing-rapprochement stage. Paul, a 38-year-old attorney, and Jenna, a 36-year-old company executive, came for couples therapy distraught over the question of whether to get married or to separate. The current dilemma had arisen after five years of an on-again/off-again relationship. In the first session Paul said, "I've finally realized that Jenna is the woman I want to spend my life with. She's everything I want—intelligent, independent, sexy, and strong enough to handle me." Jenna, on the other hand, was uncertain: "When we first met, I loved Paul more than I had ever loved anyone. I didn't know it was possible to feel that happy. I would have married him then without a moment's hesitation. But we've been through so much since then—his affairs and my promotions. I'm not sure I want to tie myself down. Also, we have so many differences about sex, religion, and parenting that maybe we're not meant for one another."

When we explored the history of their relationship, we discovered they had engaged in two years of an exclusive relationship, part of which they spent traveling around the world together. This had been a time of shared adventure and excitement in which they seemed perfectly matched. When they returned from their travels, however, Paul had seemingly abruptly decided: "Our differences are too great. You want children and a family life centered around church and community. I'm a loner. I like having lots of women in my life and am not ready for monogamy." Once back in the world of work, Paul overemphasized their differences, feeling that he would have to compromise too much of himself to resolve them. He balked and opted for his freedom. Not surprisingly, he began dating other women.

Jenna was shocked and devastated by this completely unexpected turn. She became increasingly depressed, stopped eating, threw frequent temper tantrums, and tried every method she could think of to win Paul back. After three months of this personal drama, she gave up and went into individual therapy. Jenna's next two years were ones of rapid and expansive personal development. She became more secure in both her professional and her personal identities. She received national recognition for a book she completed, changed jobs, landed two promotions, and dated several other men. Her world no longer revolved around Paul; she had come into her own.

Meanwhile, Paul was discovering that his independence was not as emotionally satisfying as it used to be. Put simply, he missed Jenna. Yes, he was a powerful, handsome, wealthy attorney who could attract many women, and yes, he could run a successful business alone—but he was still lonely. He found himself remembering Jenna and their lively conversations. Suddenly, their differences did not seem nearly as unresolvable as they had two years before. He, too, went into individual therapy to resolve his conflict. He began to date Jenna again, at first sporadically but soon consistently; he was only dating other women when he was out of town and Jenna was unavailable.

For Paul, the rapprochement phase was underway. He turned to Jenna for greater nurturance, increased intimacy, and hopes that she would be his wife. Jenna's enjoyment of her practicing phase, however, left her reluctant to relinquish it too easily. "I like my life now," Jenna stated firmly. "I'm afraid that as soon as I say yes to marriage, he'll find another woman to jump into bed with, or find another way to hurt me. It's hard for me to believe he's ready for a commitment after fighting it for so many years."

Through therapy, Paul and Jenna came to an understanding of how their relationship had evolved to the practicing-rapprochement stage, without successful differentiation. They learned how they had been unable to manage the conflict involved in mutual differentiation. Together they worked to heal the hurt caused by Paul's earlier affairs. They returned to see if they could solve the issues of differentiation which previously had led to their separation. They struggled with their religious differences and with what to do about having children. They developed mechanisms for voicing and solving conflicts. Their movement after one year in therapy led them to make a marital commitment.

Like Paul and Jenna's, most relationships do not proceed smoothly through all of the stages. In many relationships, one partner moves into the differentiation or practicing stage, while the other strives to maintain a symbiotic merger. The discomfort and frustration of this dilemma were epitomized in a 1983 *Wall Street Journal* article in which a 43-year-old divorcé was quoted as saying:

> I want a wife who isn't career oriented, who participates very little in the world outside our home, who doesn't have any high aspirations, who is useful, and whose life revolves around me. And yes, she must be a virgin.

This man found his wife in the Philippines through a mail-order bride firm. After several divorces, he spent $6,000 and traveled 5,600 miles to marry into what he hoped would be a permanent symbiotic relationship.

Whenever an individual is in a relationship with a partner who advances beyond the stage of symbiosis, while he or she does not, trouble will ensue. Indeed, we have found that many problems that occur between partners can be traced to an imbalance between developmental stages. The imbalance produces a "see-saw" effect in which the alternating pattern of conflict and withdrawal becomes dominant and is often experienced as impossible to change. It is either at this point, or at the point when both partners have remained in one stage too long and are finding it destructive, that they may turn to a therapist for help.

To determine what underlies the couple's current difficulty, we look at which developmental issues each individual is struggling to maintain or overcome. Thus, we diagnose the couple's system by looking at where we perceive each individual to be in the developmental phases of the relationship. For example, one partner may be attempting to maintain the symbiosis while the other is moving into differentiation. Therefore, we diagnose this couple as symbiotic-differentiating. If one partner is symbiotic, when the other is practicing, then we diagnose this as a symbiotic-practicing relationship. We have never found couples to be more than two stages apart. By utilizing this understanding of Mahler's developmental stages to make a primary diagnosis of the couple's system based on the individual stage of each partner, we can clearly identify the problem and work with the couple effectively. In our experience, this diagnostic model allows therapists to determine skills that are needed by each partner and to identify the joint issues that must be resolved.

In describing the stages, we want to be explicit that we see each couple as having their own unique developmental pattern. Although we will be describing each of the couple stages throughout this book as if it were a discreet entity, we do not see each stage as separate and contained in time. Development is always complex and combines periods of progression and regression. Also, as the work of one stage is being completed, an individual may simultaneously be experiencing some of the conflicts and challenges of the next stage.

It is important to stress that this model places neither partner in an "identified patient" position. It is not a medical model. Instead, it is a means by which the struggles and tensions of a couple's relationship can be viewed in the larger context of each individual's search for psychological wholeness. Thus, just as Mahler emphasized the reciprocal parent-child interaction in which the child's role is crucial in object relations development, we believe that the interaction in couples is complex and is reciprocally able to enhance the development of their object relations.

In the following chapters, we will review each of the major combinations of stages by addressing both diagnostic and treatment approaches. We will describe and illustrate how this developmental model can be used effectively to set the treatment contract, to determine the most effective type of therapy, and finally, to select therapeutic intervention strategies.

In the early chapters, we will make what is a somewhat artificial distinction between diagnosis and treatment. We will do this for the sake of clearly explaining certain methods we have developed. We trust the reader knows that in an ongoing way diagnosis always influences treatment interventions and that the impact of specific interventions enables the diagnosis to continually evolve. In fact, when the interventions are successful, the diagnosis will change. In the later chapters, we present some complete case illustrations in order to provide the reader with a greater sense of the flow, and a more integrated overview, of the entire therapy process.

CHAPTER 2

Diagnosing the Couple's Stages

In diagnosing a couple's current developmental stage, we use both specific techniques and observational approaches. By perceiving the couple's interaction, by understanding the historical development of the relationship, by learning about the presenting problem, by knowing about the unique background of each individual, and by using methods that evoke these different levels of information, a couple's therapist can gather a wealth of valuable diagnostic information.

Although there are numerous combinations of stages that are theoretically possible, it is rare to find partners who are more than two developmental levels apart. That amount of developmental discrepancy usually leads to separation or divorce. Couples seen in therapy most commonly fit into the following combinations:

Symbiotic-Symbiotic
(Two types: enmeshed
             hostile-dependent)
Symbiotic-Differentiating
Differentiating-Differentiating
Symbiotic-Practicing
Practicing-Practicing
Practicing-Rapprochement

The purpose of our initial diagnostic effort is not to saddle a couple with a negative pathological label. Rather, we are attempting to provide the couple with a starting point from which to begin therapeutic

16

work. This starting point—the stage which the couple is currently experiencing—is presented in the context of our overall developmental perspective, which means it is a stage *in flux*. Identifying this stage gives the couple a "no-blame" perspective from which to view their present turbulence. It also provides an implied "horizon" (the next stage) as a developmental inevitability.

OBSERVATIONAL APPROACHES TO DIAGNOSIS

At the basis of any diagnosis is *observation*. Our observations serve as the primary source of information about the two people in the session. Sometimes these observations are made in response to the couple's undirected interactions, and sometimes in response to structured interventions. Before we discuss the specific approaches we have created for evoking diagnostic information, it is important to comment on the fluid panorama of clues available in the couple's presenting behavior.

Climate

We look at the *climate* created within the relationship by the two partners. Is the relationship loving and growth-promoting for each partner? Or is it characterized by aggression and continual eroding of each person's self-esteem? Is intimacy allowed, or is any depth sacrificed for "looking good"? Is one partner used to promote growth in the other? Does the relationship require one partner to squelch himself or herself, inhibiting individual growth, in order to build up the other and ensure that the relationship continues? Are the partners trying to find themselves through one another? By focusing on the interactional climate created in the couple, we begin to sift through the flood of initial perceptions and to systematize and refine our observations toward the clarity of diagnosis.

Body Language

The couple's interactional climate is further revealed in their *body language*. Observing how the couple interact as individuals between themselves, and also how they interact with the therapist, provides a major source of feedback for us. The absence of eye contact, or minimal eye contact between the partners, can be an important indicator of symbiosis, as well as of the level of difficulty that might ensue in working with the couple. We have observed that couples who find it very difficult to maintain eye contact when talking to each other, or find it difficult to maintain eye contact when requested to look at each other when one is talking about the other, often change at a very slow pace. These individuals operate from an undifferentiated position in which their early experience as a child is projected onto the partner. Instead of "taking in" here-and-now cues from seeing what the partner is saying, the internal past experience dominates.

One of the results of minimal eye contact between partners is that they generally have to guess or invent their own version of how the partner is responding to them. They are completely unaware of the rich and subtle feedback cues the partner is sending out as they talk. Typically, such individuals compensate for this lack of external "data" by using their own internal stimuli to respond; their communication thus does not involve an interactive process. There are times, however, when partners are simply unaware of what they are doing and, when requested, will make more meaningful visual contact with their partners. When this happens, there is a commensurate intensification of their emotional contact as well.

Other individuals will look at their partners but continue to talk about them in the third person as though they were still talking to the therapist. For example, Jeff began telling us about some complimentary qualities in his wife, Sherry. We interrupted his third-person narration and said, "Tell that to Sherry." Jeff then turned in his chair toward Sherry but continued with, "*She* really did a pleasant thing for me by having a snack ready when I came home the other night." We then asked Jeff to substitute the word *you* for *she* and to look directly at Sherry. He found this so difficult that it took an entire session of intensive work to complete. Often, the intensity of looking directly at the partner while using his or her name or the pronoun *you* is too much for the person to tolerate, so he or she shifts into talking about the partner in the third person and either maintains eye contact with the therapist or looks somewhere between the therapist and the partner.

Eye contact can increase merger anxiety. Indeed, some clients report feeling very unbalanced or confused as they look at their partners and talk to them at the same time. This indicates the fluidity of their boundaries and how difficult it is to maintain self in the face of even a positive emotional exchange with the partner.

There is a range of behaviors that couples exhibit in their initial session, as they shift from talking to the therapist about their problem to talking to one another. To dichotomize this range, one couple may be so timid and anxious in front of a therapist that they are completely unable to interact with each other in any real way, whereas another couple might launch into a fighting tirade as if the therapist were not present.

In one way or another, most people initially are "performance conscious." Everyone wants their day in court; everyone wants to put their "best foot forward." Even the therapeutically sophisticated partners who know "in their heads" that the therapist is not judging either of them as right or wrong will fall prey to eloquent maneuvers aimed at garnering the therapist as an ally. In order to cope with the discomfort most couples feel in the beginning process of therapy, some will attempt to keep the focus on the therapist or to use the therapist as a vehicle for communicating to the partner. Some individuals are adept at conceptualizing and verbalizing and will invest their initial therapeutic efforts in articulating and abstracting about their particular situation. Others will simply complain to the therapist about the partner as if he or she were not present: "He did . . .," "She did . . .," "He said . . .," "She said . . .," and so forth.

One way to utilize complaining sessions in a diagnostic manner is to observe how partners respond to one another's complaints. Such behavioral responses can serve as an indication of how fast the couple's system of interaction is going to be changed and how readily the couple will allow the therapist to exert an influence. If couples are completely unable to receive empathically from one another (which means that they do not let the partner in emotionally in a positive way), then the chances are high that they are not going to let the therapist in emotionally in a positive way unless it is to create an ally.

Another immediate source of diagnostic data comes from the couple's body language as they choose their sitting positions. What kind of intimacy or lack of intimacy is communicated? In Ellyn's office, partners have a choice of couches or nonmobile chairs. Most often, partners sit down on the same couch. However, one couple might sit close with their bodies turned slightly toward one another, whereas other partners poise themselves stiffly at either end, with an invisible but palpable wall erected in the middle.

In Pete's office there are no couches, only two mobile chairs that roll and swivel. This allows partners to move back and forth, toward and away from each other. Whereas the couch provides a potential for more intimate exchange, the chairs allow for greater ease and subtlety in movement and, hence, in the elicitation of the couple's body language. In either setting, observing how the positions change over the course of the session is an indicator of the degree of emotional fluidity and flexibility present in the relationship. Is there a sense of emotional flow between the partners? Does their body language change in a responsive manner or remain entrenched in one or two patterns?

STRUCTURED DIAGNOSTIC TOOLS

To arrive at a clear diagnosis, in addition to the spontaneous information provided by the couple's presenting behavior and our observation of their interactional patterns and their individual personality structures, we combine several structured methods in order to evoke and constellate some other levels of information. In this section we will describe four diagnostic tools that we use when appropriate. They are:

1. The *Paper Exercise*, which provides spontaneous information about how the partners currently interact with one another;
2. The *Question of Attunement*, which elicits the level of differentiation and nurturance between partners;
3. The *Diagnostic Interview* (or questionnaire), which elicits the historical evolution of the couple's relationship; and
4. The *Individual History* interview, which reveals each partner's unique experiential and psychodynamic background.

We will now take a closer look at each diagnostic technique.

The Paper Exercise

The Paper Exercise is our adaptation of a technique developed by Susan Campbell (1980). We use this exercise both diagnostically and as an active way of engaging couples in their own process of self-evaluation. The directions we give verbally for the exercise read as follows:

> *This piece of paper represents something important to you [looking at one member of the couple], and something important to you [looking directly at the other member of the couple]. I want you to hold this paper between you, and you will have up to five minutes to decide who gets the paper without ripping or tearing it. You can do it verbally or nonverbally. You can do it any way you choose, and you will have up to five minutes to decide who gets the paper.*

No additional information is given after the directions, even if either partner asks questions. We then record the transactions that transpire over the next five minutes, signaling a one-minute warning so that the partners will know when they are approaching the end of their time. This exercise is designed to function as a projective tool and is therefore unstructured. We are interested in observing closely how the couple manages this five-minute block of time both together and individually. Specifically, we focus on the following areas:

1. Capacity for self-definition
2. Management of boundaries between self and other
3. Recognition of the separate wholeness of the partner
4. Capacity to handle conflict
5. Ability to negotiate
6. Capacity to give and receive

The content of this exercise is not as important as how the couple handles the process. By observing the couple's process in the context of the six categories listed above, it is possible to determine the skills that an individual and couple must develop in order to evolve beyond the current impasse.

It is always fascinating to witness the clear-cut and often remarkable differences that are portrayed as each couple does the Paper Exercise. For example, consider the following interaction between Ken and Ruth, who have never progressed beyond the symbiotic-enmeshed stage.

Ken: Do you want to share what it is?

Ruth: No. I figured it was something important and we would decide who would hold it. Well, go ahead. What do you think?

Ken: The thing I was thinking of was our continuing relationship. It's kind of hard to split that up and say you're going to hold it and I'm not going to have anything to do with it.

Ruth: I know. *(pause)* Yeah, I can't do it that way. I can't do it if it's just one thing. I mean if you have it, I have it too.

Ken: Yeah, that's how I feel about it too. If one of us has to hold it, it's OK with me if you hold it. When I say it's OK if you hold it, I don't mean you have to have all the responsibility for everything that's ever connected to it. It means you hold it and it's still ours.

Ruth: It just seems like it's not just one person that holds it. It's not separated from the other person. If I take it, it wouldn't mean you would never see it again.

Ken: Right.

Ruth: It doesn't matter, do you know what I mean?

Ken: Uh–huh.

Ruth: How do you want to decide?

Ken: Will you hold it then?

Ruth: Yeah, but I'd like to be able to decide to trade it back if I feel like I'm not doing a good job.

Ken: Okay.

Ruth: *(She takes the paper.)*

Individuals such as Ruth and Ken who have maintained symbiotic relationships for extended periods of time will not be able to manage the conflict or anxiety that is created by this exercise. Instead of facing the conflict, they will move into merging. They will demonstrate their lack of differentiation and their limited capacity for self-definition by how they approach what the paper is. Often they will not define what the paper represents for either of them; or if one of them defines it, the other will not. Instead they will merge and each will work with one definition of the paper, as if that definition belonged to both of them. The giving is a form of merging designed to avoid conflict rather than a genuine response to a request.

In this particular exercise, Ruth never defined what the paper represented for her, whereas Ken defined it as something joint: "our continuing relationship." Ruth began to say that she could not manage to decide if the paper represented something joint, but then her anxiety at this degree of differentiation led her to quickly reaffirm it as something joint: "I mean if you have it, I have it, too." Relieved by her willingness to keep it joint, Ken quickly moved on to decide who would hold it, while it continued to belong to both of them. Together they avoided the conflict that is inherent in this exercise. When Ruth initiated a question that could lead to more differentiated discussion ("How do you want to decide?"), Ken did not answer her. Instead he pushed the paper at her and suggested that she hold it. There is no substance to this "negotiation" and no real process being developed to resolve the conflictual situation. Instead, the observer is left with the feeling that these two people are one, and that it is totally insignificant who holds the paper.

Symbiotic hostile-dependent couples show a related pattern of interaction when doing the Paper Exercise. They, too, exhibit a very limited capacity for self-definition and an inability to respond to the other as a separate person. They are different in that the conflict is overt; often it is even dramatic! For example, one woman said, "I'd like to take this paper and stuff it down your throat!" This is in marked contrast to differentiating couples who define themselves, but become very focused on the process of "How are we going to decide when we want different things?" The content fades into the background and the process of decision making becomes primary. An example of using the Paper Exercise for diagnosis will be found in the stage-specific chapters.

Here we will give another example of a common pattern of interaction. The following couple, Dana and Carl, did this exercise in a way that is typical of the firmly defined independence of individuals in the practicing stage. For each, the paper represented a move in the opposite direction, with no middle ground available for compromise or negotiation.

Carl: What did you pick?

Dana: Moving to the country. What did you choose?

Carl: Funny, I picked moving to New York.

Dana: It seems like it is ourselves.

Carl: Ourselves in relation to each other.

Dana: So we're back to this again, either New York or the country!

Carl: When I started this exercise I said to myself, "This is just an exercise. It isn't very important how it comes out." Suddenly it's become very important, now that I hear what you want.

Dana: I want you to have what you want, but not if it means me giving up what I want.

Carl: I could give in, but I don't want to. I think this is what always happens.

Dana: Well, here is where we are stuck!

Carl: This is how we always end up!

In this example, the anxiety has shifted. It is not about defining self. The anxiety surrounds loss of self if the boundaries are not rigidly maintained. Moving too close is dangerous.

In this transcript we see Dana and Carl's differentiation. They both were able to clearly define the paper without any hesitation that this definition might lead to conflict. Their interaction was targeted but competitive, and they demonstrated no fear of the conflict once it surfaced. Each needed to totally define his or her own stand, almost like a good debater or arbitrator. Each could hardly wait for the other to finish speaking before jumping in to make a point. They both acknowledged the conflict as the way most of their interactions transpired and stated that they were angry at the conclusion of the exercise. When confronted with the actual conflict, they were at a loss as to how to proceed. The separate self of the partner is seen as strong and powerful. The other is viewed not as a separate person with his or her own wants and frailties, but as a powerful dominator capable of taking away individual gains. Instead of negotiation, Carl described his unwillingness "to give in." Negotiation and compromise are viewed as "giving in," or as loss of self. Self must be rigidly maintained, even if the cost is divorce. Thus, while Dana and Carl are well-defined in terms of their likes and dislikes, their boundaries are stubbornly maintained and their "independence" is preserved only by excluding one another.

After a couple have completed the Paper Exercise, we often explore with them whether their response is representative of their interaction patterns and whether their emotional feeling at the conclusion of the exercise represents a chronic "bad" feeling they frequently feel in the relationship. Since we record their interaction for the five minutes (video, audio, or handwritten transcript), we are then able to use our record to help the couple see where and how their process broke down. Later in therapy, this experience becomes a powerful reference point as a shorthand way to pinpoint a repetitive problem and as a model for a solution. For example, "Joan, do you remember how you felt uneasy when John pushed the paper on you and you were unable to say no and define how you wanted more discussion first? I believe that's happening again. You're squirming and saying nothing as John is expressing his desire for frequent sex."

Because the Paper Exercise is experiential and requires a time-focused interaction, it usually intensifies a couple's patterns and provides vivid, unedited material for the therapist. Current difficulties are quickly demonstrated in a "freeze-frame" manner. However, the Paper Exercise alone is not a sufficient diagnostic tool; it is also necessary to gather other data to diagnose the current problem and to create comprehensive and effective interventions.

The Question of Attunement

This technique complements the Paper Exercise by eliciting clear, behavioral indices of the partners' abilities to both differentiate from and nurture one another. In order to diagnose a couple's developmental status, it is essential to understand the amount of differentiation that has occurred in the relationship as well as the degree of nurturing behaviors that are accessible. In short, we want to know each partner's ability and willingness to identify and express important wants; we also want to know their capacity to respond to one another in an empathic, differentiated manner. In order to elicit this additional diagnostic information, we use a specific question that allows us to determine the extent of differentiation. The partners' response to the question—both verbally in the session and behaviorally throughout the following week—also serves as a simultaneous intervention that engages the couple in a therapeutic and self-informative process. Each partner is requested to ask and respond to the following Question of Attunement:

What can I do this coming week to make your week go a little bit better or make you feel more loved, valued, and appreciated?

How this question is answered by partners indicates their capacity for self-definition. Basically, the Question of Attunement is deceptively elegant in terms of the amount of information it can elicit from the client and provide for the therapist. Is there sufficient self-awareness and trust to express meaningful desires? Can partners respond to the question in a clear, understandable way? Can they allow themselves to be given to in a comfortable way? How well do they react and what do they say when they receive a negative response to their request?

We also want to know how the partners respond to the request made of them. This gives us an indication of their ability to view their partners as separate selves. Can they appreciate the significance of the request to their partner, even if it is unimportant to them? Can they agree to the request without a quid pro quo agreement? Can they agree to the request even if it requires effort on their part? Do they ask clarifying questions that will enhance the meaningfulness of the request? Can they say no to a request that exceeds their ability or desire to fulfill? The responses to all of these questions help us diagnose the current developmental stage as well as to plan future therapeutic interventions.

Some couples are so shocked by the question when we first introduce it that it has to be repeated several times before one partner is able to repeat it to the other. Others will turn to their partners and say, "Well?", as if our vocalization of it in presenting it to them was sufficient to elicit the partner's response. (We persist in having them ask the question, as it intensifies their involvement.) Often those being asked the question will make their requests in vague, nonspecific terms, such as, "I want you to pay more attention to me," or "I want you to show me more respect." Some will make requests that are minimal, "I would like you to watch a TV program with me this week," whereas others will ask aggressively for a response that they know will generate a negative reply, "I want you to have sex with me each day this week."

Because it is important to observe how partners handle this process from start to finish, we do not interrupt them or do anything to facilitate the negotiation. Observing their interaction begins to provide us with data about their level of differentiation and their capacity for empathy.

Once partners have finished their discussion, we will intervene if they have completed it with an agreement that is too vague to operationalize. "I want more attention" is an example. We then ask the partner who asked the question if he or she is clear about what exactly was agreed upon. Usually this elicits a further discussion in which the vague request is clarified: "more attention" means "a hug each day when you come in the house after work." In completing the negotiation, we ask partners if they will follow through on what they agreed to do in response to the question, even if the spouse fails to do so. We do not want to set this up as a quid pro quo agreement; rather, it is intended as a means of initiating each partner into the process of taking responsibility for making autonomous, self-directed (differentiated) changes.

Case example: Betsy and Rod

In the following case illustration, the couple is asked to report on how effective they were in responding to one another's "attunement" requests. This process provides an opportunity for us to identify specific skills and developmental milestones that need to be addressed in the therapy. Further, their responses during the week help us structure our first interventions.

Rod and Betsy were in their mid-twenties and had been living together for about one year. Their presenting problem was that of ongoing arguments that yielded no resolution. In the second session, they asked each other the Question of Attunement. Rod stated he wanted Betsy to be more supportive of his exercise program. Specifically, he wanted Betsy to encourage him when he jogged or played raquetball two or three times in the coming week. He explained that he found it difficult to generate the energy to exercise, and that he would be really appreciative if Betsy would encourage him to exercise and not make him feel guilty for leaving her. Rod was particularly angry that Betsy would spend an inordinate amount of time with her girlfriend but would become irritated or angry whenever he wanted to spend some time away from her.

When Rod posed the question to Betsy, she said that it was hard for her to answer. Then she said that she wanted to know that Rod loved her. When he asked her to elaborate, she responded, "Well, I'll know it when you do it, but I want you to be more tender and affectionate."

Betsy's initial response of "I'll know it when you do it" indicated her unrealistic expectation that Rod perceive and understand her emotional needs better than she herself was able to perceive and articulate them. When Rod pushed her to be specific about what it meant for him to be tender and affectionate, she became testy and impatient. This type of response is often one result of an individual's discomfort over his or her inability to answer the question.

When Rod and Betsy returned after the week of supposedly carrying out the exercise, they said that they had had more arguments than ever and neither was able to respond to what the other had requested. Rod said he was still vague about what Betsy meant by expressing tenderness, affection, and love to her and that he was unable to get any feedback from her as to whether or not he was "on course." Betsy said that because she didn't feel especially loved by Rod this week, it was hard for her to encourage him to exercise. This indicated that Betsy was still functioning from a symbiotic level of expectation. Differentiation for her had not yet begun to an appreciable degree. She was only vaguely aware of what she wanted in this important area and how "it" could be expressed in a way that felt appropriate.

Rod said he attempted to demonstrate his affection toward Betsy during the week through some brief physical touches, but he hadn't felt successful. He had also told her a couple of times that he cared for her, but that also felt insufficient. Nonetheless, he was still determined to be responsive to Betsy because he had an intellectual understanding that she had a problem in this area.

Rod's response to the exercise indicated that he was in the beginning phase of moving into his own process of differentiation. When he said he wanted support for his exercise program, he was asking for support in taking small steps away from Betsy. It was his way of enlisting her help with his separation and nudging his way out of what had been an intensely symbiotic relationship. Although his movement was healthy for him, it was threatening to Betsy, who felt a high level of anxiety whenever he expressed a desire to be away from her.

Using the Question of Attunement gave the therapist both diagnostic and treatment information: he was able to quickly identify Betsy's inability to manifest caring responses unless an enmeshed symbiosis was maintained; and he was able to associate this inability with an *intra*psychic issue in Betsy that was contributing significantly to this couple's developmental impasse. The therapist then focused the early phase of their treatment on Betsy's fears of being abandoned and of not being able to care for herself if Rod did not remain enmeshed with her.

The Diagnostic Interview

Our Diagnostic Interview explores the evolutionary history of the couple through a series of questions presented to each partner either verbally in a live interview, or as a questionnaire to be filled out at home (see Appendix A). The questions are arranged in a developmental sequence in order to pinpoint those phases that have been mastered by each partner and those that signal areas of impasse. Following is a list of questions we have developed, together with brief commentary about what the questions are intended to elicit.

1. *What is the problem that led you to decide to come to therapy?* How each partner initially defines the problem often gives an immediate sense about whether the couple is symbiotic or whether emerging and unresolved differences are creating the problem. Perhaps instead, the need to staunchly maintain "self" is at the root of their problem.

Do the individuals in the couple define the problem in such a way that they recognize their own responsibility in creating it? Does the description of the problem focus on the partner, or is it merged and symbiotically defined? For example, Ken initiated therapy for Ruth and himself saying, "We don't have any problems, but this is my fourth marriage and I want it to be my last. I've changed my wives when I get angry." In fact, he had begun dating Ruth the day his third wife moved out of their home and Ruth moved in three weeks later—suggesting a strong symbiotic pattern on Ken's part.

Carl and Dana, on the other hand, described their problem as "always being on opposite sides of issues." Most pressing were decisions regarding where to live, how to parent their son, and what to do about Carl's friendship with another woman. Their *differences* and independence from one another suggested a couple firmly engaged in practicing struggles.

2. *How long have you and your partner been together? In what form (i.e., married, dating, living together)?* How long the couple has been together will tell you what to expect developmentally. Our experience suggests an average of somewhere between six months and two years for a couple to define themselves stably as a couple. They then typically begin to evolve out of the symbiotic stage. When the movement toward differentiation does not occur, we look for evolution into an *enmeshed* or *hostile-dependent* symbiotic relationship (see Chapters 4 and 5).

3. *What initially attracted you to each other? How did you decide to get married or live together?* Asking about the original attraction evokes both the real elements and the fantasy illusions that were part of the couple's initial bonding experience. Such information often provides clues to aspects of the problem the couple remain unaware of or are unable to resolve between themselves. For example, one man described his wife as "my blonde-haired, blue-eyed dream girl. I love to stare at her, to eat her up with my eyes." After one year of marriage they came into therapy because the husband was depressed about losing the romance in their life. His idea of romance was being able to stare lovingly into his wife's eyes for one hour each evening before making love and going to sleep. She, on the other hand, just wanted to go to sleep!

Another woman described her initial meeting with the man who became her second husband as follows: "We met at a barbecue. My first husband did not show up for the meal I had prepared, so out of anger I shared my food with John. We got along well immediately and I accepted an invitation for dinner with him the next evening. By late that night his sexual intentions became obvious. At that point it seemed natural that we would divorce our spouses, move in together and get married."

How the decision was made about living together or getting married will often reveal the degree of a couple's orientation toward either a symbiotic or an independent style of relationship. Another couple we worked with had gone on a blind date and decided to live together by the time the woman's children awoke the next morning. Two weeks later they were married. Contrast this pattern with the couple who have been together for five years, where each partner still maintains a separate house and is unwilling to leave a robe or a toothbrush in the other's home.

4. *What do you find most fulfilling about your relationship?* The answer to this question often reveals whether the relationship is based on dependency and symbiotic elements or on growth-enhancing ones. For example, contrast "the only fulfilling part of our relationship is our daughter" with "the openness and willingness to talk to each other and not have fixed male/female roles are the best parts of how we relate."

5. *What was the very beginning of your relationship like? How long did this phase last?* This question examines the intensity and duration of the early phase. How strong was the early bond? How long did the couple maintain it? Did they allow themselves an initial time of ecstasy? Was falling in love a delight or a chore? Did they acknowledge themselves as a couple? Was there so much ambivalence about coupling that they never established a solid base of feeling and commitment to sustain them through the disillusionment of the differentiation stage?

Here are two examples from symbiotic marriages: "The first two years were intense, sexually passionate, and filled with emotional and financial dependency. We were thick as thieves and very close"; and, "The beginning of our relationship was based on our attempts to understand each other's misery. We each had suffered in previous marriages and we were going to make it all up to each other."

By contrast, a practicing-practicing couple reported on the difficulty they had with their early attachment: "We were both so afraid of losing ourselves in each other that we did silly things. Marc would suddenly get up in the middle of the night and say he had to go home for no reason. I wouldn't let him take me out. Every bill had to be divided 50–50. I think we missed out on something."

6. *What was your first disillusionment? What happened and how did you resolve it?* This is one of the most important questions to ask. When successfully mastered, the first disillusionment usually propels partners into a phase of separation/individuation. When the disillusionment is not resolved by the couple, it often leads to the emerging of a hostile-dependent relationship. The disillusionment represents the loss of the initial fantasy. Is the loss minimal or substantial, and when did it occur?

Contrast the lack of resolution for the woman who said, "My first disillusionment came after 16 years of marriage when my husband told me that he wasn't in love with me anymore; since that moment he has hardly spoken to me," with the woman who reported, "After we had been together for a year, I discovered that Earl wasn't a travel buff like I am. Since we had done so much traveling early in our relationship, I had assumed he loved being away from home as much as I did. When he changed his mind about going to Australia with me, I was devastated at first. Then, we decided I'd go anyway. Sometimes I still feel sad about not sharing all our trips together, but it doesn't stop me from enjoying myself."

7. *When do you feel least fulfilled in your relationship?* Answers to this question will pinpoint areas of conflict in a relationship as well as identify those partners who view themselves as "lily-white" victims, while considering the other as bad and blameful. For example, one man said, "I rarely feel fulfilled. I never get positive feedback. I am excluded from her thoughts and repulsed whenever I approach her."

8. *In what significant ways are the two of you similar? different? What methods have you worked out to accommodate or compromise*

on your differences? Here the therapist looks for which polarity the partners are most willing to discuss that will show whether their focus is on sameness or difference. For example, the wife who is in the differentiating stage will most likely focus her energy and feelings on the differences she experiences in relation to her husband, whereas he, who is still in the symbiotic stage, will be aware solely of the similarities. The *differences* will be a source of threat to the husband, whereas the *similarities* will aggravate the wife. If a wife responds, "He tends to be more sociable—I'm a private person and nurture myself by being alone—sometimes that creates conflict," then the therapist looks at what mechanisms the couple has developed for managing their differences. If they have not found any positive ways to work with the differences, then the therapist knows they have reached an impasse in the differentiation stage.

9. *Do you spend time in activities away from your partner? If so, how often? Do you spend time alone with people who are not mutual friends? Does this create conflict in your relationship?* Here we explore some highlights of the practicing stage. Both questions 9 and 10 are intended to elicit responses that illuminate both sides of the practicing stage: Can the partners manage their own independence? Can they manage one another's independence? What role do independent activities and friendships play in this relationship? Are they perceived as threatening? Do they lead to repetitive fights? Does *separation anxiety* occur when either goes off on his or her own?

One man reported, "My wife says it's OK for me to go out with my own friends, but when I come home she punishes me with a temper tantrum." A woman described the reverse situation: "I very much enjoy doing things away from Tom. It gives me a great sense of mastery and feeling of being in charge. It's a good time to check in with myself. I hope he gets as much joy as I do when he spends time with his friends."

10. *How comfortable are you doing activities away from your partner? How comfortable are you with your partner doing things away from you?*

11. *How safe do you feel expressing your innermost thoughts and feelings to your partner? How do you ask for emotional support from your partner when you are feeling vulnerable? Do you expect to get it?*

12. *Would your partner say that you are emotionally responsive to his/her vulnerability? Explain.*

13. *Do you take an active, energetic role in nourishing the relationship? Does your partner do the same? How?* Questions 11, 12, and 13 elicit information that will help pinpoint where the partners are in relation to the rapprochement stage. This is the stage in which the adult enjoys engaging in activities away from the partner, but also enjoys returning to the relationship to express more vulnerability and to give and receive nurturance. At this stage, however, there is still a regressive element in the nurturance, as earlier issues are in the final stages of resolution.

Contrast one individual who answered question 11 by saying, "I don't feel safe. I feel humiliated whenever I open my mouth and a feeling comes out," with the woman who said, "I feel fine expressing *very* personal things. Sometimes I hold back when I'm confused and wait until I'm sure what I'm feeling, but once I know, I feel safe sharing with him. Usually, he responds very caringly."

Also, note the difference between a woman in the symbiotic stage who answered question 13 by saying, "This is a hard question. I never thought about it before, but I think, no. Mostly I expected Bob to just nurture and protect me," with a more differentiated man who responded, "Yes, we both do. I do special things for holidays and birthdays. I want her to know our relationship is special. I also bring up new ideas to discuss or do."

14. *Do you support your partner's development as an individual? How (give example)? Do you support his/her growth as an individual even when you don't agree? How (give example)?* Many people respond negatively to both variations of this question. Partners who are able to support the other in spite of disagreement are manifesting a high level of differentiation. The emotional valence of a person's response to these questions can help identify his or her specific developmental level. For example, a symbiotic partner will tend to respond with anxiety and fear, whereas a practicing partner might evidence a subtle tone of resentment.

Contrast the following responses of individuals in three very different stages:

Symbiotic Hostile-Dependent: "I am constantly made aware by my husband that I do not support him as an individual, so I live with the feeling of guilt of not being able to do anything for him."

Differentiation: "I try to support his development, but if I don't agree with his direction, I don't support it. In fact, that's when the fighting begins."

Rapprochement: "Yes, I have recently been supporting her education and development both financially and emotionally."

15. *Do you believe that your partner is giving at least 50% to the relationship?* Very few couples believe that the partnership involves an equal give-and-take. Usually such equality does not evolve until the rapprochement or mutually interdependent stage. The major exception is found in couples who have been together for only a short time.

One woman in a practicing relationship answered it this way: "My husband has never given such a high percentage to our relationship. Soon after we got married, he started medical school, next it was law school, and then on to his career as a traveling consultant."

A man in a practicing-rapprochement relationship responded, "Absolutely, she gives much more than 50%. I'm still learning how to give."

Another man in a mutually interdependent relationship expressed the sharing in this way: "Our therapy has really paid off. It shows now since we are in the process of starting our own business. It's a time of high financial and emotional stress and we keep supporting each other!"

16. *Do the two of you have joint commitments to projects, work activities, or social causes? If so, what?*

17. *Did you deliberately decide to create something together in one of these areas?* In our experience, people who have successfully passed through all the previous stages begin to feel a desire to do something together. In the earlier stages this desire more often reflects a symbiotic movement rather than an outreach toward creating an experience of mutual creativity and sharing. It is usually obvious which vantage point a response is reflecting. Note the difference between the couple who described their joint commitment to the husband's church, and the couple who worked together in Southeast Asia after the Vietnam

War. In the first situation, the wife's commitment took the form of bringing lunch to her husband at church each day. The symbiotic overtones were made quite clear when she became upset when her husband wanted to have lunch once a week without her.

The other couple had deliberately decided to go to Southeast Asia together to aid in restoration work in Vietnam and Laos. Their jobs in Asia necessitated much separate travel and even living apart for several months. Upon their return, they described how their commitment to this work had strengthened the bond between them. The husband reported: "It was the high point of our lives together. Of course, there were difficult times—learning a new language and new customs, living a subsistence lifestyle, and getting through culture shock. We helped each other out. There was one week when all I could focus on was wanting a Coke. Instead of getting mad at me for such a stupid obsession, Mary brought some Coke back from Bangkok the next time she went."

18. *Does this project seem to add or detract from the bond between you?* It is in the later stages that a joint project will add deeply to the bond between the partners. Prior to this, joint activities may be enjoyable and satisfying but may also serve to tighten a symbiotic connection, to obscure differences, or to detract from the unfolding individuation of either partner in the practicing stage.

19. *If your marriage were a drama, movie, or book, what would it be titled? How would it end?* This is a marvelous question and will often give the therapist the most salient feeling-tone of the relationship in a few words that draw a crystal-clear picture. The following represent some responses we've received:

- Two partners in a hostile-dependent relationship called their marriage "The Tidal Wave" and "Two Prisoners in One Cell."
- A symbiotically enmeshed partner labelled his marriage "The Perfect Match" and another "A Marriage Made in Heaven."
- A differentiating partner said, "A Life Without Problems Is No Life At All."
- A practicing partner called his marriage "The Lone Ranger," while another entitled it "Drifting Along or 900 Miles Away."

Since this questionnaire unfolds in a developmental order, careful questioning usually reveals which stages have been resolved and which stages are causing difficulty for each individual in the couple. When the historical data gathered from this Diagnostic Interview are combined with the process data from either the Paper Exercise or the Question of Attunement, a fuller picture is revealed.

The Individual History and Intrapsychic Issues

Now that we have obtained clear glimpses into the couple's current interactions (via the Paper Exercise or Question of Attunement) and into their history as a couple (via the Diagnostic Interview), we turn our attention to uncovering those feelings out of each person's past history that are being displaced or projected onto the spouse. These lead to rigid, unchanging, and self-defeating patterns of interaction. By identifying the particular childhood issues that are contributing to the current developmental impasse, we are able to work far more quickly than if we examined all elements of an individual's early history.

We have found the work of the Gouldings (1979) to be particularly effective in identifying the chronic negative feelings underlying the problem. The Gouldings give many examples of how to trace current chronic negative feelings back to the original childhood traumas that spawned them. They then combine TA and Gestalt techniques to resolve the current impasse. Following is our adaptation of one of their exercises, "The short script," as we apply it to uncover each individual's intrapsychic impasse in the context of couples therapy:

Close your eyes and allow yourself to go back to a time when you were a young child growing up in your own family. And as you go back, allow yourself to remember the time when either your mother or your father treated you the worst or meanest you can remember. And as you're back in that scene, allow yourself to see what is happening, to know what you are feeling, and to see what you are deciding about how to cope with the situation. Also, let yourself know what demand you would like to have made of either of your parents.* Then, after you have discovered the

---

*Using *demand* as a therapeutic technique is described by John McNeel (1980).

*answer to these questions, slowly grow yourself up and come
back into the room, once again being your own age now.*

Each partner is then asked to describe the scene that was imaged.

Case example: "The short script"

Cindy and Burt had entered couples therapy because of her depression and agoraphobia and his incipient drinking problem. The therapist (Ellyn) used "the short script" exercise to reveal how early life
decisions made in relation to particular traumatic events had been
impeding the couple's ability to move beyond the symbiotic stage in
their current relationship.

When Cindy was given "the short script," she reported an experience that had occurred when she was 16 years old. She was staying at a
friend's house, and together they sneaked out to meet other friends at
the school dance. On that night they were both raped by strange boys.
When Cindy's father found out, he became very angry at Cindy and
blamed her for being out alone in the evening. Cindy's response to his
attack was to feel very sad and to decide, "I'll never go out alone
again." Her demand as an adult was to wish that her father would
protect her and take better care of her.

Burt reported his childhood scene: When he was 14, it was his job to
come home after school and look after his sister, who was seriously ill
in bed. He was given the responsibility of watching her from the time
when his mother went to work at 3:00 p.m. until his father came home
at 5:30 p.m. each evening. On several occasions, Burt neglected his
responsibility to his sister, and one day while he was playing ball, she
died. He felt very guilty and decided that since it had been his
responsibility, he should have looked after her better. Over the years,
his guilt had become an enormous burden. His demand as an adult was
to be angry at his parents for putting him in such a responsible position
at such a young age.

At the age of 20 Cindy had married Burt, a police officer, who was
then 27 years old. It is not surprising that Cindy married a police
officer to protect her and that she had difficulty going anywhere alone.
It is also not surprising that Burt had become a police officer, and that
he felt a strong obligation to protect Cindy—indeed, to smother her

with protective attention—and yet at the same time to feel angry that he was constantly put in that position. Because of early decisions made by both Cindy and Burt, they had been unable to move their relationship beyond the symbiotic stage. By working through the early underlying traumas and developing empathy and respect for each other's difficulties, they were able to successfully move into the differentiation stage.

Case example: Tracing chronic negative feelings to uncover intra- psychic impasses

Jim and Sally had been married for four years. They had come for couples therapy because Sally was depressed that Jim was spending so much time away from home. In fact, she called him "a hippie runaway." He would leave home for days at a time, often to play with his band or to act with a theater group, and was unwilling to tell Sally when he was coming or going. In an early session, Jim and the therapist (Ellyn) had the following exchange:

Ellyn: What do you feel before you leave home?

Jim: Angry.

Ellyn: What does your anger say?

Jim: "No one is going to tie me down."

Ellyn: When else in your life did you feel this way?

Jim: When I was 16, with my mother. We used to be close but then I got tired of her trying to control me and keep me close to home.

Ellyn: What did you do with your anger then?

Jim: I ran away.

Ellyn: And what did you tell yourself inside your head as you ran away?

Jim: The only way to get away is to run away.

Ellyn: Is that what you do now with Sally?

Jim: (sighs) I hadn't realized it before, but that's exactly what I do with her.

Ellyn then traced Jim's feelings back to an earlier scene when he was in the eighth grade. Each day his mother would pick him up after school, often saying to him as he got into the car, "It's too bad you don't like to play with your friends after school." To himself Jim would angrily retort, "It's too bad you won't let me—someday I'll get away from here."

As an adult Jim now equated independence with angrily leaving a woman behind and running away. At the time he came to therapy, he did not know how to take his independence directly without first setting up a woman at whom he could be angry. After enjoying an initial period of closeness with Sally, he had begun acting with a local theater company and wanted more time away to develop himself. He would go to evening rehearsals and then to cast parties until late at night. He refused to include her and wouldn't let her know how late he would be out. He left her wondering what he was doing backstage. The only way he knew how to get what he wanted was to get angry at Sally's wants and run away from her, leaving her scared and him angry.

Earlier, Jim and Sally's presenting problem, Diagnostic Interview, and Paper Exercise pointed to their relationship having reached an impasse at the symbiotic-practicing stage. From the information obtained by tracing Jim's individual history, it became clear why Jim and Sally had been unable to evolve beyond this point on their own.

Jim's early history revealed a childhood problem which had surfaced during adolescence. Jim felt repeatedly impeded from developing his independence by his mother. In fact, over the years he had become increasingly angry with her for interfering with his own growth. His silent rage had erupted at the age of 16 and, instead of being resolved, culminated in his running away from home. This unresolved childhood drama was now being replayed with Sally and was serving to solidify a symbiotic-practicing relationship without differentiation. Any attempt on Sally's part to begin to define her own desires threatened Jim. From his fear of being controlled by Sally and his inability to differentiate, Jim angrily demanded independence and took it in a way that led Sally to become increasingly clinging. Her dependence only increased as she became more fearful of losing Jim permanently.

By knowing about Jim's early history, Ellyn was able to select treatment interventions to accomplish the following:

1. Help Jim recognize that he was displacing anger at his mother onto Sally and then treating Sally in an angry, abusive manner;
2. Help Jim resolve his earlier anger while learning how to resolve conflicts directly with his wife so that his independence could be taken in a positive and mature way;
3. Help Sally tolerate her discomfort at Jim's independence while simultaneously developing a stronger, more differentiated sense of herself.

The diagnostic process with Jim and Sally made it possible to target therapeutic interventions that helped both of them to move through differentiation into a healthy, direct practicing stage.

These poignant examples demonstrate the impact of specific early decisions on an adult's capacity to manage the developmental tasks of a couple's relationship. Such longstanding, fundamental problems inhibit a couple's ability to deal with differences and to accept each other's individual identities without demanding large sacrifices from one another. Those intrapsychic conflicts that are directly impinging on the partners' abilities to relate effectively with one another must be resolved in order to allow the relationship to unfold and in order to develop real, ongoing solutions to the couple's conflict.

Now that we have considered the various diagnostic tools we use, we will turn our attention to providing an overview of the treatment process as it unfolds in couples therapy. In the following chapters we will describe comprehensive profiles of each major couple-combination. These profiles demonstrate how we apply the techniques to the diverse types of couples we have encountered, and how we use the accessed information to create effective therapeutic interventions. We will also highlight the unique difficulties inherent in each diagnostic category. In most instances, we have chosen to present case examples that had positive outcomes in order to emphasize the ways in which we have used the developmental approach successfully. However, needless to say, we have also had negative outcomes in which couples either chose to divorce or were simply unable to resolve their developmental impasses.

CHAPTER 3

Treating Couples in a Developmental Model

"Couples are more than the sum of their parts"

Although many people are propelled into therapy as a result of problems in their intimate relationships, few therapists have been trained as couples specialists. Couples therapy is not simply individual therapy with two people. It is a different entity and thus requires a different theory and perspective. The focus of treatment must be on the relationship rather than on curing or changing all of the pathology within each individual. Because there are two people in the room, and because most therapists have been trained initially and most thoroughly as individual therapists, there is a strong tendency to focus primarily on individual symptomatology. In doing so, the process of couples therapy often takes the form of ventilation and exploration of past motivations: "What is each partner's problem?" "Who's doing what to whom?" "Why are they doing it?" "What are the points of intersection between partners' problems?"

In the field of psychotherapy, complex and sophisticated methods have been created for asking and answering the question "Why?" Inherent in this particular questioning process is the belief that by focusing directly on the problem and its historical antecedents, one will discover why an individual is acting in a particular way. To achieve this insight implies that the individual will change and this, in turn, will automatically net a positive change in the relationship. Unfortunately, in couples therapy such individualized insight does not always lead to positive relational changes.

A time when focusing on *why* is particularly ineffective is when one partner is present against his or her will and is being asked to change

42

something that is ego-syntonic. Such an individual may develop insight into *why* he or she is behaving in a particular way, yet make no changes that impact the relationship in a successful direction. In fact, analyzing and discussing problems for highly distressed couples will produce neither relief nor change until the partners have committed themselves to making some specific attitudinal and behavioral alterations in how they interact with and support one another.

Sometimes, however, specific intrapsychic conflicts originating in childhood traumas are at the basis of a couple's developmental impasse. Then "Why?" becomes a critical question. When this appears to be the case, we work in a highly focused way to uncover and resolve the personal trauma (as described in Chapter 2). It is important to note that even when an intrapsychic issue is being addressed, we work from the larger perspective of the relationship. We do this by carefully bridging the impact of each individual's insights to how they affect the fabric of the ongoing relationship.

Because our model of treatment focuses on the *relationship*, we design interventions to help couples create more effective, mature, and flourishing interactions that can be sustained over time. After diagnosing the developmental stage or impasse, our interventions are intended to facilitate movement of the couple into the next stage. We do this by creating experiences between the two individuals that allow for the unfolding of a more normal developmental process. We do not want to foster an unhealthy dependency on us as therapists, nor do we want to stabilize the system by establishing a situation in which the couple needs us in order for any intimacy to occur. Rather, we attempt to find the target or nodal point of intervention that will enable the couple to *move themselves* into the next phase of their own developmental cycle.

PRINCIPLES FOR INTERVENTION

The following principles guide our interventions at all stages of impasse and will be demonstrated in greater depth in the following chapters.

Actively Providing Structure ✓

We are active therapists and believe it is our job to structure the therapeutic process in a way that provides meaning to the couple's experience. At the same time, we carefully monitor our activity level so that it does not interfere with the client's autonomy. While creating a safe therapeutic environment in the office, we encourage risk taking that pushes the boundaries of each partner's development in a manner that stimulates the couple's movement to a healthier developmental level.

Making Partners Responsible for Autonomous Change

It is not uncommon for one partner in the couple to attempt to negotiate a reciprocal change of behaviors. However, the common attitude of "I will change if you will change" gives the less motivated member of the couple the most power, while leaving the therapist in a position of minimal influence. We encourage autonomous changes in the partner who is feeling the most relationship stress and who is demanding change in the system. Because this individual is experiencing more discomfort, he or she is the one who often has the belief that "the only way I am going to feel better is if my partner does most of the changing." Such individuals may believe that simply because they want their partner to change, the partner is obligated to make the requested change. This attitude maintains a symbiosis in which a want from one person becomes an automatic demand for compliance. Other individuals find it emotionally difficult to manifest their vulnerability by openly and nonblamefully making a request of their partner. Once the difficult task is done, there is the hope that their job is finished and it is now up to the partner to comply with this request. We frequently surprise one of the partners by refusing automatically to support a request for change when it comes from a symbiotic position.

Autonomous change can be facilitated on both external and internal levels in the distressed individual. External autonomous change requires the distressed partner to change his or her behavior, thereby creating a physical or emotional environment that is conducive to generating change in the mate. Sometimes, individuals are reluctant or unwilling to do anything to encourage a desired change in their partner. This reluctance is usually reflective of an entrenched symbiotic position. When we ask the requestors to support their partners' change, we are helping them learn that childlike demanding and parental nagging are not facilitative of an effective relationship. Interestingly, when couples make changes autonomously rather than in a tit-for-tat fashion, they are actually more effective in helping each other to resolve past hurts.

Case example: External autonomous change

Kip and Lana both worked at demanding jobs. Lana did most of the household chores and arranged child-care responsibilities. Lana wanted Kip to pitch in, to take more initiative with the kids and the house. Kip agreed in principle that he should do more, but only responded to high-pressure nagging. Examining Kip's motivation for not participating more fully provided some insight and illumination about his noninvolvement, but did not yield a protracted change. Lana was sharp enough to know that when Kip responded periodically to her nagging, it only reinforced her to nag more. She said her dilemma was whether to continue nagging or not to say anything and do all the work and end up feeling enormously resentful.

During this discussion, the therapist (Pete) said to Lana that generally there are two ways to influence someone else to change. One is through fear, and the other is to make that person want to change. Lana acknowledged she had some intermittent success with using fear. Indeed, Kip, in an attempt to avoid future harangues, would pitch in occasionally to help out. When Kip did this, Lana saw no reason to compliment him for it: "You don't compliment someone for what they should be doing anyway. Besides, it would probably go to his head and he would stop helping."

Pete asked Kip if Lana's opinion of him was important. He replied that, in fact, it was quite important to him. It was exactly because he cared about her opinion that, contrary to her belief, the nagging really bothered him. He ended up feeling that she would never be satisfied, and she would always be harping and parental. Kip said he would really enjoy having a lot more "gee, you're wonderful compliments" from Lana. Lana responded, "Well, if you would grow up, I'd be glad to tell you that you're wonderful." Lana was gently reminded that the task at hand was to create an atmosphere that increased Kip's desire to pitch in and become more active around the house.

Lana was then asked what she felt when Kip commented on the importance of her compliments to him. She said she liked that and would be glad to tell him more of those things if he would just be more responsible. Knowing that Lana liked to fish, Pete then asked her this question, "Lana, when you go fishing, have you ever considered using chocolate truffles as bait?" She responded, "Why, of course not, fish don't like chocolate truffles!" And then the light went on for Lana! Trying to suppress a chuckle, she said, "You mean I've got to change my bait?" In that session Pete explored Lana's reluctance to give compliments to Kip and then also looked at what the benefits would be for Lana to increase her level of positive support. Kip said, "The key to my heart is a plentitude of compliments." He then gave some examples of the kind that had the most meaning for him. Lana wrote these down so she would be able to remember them. At the end of the session, each reaffirmed the level of effort they would put out during the coming week. Kip was able to understand the difference between asking Lana, "What do you want me to do, dear?" versus his initiating a conversation with, "Let's draw up a list of things that need to be done this weekend and assign specific chores to each of us." They were asked not to look for perfection in the coming week, but rather to be aware of the effort that each was making.

When they came back for the next session, things were not perfect but were improving. Lana stated she had given Kip encouragement grudgingly for more participation, but felt she was being maternal by saying "good boy" when he was doing more. Pete described the difference between giving Kip a pat on the head and telling him about the positive impact he was having on her when he took the initiative. If, in fact, Lana said to Kip, "You've lived up to my standards," then this interaction would feel maternal to both of them. However, if she would express her relief and positive feelings at seeing the kitchen table free of his clutter, then they both would feel good about the interchange. Before this, Lana believed that the appreciation would have to come from a pseudonurturing parental position. She knew intuitively that would not be effective. She also revealed how vulnerable she felt when she expressed what she wanted from a nonparental position.

Over the next weeks Kip began to recognize that by being more involved around the house, he wasn't doing it "for Lana," but he was really doing it "for us." If the problem had been defined as "Kip has to help out," then both Lana and the therapist would be at the mercy of Kip's willingness to participate. When the problem was put into a much larger context of supporting one another's wants, Lana was not stuck in the parental nagging position.

In addition to an external autonomous change, one partner can make an internal autonomous change to facilitate relationship growth. In this case the individual accepts responsibility for his or her own intrapsychic problem that is creating stress in the relationship. Then the emphasis shifts to resolving the intrapsychic issue to facilitate growth in both the individual and the relationship.

Case example: Internal autonomous change

If John tells Sue that he would like to spend more intimate time with her, and Sue is reluctant to do so, then it is fairly typical for men like John to either withdraw, get angry, or escalate the request into needy demands. Often John will balk at the idea that it is important for him to go beyond his verbal request for more intimate time to create the conditions under which Sue would like to spend more time with him. It is easy for John to complain that Sue is not spending enough time with him; however, it is far more difficult for him to relinquish his own egocentric needs in an effort to understand Sue's feelings as a separate, distinct person. It is even more difficult for John to understand the impact of his requests on Sue and begin thinking about the conditions that would make it easier and more desirable for Sue to spend more close time with him.

If John is unwilling to create an external atmosphere in which Sue would like to spend more intimate time with him, then we seek to evaluate the reasons. John's reluctance might be based on environmental stress: there may be so many pulls on his emotional resources that he simply feels unable to go beyond requesting the type of time and intimacy that he would like from Sue. An intrapsychic impasse might underlie his unwillingness. For example, John might have been raised by a doting mother who did not expect him to grow up or to give much. John might resent being put in the position of extending himself to his wife when he wants her to take care of him. A third factor contributing to John's reluctance might be a maturational deficit. If John was not responded to in an empathically effective way in his family of origin, then he would have a diminished capacity to approach Sue as anything other than an extension of himself.

Once we uncover the reason for the reluctance, we explore with the individual ways to heal the problem and promote change. In this particular example, John discovered that his compelling need for greater intimacy with his wife was primarily a sophistication of the emptiness he felt as a young boy and prior to his marriage. He realized that as long as he was driven by the buried feelings of the hurt and needy little boy, no amount of attention from Sue would ever satisfy him. As John recognized the significance of his problem, he requested individual therapy. We then combined individual and couples therapy to help him resolve these issues. By seeing that a major source of the problem in the relationship stemmed from a dynamic within him, John became motivated to resolve his personal issues and then was able to make individual changes that enhanced their relationship.

Creating a Future Focus

This approach provides a specific way to structure treatment that shifts the couple away from focusing on present blame or projection and asks them to focus on how they would like to create their future together. By looking forward rather than backward, the couple become excited about and involved in planning for their own future.

How far into the future we focus with a couple depends on the level of their development. The ability to think ahead and plan for what each individual wants in a cooperative way that incorporates relationship goals requires a high level of sophistication. Couples in the earlier stages of development are often confused and vague about what it is they would like to create together. In these cases, the future focus may be as limited as a one-month time frame, or from session to session. The emphasis, then, is on helping partners learn to think about what it is they want to direct themselves toward in order to generate good feelings beyond the appetite level of self-indulgence and self-centeredness. This type of focus also asks each partner to develop ways of making his or her behavior consistent with the goals they both want for the relationship.

Helping couples identify what it is they want to create together beyond the appetite level is as crucial to the process of differentiation as it is to the process of learning to set mutual goals. Most partners in the early developmental stages need to be coaxed and even pushed into developing this level of self-awareness. Without some kind of outside pressure or stimulus, such individuals will typically pull for symbiotic solutions. In one way or another, they will manipulate their partner into figuring out for them the difficult questions and answers about what will create a life that is satisfying.

When one or both partners have a poorly developed sense of self, it is especially difficult for the couple to visualize with much clarity the type of future they would like to create. Often their confusion will be reflected in the vagueness of their desires. For example, a partner might respond: "I want to be happy together," "I would like to be rich," "I would like us to have fun," or "I just want a little respect." Usually this individual will respond with frustration when pressed to clarify or be more specific about what is meant by being "happy." At this point, it is necessary for the therapist to bypass the frustration and pursue the future focus until each partner has vividly and clearly described the behaviors and activities that will help move them forward as a couple. Understanding future focus on an intellectual level is fairly easy for most couples. However, experiencing it on an emotional level that gives it its potency is another level of work altogether.

A future focus, rather than a problem-solving focus, is especially fruitful for couples in the later developmental stages; it enables them to progress rapidly both as individuals and as a couple. Partners begin to feel excited about working in concert toward the achievement of specific objectives and ideals. We have found that partners at these stages sometimes change more rapidly than individuals working toward the same goals. Couples, when they are in agreement and working in a mutually supportive way, develop a momentum that helps keep each "on track" when one or the other falters.

The Principle of "Selling Change"

We have found that clients will often agree in principle about the importance of placing their struggles in a larger context by looking at what they want to create in their relationship. What often happens in the session, however, is a retreat to complaining and accusatory behaviors. We explain to clients that most important changes do not take place without *enthusiasm, desire, energy,* or *acceptance of individual responsibility for* change. While the process of psychotherapy involves awareness, insight, understanding, and the exploration of feelings, these will not *in themselves* produce change unless they are enlivened by a partner's enthusiasm and motivation. As a way of increasing motivation for change, we introduce the partners to the principle of "selling change."

This process is important when one partner makes a demand or request of the other which that person is unwilling or reluctant to fulfill. In this situation, the therapist usually feels pressure to provide relief to the distressed partner wanting the change. However, the least effective response is for the therapist to align with the distressed partner and begin pressuring the apathetic/reluctant spouse to change.

In order to relieve some of this pressure, we describe to the couple the benefits that can occur when they learn to "sell change" rather than nag one another. This principle is illustrated in the following case.

Case example: Sheila and Rocky

During the fourth session with Rocky and Sheila, Rocky mentioned his strong desire to move to a larger house but that Sheila liked the coziness and cottage charm of their present home. Rocky had grown up in a family of six, living in a two-bedroom house. The coziness that Sheila adored created claustrophobic feelings for Rocky. Repeatedly he pushed her to move to a larger home. Sheila reported two major obstacles to moving. Rocky was apparently unable to see the clutter in the house until Sheila exploded about the house looking like a war zone. Then Rocky would do a whirlwind cleanup to eliminate the visual disarray. Sheila felt frightened that moving would mean only more expansive messes for her to clean or more frequent outbursts to mobilize Rocky! Neither of these outcomes made it desirable for her to leave a home she enjoyed. Also, she did not want to work longer hours to meet a larger mortgage payment.

Prior to this session their arguments had been circular, with no measurable progress toward arriving at a solution. To help Rocky develop a larger perspective, the therapist (Pete) offered him the following concepts:

Pete: When we desire a change in our partner's behavior, we think about how we are going to be better off after they make the desired change. So, we ask them to change *for us*, and even tell them how much better we will feel if they do. This may or may not be successful, depending on the altruism of your partner or the amount of guilt you use to get your way.

A strong desire for change does not come mainly from *understanding* that there is a need for the change. The strong desire comes from our partner's *deeper realization* that "Oh, wow, if I agree to this, then this is how I am (we are) going to benefit!" The desire for change comes as a moment of emotional enlightenment in which it dawns on our partner that "I am and we are going to be so much better off if I make this change."

What most individuals don't do is try to sell their partner on the value of change. For example, any top-notch salesperson, when selling a product or service, has to focus on the benefits to the customer—how the customer will profit by spending time and money to purchase this product or service. Problems in a marriage can be resolved faster when the focus is on the benefits of change. Do you really understand how Sheila will be better off if she moves, given the constraints on her time, energy, and emotions? Now here's the hook: if you want Sheila to change, you truly must understand her needs and honestly believe she will be better off by making the change. Otherwise, you will come across as a manipulating, used-car salesman. As the emotional benefits become more clearly articulated to her and especially as she sees how they are related to her unique wants, then she may have a desire to change in the manner you are requesting. And when her desire is aroused, she may want it and want it now. Action results from our desires, and the stronger the desire, the stronger will be the accompanying action.

This is an incredibly powerful concept to introduce change into your marriage. In short, if you don't like certain aspects of your relationship, then you can change the way you think about the problems and begin to reap some of the harvest that so far has been lying around sight unseen. So Rocky, is it clear to you why Sheila doesn't want to move?

Rocky: Sure. But if we move, I'll pick up after myself so she won't have that complaint. I can earn more money by working smarter and not harder [he was a salesman on commission], so the money shouldn't have to be that big of a deal.

Sheila: I'll believe it when I see it.

Rocky: Be glad to prove it to you when we move.

Pete: ~~I don't think~~ you will convince Sheila by good intentions. You've had good intentions in the past and nothing has come of them. How will Sheila know she will be better off if you move?

Rocky: *(long pause)* She will have a neater house which she values so highly. We can find one that she also enjoys. It will force me to find better ways to manage my time, which will profit both of us.

Pete: What are your thoughts and feelings about what Rocky said?

Sheila: I'm glad he recognizes my level of discomfort about the mess and I would feel better if he was more organized, but I'm very skeptical and don't want to do anything until I see some proof.

Pete: What kind of evidence do you want?

Sheila: I'd be glad to say after Rocky tells me what he is willing to do in our present condition to make things better.

Rocky: Tell you what—give me two months to establish a record of keeping the house neat and increasing my income. Then, if things are moving in a satisfactory direction, you will begin looking at houses with me. I know we will need to find one that has charm and coziness to make you happy. I'll keep the new place at an acceptable level of neatness, because it is easier for me to pick up after myself than to pay therapy bills to understand why I am a slob. I won't expect you to move until you feel the change is substantial and lasting. *(Rocky was beginning to understand the concept of getting outside his frame of reference to view the problem from Sheila's eyes. He was making it difficult for Sheila to say no to him.)*

Sheila: Will you do it for three months before we look at houses?

Rocky: Three months it is! *(Again Rocky understood the importance of not haggling over Sheila's time frame so it would seem that his change would be only a temporary adaptation to get his selfish way.)*

Pete: Rocky, is there a part of you that would like to make these changes even if Sheila was not a significant catalyst pushing for change? *(Lasting change that requires significant effort must also ~~include some~~ intrinsic motivation for the individual.)*

Rocky: This is something I want to do, but usually it falls under the category of my New Year's resolutions which only last until the middle of January. So yes, I do want to change this within myself *and for Sheila.*

In fact, eight months later Sheila and Rocky were in a new house and reported an acceptable level of satisfaction in solving the messiness problem.

Using Individual Therapy as an Adjunct

When it is clear that either or both individuals have major early structural deficits, we use individual therapy as an adjunct to the couples work. This is most commonly the situation with symbiotic-enmeshed couples. Here, we often recommend that the couple work with a team of cotherapists, and that each individual have one therapist from the team available to himself or herself as an individual therapist. In this way, each member of the couple has one defined therapist available as a source of support when the anxiety surrounding differentiation begins to surface. Also, the therapists are aware of the couple's interactions in an ongoing way and can balance time spent in individual and couples sessions. This arrangement provides necessary coordination of the therapy process and prevents unnecessary stress for the client attempting to manage different perspectives from two unrelated therapists. Undifferentiated, symbiotic individuals will regress unnecessarily when faced with therapeutic disparities.

Also, when there are large discrepancies in the psychological development of the partners, individual therapy often will be beneficial for the lesser developed partner as an adjunct to couples therapy. Usually, couples cannot move any faster than the progress of the slower partners; thus, a couple's therapeutic goals must be tempered to fit the developmental resources of both partners.

Here is a summary of the overarching principles we utilize in doing couples therapy:

1. We structure the therapeutic process in an active manner that seeks to facilitate positive risk taking, while respecting the couple's autonomy.

2. We ask partners to move autonomously in making changes without relying on a simultaneous change in the other. This request interrupts the symbiotic connection between the two partners and gives each an opportunity to experience growth that is self-directed.

3. We direct our emphasis *away from* the content of the specific problems—away from blame and rationalizations—and *toward* a future focus involving the development of new skills and the realization of personal, heartfelt goals.

4. We also ask each individual to create the environment that is conducive to the change that is being requested of the partner. As a general rule of thumb, the greater the developmental change that is being requested, the more the requestor needs to be involved in creating the conditions to facilitate the change.

5. We introduce the concept of "selling change" to partners as a means of evoking motivation and enthusiasm for creating change in the relationship.

6. When indicated, we use individual therapy as an adjunct to the therapeutic work with the couple.

THE CONTRACTUAL PROCESS

The way in which a therapist approaches the initial sessions will act as a powerful factor in determining the course of treatment and in focusing the direction and intensity of the couple's motivation. The range of possible interventions is vast and the therapist's agenda is full. Deciding where to begin requires a great deal of balancing and flexibility, depending on how the partners present themselves as a couple. The facet of the agenda on which the therapist initially focuses will be determined by the skill of the therapist and on how the couple's history unfolds.

Included in this initial phase is: 1) making a stage diagnosis and determining what is causing the impasse (discussed in Chapter 2); 2) structuring the treatment contract to involve and motivate both members of the couple and to create a safe therapeutic environment (discussed below); 3) developing a future focus (previously discussed); 4) identifying intrapsychic conflicts (discussed in Chapter 2); and 5) establishing the business aspects of the treatment contract (fees, policy, scheduling, billing, insurance, etc.).

Structuring the treatment contract to motivate both partners to begin therapy feeling emotionally connected to the work requires skill and sensitivity on the part of the therapist. Often, one partner drags the other into treatment. When this is the case, the therapist must help to stimulate motivation in the reluctant partner before significant change in the relationship can take place.

In developing the contract, we ask partners to focus on the outcomes they desire. It is difficult to be enthusiastic about changing oneself and altering lifelong patterns if one is responding primarily out of intimidation, pressure, or a "should" mentality. Changing a significant affect, belief, or behavior pattern with the sole goal of reducing the partner's nagging is a prescription for failure. As we discussed earlier in this chapter, the impetus for change must arise within each partner in a uniquely self-connected and autonomous manner.

When a couple first arrives for therapy, we generally ask the partners to describe their reasons for coming to us. After listening and clarifying their presenting problem(s), we begin to think about the focus of change: *Where are we going? Why are we going there? How are we going to get there? What were the conditions that helped shape the couple's present situation?* These are the basic questions we ponder and pose to the couple in setting a direction. Although we begin with these questions in order to set the direction, we also recognize that the contractual process is ongoing throughout the course of therapy and often requires periodic reevaluation and readjustment.

In order to create an effective contract, the end goals, the methods for achieving the goals, and the levels of motivation in each partner must be considered and balanced. Ideal contracts will have 1) mutually agreed-upon objectives with a high motivation for achieving them. However, reality intrudes upon the ideal with the result that many couples will have less desirable combinations of elements. They may have: 2) clear objectives with little motivation for achievement; 3) unclear objectives but high motivation for change; 4) unclear objectives with little motivation for change; 5) conflicting or incompatible objectives. We will exemplify each of the combinations briefly.

1. *Mutually agreed upon objectives with high motivation for achievement.* Morgan and Samantha came for couples therapy to improve their sexual relationship. Both were clear about this goal and

both were motivated to succeed. Their motivation was especially strong because they were anticipating an upcoming vacation to Tahiti. In the past their sexual desire discrepancy had led to intense arguments on vacations and neither wanted to repeat those painful interactions on this special romantic holiday.

2. *Clear objectives with little motivation for achievement.* These couples will know what they want but do not want to expend the necessary energy to bring about the desired objective. Luke and Jana were a married couple living apart. They came for therapy with the clear objective of wanting to get back together again and having a "good marriage." Although their reunion was an agreed-upon goal they both stated they wanted, it quickly became apparent that Luke's motivation was weak and uncommitted. He was not following through with any of his agreements or homework assignments, and his rationalizations were only halfhearted attempts to maintain a façade of being motivated. When we looked at the process of how Luke wanted to go from the current situation to getting back together with his wife, he finally stated that his true intention was "to make the minimal possible change and even that feels like a burden — it's just so easy and natural for me to be passive." (See Chapter 6 for how this problem was resolved.)

3. *Unclear objectives but high motivation for change.* This combination usually surfaces in couples who try very hard, yet nothing positive or substantial seems to happen. They lose sight of their focus and goals but redouble their efforts. Typically such couples have difficulty focusing on one particular problem; they say they want a better marriage but they cannot identify what a "better marriage" means in clear, behavioral terms. They also have difficulty identifying and articulating the problems they feel on an emotional level, yet they know clearly that they want to stay together. They can understand the dynamics of one problem but will shift to another before creating a resolution to the first. This process occurs frequently with enmeshed and hostile-dependent symbiotic couples. (See the treatment sections of Chapters 4 and 5.)

4. *Unclear objectives with little motivation for change.* This combination often occurs as a couple's "last-gasp-attempt" to hold together a

failing marriage. It allows partners to say that they have gone through the process of trying to salvage their marriage and thus exit with reduced guilt. In this situation, it is best to expose their lack of commitment to the marriage and to form a new contract to help them separate with dignity.

5. *Conflicting or incompatible objectives.* This dynamic will occur in three major arenas: *inter*personally, *intra*personally, and psycho-dynamically. When *inter*personal incompatibility exists, each person has an objective that is disagreeable to the other. This situation often develops in the symbiotic-practicing couple where partners typically want the opposite change: "I want more time together" versus "I want more time apart." Even though the objectives are incompatible, a suitable contract reflecting both sets of needs can still be created. We do not force the contract to fit one person's objectives but, rather, ask partners if they would be willing to work toward the accomplishment of one another's goals. For example, we might ask the symbiotic partner to help create more time apart, and the practicing partner to create more time together.

*Intra*personal incompatibility occurs when one individual has conflicting objectives. Henry was clear that he wanted more intimacy in his marriage with Jan, and he was also clear that he wanted to increase his income 45% in the coming year. To reach his monetary goals, Henry would have to travel away from home approximately 212 days —certainly not an arrangement conducive to the experience of greater intimacy! When these types of incongruities develop, we often help the person clarify and prioritize his or her individual goals in the context of the couple's therapy.

The third arena of incompatibility occurs when there is a request for a change in a partner that is reasonable, yet because of compounding psychodynamic issues, it is also unrealistic. Creating mutually agreeable and supportable goals can be a difficult and delicate task, especially if one individual is carrying a burden of past resentments. Often it is necessary to resolve these issues before this partner can generate motivation and enthusiasm about a positive future for the couple to create together.

For example, Jill and Ben both worked at demanding jobs. After six weeks in therapy, Jill requested that Ben take more initiative in making their frequent travel arrangements, in identifying and procuring needed supplies around the house, and in paying their ongoing bills. These were all reasonable requests, especially considering the fact that Jill was handling the vast majority of household and mutual responsibilities. However, Ben's level of development was such that it took all his energy merely to survive his workday; he had no reserves left over with which to function as a more equal partner around the house. Although he realized that he should share more responsibility, he felt that he was unable to generate the emotional resources needed to be more responsive. At that point in time, Jill's request was unrealistic though perfectly reasonable. Once she understood the underlying dynamics that were involved, she was willing to continue shouldering extra household responsibilities if Ben was willing to work intensively on his personal issues.

When mutually agreed-upon and supportable objectives are identified, the therapeutic process becomes more of a collaboration between the couple and the therapist. Whenever this process begins to feel "bogged down," it is helpful to review the original contract to see if it needs to be changed or reclarified in terms of either the means or the ends.

MATURATIONAL MILESTONES

Effective relationships are more than the sum total of positive behavioral interchanges and clear, effective communication skills. We believe that there are certain maturational milestones which promote a deeper bonding in the relationship. These milestones provide the experiential backdrop for the development of relationship skills, which emerge over time as the couple passes through the normal phases of couple development. Relationships flourish as this development occurs and the skills are honed.

When maturation is impeded in one or both partners, problems are inevitably triggered by the chafing constraints of the interaction. The problems, often called neurotic symptoms, occur when the individuals have little idea about how to bring about positive connection and intimacy. Fights then erupt and endure as a way to provide ongoing contact and stimulation.

In order to influence the development of a couple's system, we must identify the maturational deficits. As we intervene to promote maturation of both the individuals and the relationship, there follows an unfolding and strengthening of the bond. In the following chapters, we will describe a variety of methods we have created to help couples mature and move from one stage to another. For now, let us consider these milestones briefly:

1. *Empathy for one another.* Empathy is the ability to "get inside each other's skin" and understand how another person experiences life. Or, as Pine (1985) defines it, the goal of an empathic statement is "to provide a clarifying description of some inner state" (p. 168). These statements "potentially promote a feeling of being understood, of self-acceptance, of greater affect tolerance in the region of what has been stated so that higher levels of function can be built" (p. 169). For couples to be able to make empathic statements to one another requires the capacity to view and understand the partner as a separate person. Indeed, understanding someone else's feelings is the basis and foundation of unselfishness.

Without this maturational milestone of empathy, the relationship has severe limitations in how far it can evolve. Under stress and without empathy, one partner will usually blame the other for not responding emotionally and not meeting his or her needs at a particular moment. With empathy, an individual can have compassion for his partner's emotional distress and periodic inability to be responsive. With empathy, a partner can put her needs "on hold" or pause until her partner is more willing or capable of responding. With empathy, an individual will not expect his partner to be able to read his mind and respond accordingly. With empathy, an individual will not express herself in a demanding and whining manner, oblivious to the impact of such behavior on her mate. Simply put, the relationship cannot progress beyond the symbiotic stage without the beginning development of empathy.

With empathy, soothing moments can occur within the relationship that provide healing and promote closeness. Pine (1985) discusses the distinction between making *interpretations* versus *empathic statements* on the part of the therapist (pp. 162–172). We believe that the same is true for partners in a relationship. When one partner goes to the other to express strong inner feelings, the response that is hoped for is an empathic one. Often what is received instead is either a defensive response or an interpretation such as, "You are feeling that way because you are really angry at something that happened at work." Although these interpretations can provide useful information, they do not promote moments of connection between couples.

With empathy, individuals are able to search for and generate long-term solutions to complex emotional difficulties. And with empathy, individuals can develop committed, ongoing, flourishing relationships because there is a desire to discover what the partner wants and a willingness to help in its achievement. In the most fundamental way, the cultivation of empathy is absolutely necessary if couples are to move beyond the early stages. In later chapters, we will give examples of how to facilitate the growth of empathic responses within the couple's relationship.

2. *The ability to identify and express desires, thoughts, values, and feelings.* This ability is the hallmark of the differentiation stage. It requires a willingness to be vulnerable and the effort to take time to focus inward. It also often requires that one or both partners surmount long-held feelings of inadequacy in verbalizing what they are experiencing. Without this ability, individuals are perpetually locked into a symbiotic relationship in which they tend to pull for symbiotic solutions by attempting to pressure their partners to do this complex emotional work for them. With the ability to identify and express desires, thoughts, values, and feelings, however, it becomes possible to promote ongoing differentiation between partners and to generate a clear future focus for the relationship.

3. *The capacity to complete interactions in a satisfying manner.* This skill requires a consistent perseverance in the face of strong, regressive tendencies to walk out, slam doors, throw tantrums, or to be *right* while proving the partner is *wrong*. It also requires the capacity to tolerate the fear that is aroused when differences surface and are acknowledged.

4. *The willingness to give to the other person, even when it is not convenient.* This quality requires the developmental capacity to put one's own impulses and desires "on hold" in order to respond to the

partner's needs. Once developed, this capacity forms a cornerstone of enduring trust and safety in the relationship.

5. *An ongoing commitment to each other and to the relationship.* This is the most difficult level of maturation and usually it does not emerge until the later stages. Some couples feel a commitment to the relationship earlier but are unable to commit themselves to enhancing their partners' lives. To live in accordance with this principle involves compromise, give-and-take, effective negotiation, an ongoing recognition of the partner's "growing edge," and a genuine willingness (not just "lip service") to help in its achievement. Here, the understanding that "when I give to you, I get back" is experienced repeatedly and thereby incorporated into daily feelings and behavior.

We have found that by assisting a couple's movement forward, we simultaneously activate their strengths and resources as individuals. When we effectively diagnose the stage where forward movement has stopped, we can establish a contract and intervene with the couple to enable them to move forward once again. Education about the developmental stages also reduces the stress of ongoing struggles and provides a facilitative treatment tool whereby couples are able to view their conflicts as part of a normal relationship process.

CHAPTER 4

The Symbiotic-Symbiotic Couple: Enmeshed Type

"We are one"

When two people fall in love and go through the intense merging of boundaries that occurs at the beginning of the relationship, they are establishing themselves as a couple. Although not every couple comes together in the same way, some kind of initial bonding phase—of falling in love and establishing "coupleness"—is crucial for weathering the tasks ahead. This is a very important time; it sets the stage for how the partners feel about each other and provides a foundation for the couple to fall back on during times of conflict and stress.

As individuals join together to form a relationship with intensity, they engage in a symbiosis—a merger in which the "I" is not clearly differentiated from the "not I." Because the couple is being established as an entity during this time, each partner often disengages from friends and family in order to spend all available time with the loved one. Both become so wrapped up in one another that they forget about things they previously considered important. It feels as if they are one. They read each other's minds; they spend most of their time together; they focus mostly on their similarities. This is as it should be, for the function and developmental task of this stage is that of bonding, attachment, and the establishment of "the two of us are a couple." When each partner indulges in and enjoys the nurturance of this period, the relationship can begin with a strong foundation.

Although not representative of the norm, Tia and Norm demonstrate the extreme with which this symbiosis can occur. They fell in love on a blind date. Norm's friends told him that Tia would be the perfect woman for him. They were right; he knew it the minute he laid eyes on her. By midnight he had convinced her. They spent that night together, and by the time Tia's children awakened the next morning, the decision had been made for Norm to move in.

Although most couples do not get together with the same speed and intensity as Tia and Norm, we see an initial phase of merging—of falling in love and establishing coupleness—as essential. This stage may occur rapidly or evolve more slowly. After this initial phase, new elements will begin to unfold in the relationship: either the partners will progress to the next stage by beginning to differentiate, or they will stagnate at this first stage of symbiosis. The stalemated symbiosis then tends to grow into one of two variations: *symbiotic-enmeshed* or *symbiotic hostile-dependent*. In both of these systems, each of the partners continues to experience a consuming need to merge with the spouse. They become more dependent, less able to establish trust, and more fearful of abandonment. While the behavioral characteristics of each type are strikingly different, the interaction of both types increasingly serves the same end: to keep the other partner nearby. As time passes, the couple functions more and more like a *we* and less and less like two *I's*. In the remainder of this chapter, we will focus on the symbiotic-enmeshed couple. In Chapter 5, we will describe the hostile-dependent couple.

DESCRIPTION AND DIAGNOSIS OF THE SYMBIOTIC-ENMESHED COUPLE

By the time Tia and Norm came for therapy, their relationship had become severely enmeshed. They had spent four years of extreme togetherness and they were inseparable—so much so that Tia had not been to the grocery store without Norm! They ate all their meals together except dinner, at which they included Tia's parents who lived two houses away. Tia and Norm, like other long-term enmeshed couples, find the merging and diffuseness of their boundaries to be ego-syntonic. The strength of this attachment not only is anxiety free, but also provides a mechanism for each person to know himself or herself through converging with the other. The individual's identity is formed only in relation to the other. Thus, any threat of losing the partner will trigger the extreme anxiety of loss of self and/or psychic disintegration.

What led to this degree of overdependence in Norm and Tia? Both had had extremely deprived childhoods, and both were grieving over intense losses at the time they met. Norm's first wife had left him rather suddenly for another man, while Tia's fiancé had died suddenly from a coronary just days before their wedding. Neither wanted to experience such severe loss again. So what change in their life was significant enough to topple their entrenched symbiosis and propel them into therapy? Norm received a job promotion that required him to travel away from home two nights a week. Tia became enraged in response: she became obsessed with the belief that Norm was having an affair or squandering their money gambling when he was away from her.

When two people evolve into a symbiotic-enmeshed relationship such as Tia and Norm's, they view the maintenance of the relationship as the primary goal of their lives and will do *anything* at any cost to ensure it survives. Usually the cost comes in the form of lost individuality: personal identities become defined only through being reflected in the other's eyes. Interactions become characterized by high levels of passivity and adaptation. Symbiotic partners try to read each other's minds and do what they imagine the other wants. As these patterns repeat themselves over the years, each partner becomes less aware of his or her own thoughts and feelings; each partner's behavior becomes almost entirely reactive in nature. The symbiotic system evolves to prevent the expression of feelings, except for those that affirm or increase the unity; anxiety only emerges when an interaction or an activity precipitates a possibility of seeing the self or other as different.

Since most of the couple's interaction patterns are designed to mask the differences, it usually is unnecessary for the anxiety to be felt. Instead, the partners' prevailing behaviors continue to be designed to meet each other's needs and to be the "one and only" other person in the world who does so. Because of the underlying anxiety and the inability on the part of these individuals to establish any sense of identity, these couples often produce children who have psychosomatic, anorexic, or schizophrenic type problems (see Beavers, 1977; Minuchin, 1974; Minuchin, Rosman, & Baker, 1978).

In a session with a couple who had an anorexic daughter, the 45-year-old wife said to her 50-year-old husband: "You know, I think I would like to drive the car by myself one day soon. I don't always need for you to come along." She had never driven the car without him.

"But dear," he responded, "if you do that, I know what will happen. The car will break down on the freeway and somebody will come along and pretend to help you but instead you'll be raped. I'm sure of it—you'll be stuck on the freeway and you're going to get hurt!" Feeling frightened himself by his wife's proposed independence, the husband immediately attempted to scare his wife into believing that something catastrophic would occur if she ventured out on her own.

Another man was so threatened by the possibility of his wife acting as an individual that he responded as follows (when the therapist, Ellyn, asked him to let his wife speak for herself rather than saying "we"): "I speak for *both* of us! I always speak for both of us, and you will never address her again!" The couple had come to family therapy at Ellyn's request to discuss the possible admission of their 19-year-old daughter to a halfway house. Currently she was living in a residential treatment facility as a result of her second psychotic episode. The daughter wanted to move to the halfway house, but her father's response was so enticing that she was unable to hold onto her resolve to move away. He said: "Remember, Sarah, if you come home, I'll buy you a new car and I'll love you forever. How about that convertible you've had your eye on?" No price was too high to keep this family intact, even when the mental health of his daughter clearly was at stake.

For a couple to be diagnosed as symbiotic-enmeshed, their relationship must have remained merged beyond the initial phase of "falling in love." They must demonstrate that they have resisted differentiation in themselves and in each other or become less defined over time. The resistance will be evident to the therapist through their communication patterns, their behavioral interactions, their routine lifestyle, and in how they manipulate one another emotionally.

The merging so characteristic of these couples will be particularly evident in their verbal styles of communication. It is common for enmeshed partners to speak in terms of *we* and *us* even when they mean *I.* One woman attending a session alone carried this habit to the extreme by beginning the session with, "We want to tell you about our daughter," and ending the session with, "We want to say goodbye now." These partners do indeed believe they can talk for one another, and that talking to one of them is as good as talking to them both. It is unusual for either to ask the other what he or she wants, thinks, or feels.

The nonverbal behavior of an enmeshed couple is also designed to avoid conflict. Anger and differences of opinion or emotion are viewed as maximum threats capable of dissolving the relationship at a moment's notice. Often it takes only a look or glance to rapidly silence one another. Since the couple do not know how to negotiate differences, they become extremely sophisticated at obscuring their differences. When a therapist begins a meeting with this type of couple, he or she must learn their nonverbal language or risk missing significant transactions.

The diagnostic tools described in Chapter 2 can form the starting point for developing interventions that help symbiotic partners understand the limitations of their behavior. As is typical of the Paper Exercise, it swiftly evokes a clear pattern of interaction that is easily identified as enmeshed. Marilyn and Bill quickly revealed the extent of their enmeshment.

Bill: (begins speaking after a two-minute silence during which they each scrutinize one another) What did you choose?

Marilyn: Nothing. I couldn't think of anything. I was waiting to hear your choice.

Bill: I thought I'd let you have it. In this case, I'd rather have you take it than have you mad at me. Here, you take it *(pushes paper toward her).*

Marilyn: (pushes paper back) No. I want you to have it.

Bill: (takes paper) I guess we decided that quickly.

This Paper Exercise is illustrative of the lack of self-definition in enmeshed couples. During the long silence at the beginning, each seemed to try to read the other's thoughts. Even the minimal definition of one holding the paper seemed to create anxiety. As soon as they began speaking, Marilyn and Bill rushed to solve the problem without creating conflict.

The Diagnostic Questionnaire, which the couple completed after their first therapy session, exposed the unfolding of their enmeshment over time. Through the questionnaire, Marilyn revealed the extent of her dependency and lack of self-definition. After 17 years of marriage, she began to recognize how suffocating her relationship had become only when confronted with the necessity of answering the questions on the questionnaire (see Appendix D for her verbatim answers). Amazing as it may seem, Marilyn reported that her first disillusionment with her marriage occurred the week before her first therapy appointment, when her husband told her he did not love her anymore. Up until that time, she had viewed her marriage as perfect. Now, confronted with the devastating reality that her "marriage made in heaven" might be in serious trouble, Marilyn had agreed to come in for therapy.

This couple's symbiosis had been thorough and all-encompassing. When Bill wanted to engage in a weekend activity without her, Marilyn would beg him to go somewhere with her instead. She missed him whenever he wasn't with her, and wasn't comfortable doing any fun activities away from him. If she wanted to watch TV, she urged him to bring his book and sit on the couch with her while she watched TV. After 17 years of total togetherness, this was the first time she had ever considered the possibility that, "My ideas of so much togetherness are probably wrong—I see how suffocating I have been."

THERAPEUTIC TREATMENT OF THE SYMBIOTIC-ENMESHED COUPLE

Long-Term Enmeshed Couples

Doing therapy with long-term symbiotic-enmeshed couples is considerably more difficult than working with enmeshed couples who request therapy early in their relationship. Long-term symbiotic-enmeshed couples rarely present themselves requesting couples therapy. It is much more common for them to arrive with a severely symptomatic child, or with depression in one partner who appears to be the identified patient. Because of the severity of the disturbance in the family and the level of fear in the couple, we usually begin by addressing the symptom. In doing so we align with the couple, even to the extent of accepting their definition of the problem. Initially confronting them with their dysfunction or becoming embroiled in a power struggle with the couple usually proves fruitless. We begin with the family and accept their definition of symptom-alleviation as the targeted goal. This results in establishing treatment contracts that focus, for example, on treating the anorexic or psychosomatic child, alleviating the depression, or creating more closeness in the family as a whole. While we remain cognizant of our longer-term goals of enhancing and facilitating differentiation in the couple, we know this cannot be accomplished without our first addressing the symptom and establishing an alliance between ourselves and the couple. We want to join with them rather than threaten them, and in so doing, provide a support system that allows them to loosen their grip on one another as they experience a new source of support from the "outside."

Once we are able to shift from the family to the couple, effective therapy with these couples requires intervening in a way that promotes movement into the differentiation stage for each partner. Ironically, this involves increasing the couple's bonding first before facilitating differentiation. To do this we must be adept at interrupting the symbiotic transactions and facilitating personal responsibility. Note how these methods unfold with the O'Neill family.

Case example: The O'Neill family

First family therapy session with the O'Neills. The O'Neills (Dr. Joe O'Neill, the father; his wife, Lillian; Tina, their anorexic daughter; and Sarah, their other daughter) arrived in Ellyn's office looking frightened and doubtful. Dr. Joe began the session with, "We're here because Dr. Jones said you were the one who could help us. I've never believed in psychotherapy, but I'll hear what you have to say."

Ellyn: (refusing to be set up in a passive-symbiotic position) With what might you want my help?

Dr. Joe: (again, it was he who responded) Tina is anorexic. She's been in the hospital for the past six weeks. We want her to get better! We want her to start eating and we want her to see how she is hurting herself.

Ellyn: And how is Tina's anorexia hurting each of you?

Dr. Joe: We worry about her every day. My wife and I drive to see her five times a week, or we talk to her on the phone in between. We talk a lot about her. We don't seem to be able to get her out of our minds. We just don't know what to do.

Sarah: I used to like having Tina spend time with my friends, but now I'm embarrassed. She looks like a scarecrow, even like a boy! She also looks much younger than she is. I don't really like to take her with me to parties or to hang out with my friends.

Ellyn: Lillian, what about you?

Lillian: Dr. Joe said it all.

Ellyn: And, Tina, what about you?

Tina: I'm fine, I'm doing great. I've put on 10 pounds since I've been in the hospital, and I'm fine. I'm not worried about myself anymore.

The remainder of this first session was used to learn more about the family. Most of the information was provided by Dr. Joe, who answered for the family:

Dr. Joe: We've been married for 28 years [Dr. Joe is 55; Lillian is 50]. I met Lillian just as I was finishing medical school and about to start my surgical residency. She was a nurse on the last unit where I worked. I liked the way she looked. She came from a good family, and I knew the time was right for me to get married. We married quickly, and Lillian helped support us while I finished my residency. As soon as I was in private practice, we decided to have a family, and before long, Sarah was born. Three years later, Tina, whom we hoped would be a boy, came along. After Tina's birth, Lillian was hospitalized for about six weeks with postpartum depression. I realized then that she was not as strong as I had first thought: she needed me, and I would need to take better care of her. It felt good for me to be needed, and between my patients, my wife, and my daughters, I was very satisfied with my life.

During the years Lillian spent at home raising her two daughters, she also structured her life around her husband. She joined the hospital guild and the ladies auxiliary and supported her husband's career whenever possible. Together, they worked for the betterment of his career and the betterment of their family. They moved several times, ending up in their present home when Sarah was 13 and Tina was 10. Their continual experience of uprooting the family and moving made it clear to them that establishing outside friendships was pointless; it only resulted in the inevitable pain of separation when it came time for the next move. They had therefore begun to rely almost totally on each other and the two children. Except for occasional visits with relatives, their social life came to a standstill.

The first family trauma since Lillian's severe bout with postpartum depression occurred when Tina was 13 and Sarah 16. Sarah was raped by boys "from the wrong side of the tracks" in her high school class. Tina was never directly told about the incident, but she could sense the shock and distress permeating the emotional atmosphere of the family. She knew that something horrible having to do with boys had happened. She began to have nightmares, and for a period of time she became fearful of even going out of the house. Her most recurrent nightmare was of being stabbed.

At this point Sarah was sent off to boarding school and would come home only on weekends. Things at home settled down once again, and Tina, Dr. Joe, and Lillian engaged in their life together without much contact with the outside world. When Sarah returned home for weekends, she and her father would go to baseball games or go golfing; Tina would stay home and keep her mother company.

As time progressed and this family routine continued, Lillian began to show signs of chronic depression, and Tina's eating habits deteriorated. By the time Tina was 16 years old, she was maintaining her weight at about 85 pounds. Meanwhile Lillian's depression had steadily worsened, and around the time of Tina's 16th birthday she had a psychotic episode and was hospitalized and eventually treated with electroshock therapy. This dismal turn of events left Tina with a feeling that marriage, sex, and femaleness were all dangerous and resulted in either violence or psychosis. She believed her best bet in life was to stay home, look after her mother, appear as boylike as possible for her father, and hope that she would eventually get some recognition from him.

Meanwhile, the dependency between Dr. Joe and Lillian increased dramatically. Lillian stopped driving and would not even shop for her own clothes without her husband. His daily routine evolved into spending 8 to 10 hours at the hospital and then providing for his wife's physical care. Most evenings he would take her out to dinner so that she would not need to cook. During the afterschool hours, he relied on Tina to check on her mother and make sure that her depression was not getting out of hand. Tina's anorexia remained constant at about 85 pounds until she left home at the age of 19 to attend college. Rapidly, she lost another 10 pounds and was soon hospitalized.

This initial two-hour session ended with an agreement among the family members to spend six weeks in family therapy, with a possible renewal of another six weeks if they believed progress was being made on Tina's anorexic condition. They also agreed that during the course of therapy, neither parent would threaten divorce or separation. "No-suicide contracts" were also made with each member of the family.

Second family therapy session. Ellyn began the second session by asking each member of the family to portray the family relationships through a family sculpture. With this technique, each member takes a turn in arranging and positioning everyone in a kind of tableau that epitomizes how the family is experienced by that member. While all the sculptures were different, each in one way or another depicted Lillian in an invalid role, with Dr. Joe as the kindly caretaker. Tina's picture was perhaps the most poignant. She seated her father in a large, comfortable chair, holding her mother on his lap. Standing next to him and holding his hand was Sarah, making eye contact and smiling warmly at her father. Tina seated herself on the floor at her mother's feet, looking up fearfully at her mother, with arms open, pleading, as if she wanted her mother to do something.

This session concluded with both daughters talking about how they worried about their mother. Lillian was reluctant to talk about the effect of her illness on either herself or her daughters, and she denied the impact her depression might be having on other family members.

Tina's suicide attempt. Therapy with the O'Neill family took a dramatic turn between the second and third sessions. Tina, while on a pass from the hospital, made a serious suicide attempt. She called the hospital, was picked up by the police, and was readmitted through the emergency room. She came close to dying and seriously scared both herself and the other members of the family. The next few sessions focused on Tina's suicide attempt, the meaning of it, and the effect it had on each of the family members.

Sarah was grief-stricken. With deep, heartfelt sobs, she told Tina that she wanted her to stay alive. She wanted to be her friend; she wanted to be close to her; but she did not always want to be afraid that the next time she turned around, Tina would be dead.

Dr. Joe also expressed his love for his daughter: "Tina, I love you. I know we've never been as close as Sarah and I have. I know that I never showed interest in your activities, that I was disappointed that you weren't a boy. But even with all that, I do love you, and I want you to stay alive. I want you to find a way to be part of the family and for you and me to find another way to be together."

Tina was then asked to resculpt the family, finding a different position for herself. She tried to do this but became immobilized saying, "I can't find a new place for myself until something happens to my mother. I'm afraid if I change, my parents will divorce. If I leave home, my mother will be lonely and my father won't have anyone to look after my mother. Maybe my mother will die. Also, Sarah and Dad are so tight that I don't think they'll let me in." Ellyn then told Tina to make a request of her mother. Instead, she spontaneously addressed her mother.

Tina: Mother, I want you to *do something*. I want you to stop sitting around and just *do something*. Even making me clean up my room would be better than sitting there staring into space and doing nothing. I want you to get better!

Couples therapy begins. After six two-hour family sessions, Ellyn then asked Lillian and Joe to come in for one session as a couple. She began the session by asking, "How helpless is Lillian, really?"

Dr. Joe: Very! She used to be a vital woman, but now she is dour, critical, and unable to do much to fend for herself.

Lillian: (suddenly angry) I'm not as helpless as he or Tina thinks! I'm angry! I'm just plain angry, that's what I am. I haven't wanted to say so, but I'm sick of this whole family. I've given up myself to be Joe's patient. I moved with him, gave up my friends, my social life, and finally my independence. I always thought if I got angry, he'd leave me, and then I'd have nothing. Now, in the last few years, I've even given up sex. I feel like a little girl living in a doctor's office. I hate it, and right now I hate you *(addressing Joe)*!

Dr. Joe: Calm down, dear. You don't know what you're saying. You'll be sorry later, I know. Did you take your medication today?

Ellyn: Joe, I think Lillian means what she's saying. Will you listen to her and at the same time do your best not to interpret what she is saying as meaning that you've been bad?

Lillian: I've said enough. I'm just angry and tired of this life, the way I've been leading it.

Ellyn: Last week, Tina asked you for a change. Now you seem to be saying that you, too, are ready for a change.

Lillian: You bet! I'd like to have our sexual relationship back again.

The session terminated with a reaffirmation of the agreement that neither partner would threaten divorce or separation; and with some new agreements, including a decision to work on reestablishing their sexual relationship, and for Lillian to discuss with her physician a possible reduction in her antidepressant medication.

What followed with Joe and Lillian was a series of sessions that integrated personal history and family-of-origin work with a modified form of sex therapy. Both wanted to resume their sexual relationship, and both reported having had a very active, satisfying sexual past with one another. At the present time, each was fearful of initiating, and each anticipated rejection from the other. They began bridging this problem by having each initiate brief periods of physical intimacy without it leading to sexual intercourse. Simultaneously, we reviewed the history that led them to dissolve into a doctor-patient relationship with one another.

Joe described his childhood as very cold and bleak. He had grown up in the city slums and spent most of his childhood in a cold, unheated bedroom in the attic of the house. He remembered lying in bed shivering on many winter nights and saying to himself, "This family doesn't need me. When I grow up, I'll find people who need me. I'll make myself matter." It was out of this decision that he positioned himself as a rescuer and established both a professional and a family life in which he was desperately needed.

Lillian, on the other hand, was an adopted child in a wealthy family. She felt unwanted, first of all, by the parents who gave her up for adoption, and, second, by the family into which she was adopted. Soon after she had been adopted, her adoptive mother became pregnant and Lillian was "replaced" by another girl, a natural child. From the time she was two years of age, she felt unwanted by her adoptive family. She remembered saying to herself as a little girl, "Someday I'll find someone who wants me." With Joe, she felt secure and wanted. Early on, she recognized that he thrived on her needing him. Indeed, far from scaring him, her dependency seemed to increase his attentiveness to her. Over time, she became caught in a vicious circle in which she placed herself in a progressively needier position in relation to her husband. Her identity and self-confidence dwindled commensurately.

As Lillian gradually connected her past experiences with her present situation, she began expressing her own wants and desires to Joe. By the time they terminated therapy, she had reduced her antidepressant medication, had begun driving again, had resumed her work with the hospital auxiliary, and was contemplating returning to school to reestablish her nursing license. Joe, with his growing understanding about his own inner influences from his childhood experience, began moving out of the caretaker position. He realized that since he could continue this role appropriately with his patients, he did not need to occupy the same role with his wife and daughters. He began to set more limits with Tina, and also to view his wife as a companion rather than an invalid. At the end of another two months of therapy, he and Lillian had successfully resumed their sexual relationship to a level where it was mutually satisfying. The warmth and reconnection they experienced in the bedroom allowed them to begin to differentiate from their long-established, symbiotic past.

Family therapy resumes. After three months of couples therapy, family therapy was resumed with the primary goal of helping Tina to leave home. She had gained weight in the hospital (she checked out weighing 98 pounds) and was once again living at home. Lillian and Joe realigned themselves as her parents. They set clear goals for her to return to college, agreeing to aid her financially with both school and therapy expenses as long as she kept her grades above a C level. Before Tina left for school, her father started treating her more like a daughter and even went with her to a rock concert.

In one of the final family sessions, Tina was told the truth about

Sarah having been raped and the family's incapacity to deal with the trauma at that time. Tina's sympathy for Sarah was useful in helping the two of them feel closer to one another. Lillian also became effectively angry at Tina in one of these sessions and told her, "I'm angry you're letting your life pass by. I've done too much of that. I want you to figure out what you want to do and do it. Worst of all, do not stay home and take care of me. I'm going to be all right. I'm not going to kill myself. I'm not going to lose your father. I'm going to do now what I should have done years ago. *I'm going to find my way, and it's time for you to find yours!"*

In the final session, they were asked to do another family picture — this time with all of them working on it together until they could agree on an acceptable family portrait. They ended with Joe and Lillian arm-in-arm, each looking off in their own directions and waving to Sarah and Tina, who were off in two different corners of the room, each completing their college education. A one-year follow-up found Tina to be well involved in a college program in another state, where she was continuing in group therapy to work on her issues of dating and sexuality.

Case example: Gail and Webster

Not all long-term enmeshed couples are able to move as quickly or as far as Lillian and Dr. Joe. Gail, 40, and Webster, 50, began couples therapy after Gail was hospitalized in an acutely suicidal state. Gail became severely depressed four months after the birth of her third child. She had been hoping to return to work after her first two children and now resented the need to stay home once again. Since she was unable to express these feelings or to express her desire to work, she became increasingly depressed.

During her hospitalization, she did not respond to antidepressant medication or individual therapy. The hospital staff referred her for couples therapy to a psychiatrist who had trained with us. The therapist began the work by asking Gail to make a weekly-renewable, no-suicide contract.

The psychiatrist decided to have Gail attend group therapy as well as couples therapy. The group setting was used as a specific vehicle for resolving Gail's personal issues relevant to her depression. The couples therapy initially was used to manage decisions about care of the children.

The group therapy time for Gail alone revealed her desire to work and her fear of upsetting Webster. She believed Webster also wanted her to remain at home. As Gail began to bring these awarenesses from her group therapy into the couples work, Webster became increasingly frightened. He stopped allowing his wife to drive to the sessions alone and insisted on taking time away from his job to escort her. Later, when the group had a weekend workshop, he objected so strenuously that Gail was reluctant to assert herself even though she wished to attend. The more desire for independence Gail expressed, the more Webster's dependence surfaced. He began to gain weight and to drink. Over time, Gail recognized that his behavior was designed to keep her at home. In couples therapy, she identified how she was continuing to stay depressed in order not to upset her husband while simultaneously keeping Webster committed to attending treatment. As Gail became clearer about her motives, she decided to find baby-sitting and return to work. She was able to relinquish her depression, allowing more of the focus of the couples therapy to shift to Webster. Webster dealt briefly with issues related to his own physical health and made sporadic improvements in this area. However, he decided to discontinue the couples therapy after Gail started working.

A two-year follow-up showed no recurrence in Gail's depression and Webster begrudgingly tolerating his wife's working away from home. However, this couple remained caught in a predominantly symbiotic relationship due primarily to the lack of differentiation of both partners from their families of origin. Gail's obvious psychiatric symptoms of severe depression initially hid her husband's enormous dependence on her. This dependency, while mildly modified, continued to block the partners from moving clearly beyond the symbiotic stage into an active mutual differentiation process.

Short-Term Enmeshed Couples

Lillian and Joe, and Gail and Webster, are both representative of couples who have been enmeshed for long periods of time. Although in the long-term symbiotic-enmeshed couple, the merging is ego-syntonic and the attachment provides a means for each person to know himself or herself, this extreme is not found in short-term enmeshed couples.

Short-term enmeshed couples who come for therapy usually enjoy the dependency and caretaking they provide for one another, but they are uncomfortable with the amount of togetherness and uniformity of ideas required to maintain the closeness. It is usually much easier to move short-term enmeshed couples into the differentiation stage because their primary difficulty is fear of losing the relationship if the conflict surfaces. Once they feel assured that each of them is committed to seeing whether the differences are resolvable, they no longer hold on so tenaciously to the symbiotic stage.

Case example: Vera and Mark

Vera and Mark are an example of a short-term enmeshed couple who came to therapy after being married for only one year. The presenting problem was diminished sexual involvement with one another, and Vera's withdrawal from Mark. At the beginning of their relationship, Vera reported having tried to describe what it was she liked sexually, because what pleased her was so different from what pleased Mark. Initially, Mark experienced her description as critical and controlling and he responded angrily. This led Vera to feel afraid and withdraw.

In therapy, Ellyn helped Vera and Mark to talk openly about their sexual differences. At first, they were only able to talk about these differences in the office because they were so frightened that talking about them at home would lead to a catastrophic conclusion. Indeed, when they would plan time at home to talk to one another about sex, something would always interfere! This led to an awareness about how frightened each of them was to encounter conflict.

In exploring Vera's childhood experiences, it became clear that Vera was frightened to raise any of her differences with Mark because she had grown up with parents who were extremely volatile. Watching their fighting led her to vow to herself as a child that she would not repeat the same destructive behavior in her own marriage. In therapy Mark gradually came to appreciate the fact that she was actually wanting to communicate with him rather than control him. Mark, on the other hand, had grown up in a family where conflict was taboo. Although his parents were not emotionally close, they never discussed anything difficult or substantive in his presence. Vera and Mark reinforced each other's fears and strong desires to shy away from problems. Once this problem was recognized, Ellyn spent time helping them reframe the value of conflict within a relationship. She also helped the couple establish an agreement that if they did not solve initial conflicts within 30 minutes, these would be put aside until their next therapy session.

To desensitize them initially to disagreement, Ellyn set up some playful exchanges in the office. Vera was asked to say no, while Mark simultaneously said yes. Ellyn asked them alternately to whisper, to yell, and to talk in a normal voice tone, while only using their allotted one word. During the first attempt to complete this exercise, Vera dissolved in tears saying the tension was too much for her. However, by proceeding slowly, with gentle support, she was able to complete the exercise. By the next session, she was able to have fun being assertively loud with Mark. They then progressed to one partner saying "I will" and the other partner saying "I won't," while they experimented with different physical space distances between them. Soon they enjoyed this banter and said that Ellyn's comfort with disagreement helped them tame their fears.

After eight sessions spent on conflict, they decided to resume discussions about sexuality. They agreed to spend one period of time at home each week where only one of them would be responsible for deciding what they would do sexually. This plan was successful in helping them reestablish their sexual relationship. They remained in couples therapy for another six months, during which time they established more open communication, built a stronger foundation for managing disagreement, clarified how they wanted their marriage to differ from those of their parents, and developed a sexual relationship that was mutually gratifying.

Vera and Mark are typical of short-term enmeshed couples, not so much in the content of their problem but in the fear that each of them experienced about their potential differences. One main distinction between short-term and long-term symbiotic-enmeshed couples is that the former are far easier to treat. They recognize that there is a problem and feel uncomfortable, even if they are unable to verbalize exactly what the problem is. Long-term enmeshed couples, by contrast, find their methods of relating to be ego-syntonic. For many years, their patterns of adult interaction and their unresolved childhood issues have been reinforced, compounded, and exacerbated, making it an extremely difficult system to penetrate.

CHAPTER 5

The Symbiotic-Symbiotic Couple: Hostile-Dependent Type

"I can't live with you and I can't live without you"

Who could ever forget the experience of watching Elizabeth Taylor and Richard Burton's film rendition of Edward Albee's play, *Who's Afraid of Virginia Wolfe?* The viewer leaves the movie exhausted from the battering that never stops and sickened by the violent intimacy that somehow cleaves one character to the other.

Albee's play provides a dramatic portrayal of the symbiotic hostile-dependent couple. These couples are easy to identify when they first enter a therapist's office. Their voices and body movements communicate ongoing anger, bitterness, and blame. Often, even the usual social amenities of exchanging greetings and getting comfortably seated are foregone in favor of bickering. In the case of one couple, the husband walked through the door first, saying over his shoulder, "In 10 years of marriage we haven't been able to agree on one thing!" To this the wife quickly retorted as she bustled in after him, "It's been 11 years!"

This type of hostile, competitive, escalating transaction is typical of these couples. The saying, "I can't live with you and I can't live without you" summarizes the dilemma faced by couples stuck in this stage of development: it is impossible to be close and it is equally impossible to move away. Behaviorists describe these couples as being "conflict-habituated." Indeed they are!

DESCRIPTION AND DIAGNOSIS OF THE SYMBIOTIC HOSTILE-DEPENDENT COUPLE

In this kind of partnership, each clings to the fantasy that the partner is finally *the one and only person* who can make up for everything their parents and family did not provide for them as children. Over time, however, reality sets in and it becomes clear that neither partner is the all-gratifying need-fulfiller. As the betrayal of the fantasy becomes more pronounced, the anger in each person increases. It is common for this pattern to emerge in couples in which one or both partners are borderline or narcissistic. In their own childhoods, the symbiotic stage was either insufficient or prematurely lost. A borderline individual often starts out idealizing his or her partner and looking to the partner to fill unmet symbiotic needs. However, the "perfect partner" does not stay perfect for long. What began as clinging may rapidly turn into rageful, acting-out behavior. The narcissistic individual becomes angry for other reasons. The narcissist is usually totally other-oriented, being dependent on the partner to build up his self-esteem. Since it is impossible for that to occur on an ongoing daily basis, he becomes angry and despairing when the partner does not come through. He is so unable to see the partner as a separate individual that he will not want the partner to have her own interests or activities. These only interfere with the partner's availability and come into direct competition with the need to be bolstered and glorified. The narcissistic partner will denigrate and berate the spouse for not providing perfect mirroring or move on quickly to find a more perfect partner.

The pattern seen in hostile-dependent relationships is a complex one in which contradictory expectations and beliefs coexist. On the one hand, each believes the partner should provide total nurturance; on the other hand, each believes he or she does not deserve to receive such nurturance. So, ironically, partners expect nurturance, demand nurturance, and yet also push it away when it is offered. Compounding this double-binding pattern is the problem of pronounced separation anxiety, which is adamantly denied; there is a refusal to show much vulnerability or to admit need of any kind. The narcissistic and borderline individuals described above typically establish hostile-dependent relationships in which they come to view their partner as all bad. Previous positive interactions are forgotten and each begins to view the other as more and more withholding, which in turn justifies their own competitive, childlike behavior.

Confrontations, even small ones, are perceived as global attacks. Quick escalations occur once arguments have arisen. It is common for each transaction to spiral toward a more extreme position than the previous one; it is not uncommon for it to culminate in physical violence. Any kind of positive response given by one partner is often seen as manipulative by the other, and thus is not effective in developing trust or support within the relationship. When one partner responds empathically to the other, it is common to hear a retort of, "Why couldn't you have done that sooner?" Instead of accepting positive support when it is given, it is rudely rejected. Each sees himself or herself as being helpless, victimized, and at the mercy of the other, who is all-powerful.

In the hostile-dependent couple, each partner experiences the urgency of his or her own needs and believes he or she should take precedence over any discomfort felt by the other. Both are unable to appreciate the impact of their behavior on each other; instead, the primary focus stays on "what *you* are doing to *me*." In the absence of any genuine giving between partners, feelings of desperation increase. Both individuals have a poorly developed sense of self and, therefore, are unable to tolerate criticism. Even the most constructive criticism cannot be successfully internalized and instead will activate a defensive threat in the partner, such as, "I don't like you and I will leave you!" Insight into this pattern rarely leads to behavioral change.

Communication patterns for the hostile-dependent couple are confusing and destructive. She will intend to say *a-b-c* but actually end up expressing *h-i-j*. He hears *m-n-o* and then responds with *x-y-z*. It feels as if both have walked willingly into a swamp, out of which there is no exit. Adding to the confusion is the fact that partners typically project their own feelings and assumptions onto each other and rarely confirm the validity of the assumptions that are made. Since they also have extremely limited capacities for negotiation, a fight rarely proceeds to a point of closure and resolution. During an argument they have an enormous capacity to stack related and unrelated problems on top of each other, until they all become grist for the mill in future fights as well.

When a hostile-dependent symbiotic couple executes the Paper Exercise, conflict is exaggerated rather than obscured, as it is with the symbiotic-enmeshed couple. It is common to hear angry, aggressive, and escalating transactions without any trace of negotiation, discussion, or give-and-take. One example is the "Here, I want it"–"No, I want it" sequence. In the example that follows, the husband escalates his needs over his wife's by proclaiming, "It's fundamentally more important to me than it is to you!" This is said with no knowledge of what the wife has chosen, or without letting her know what the paper means to him. The capacity for self-definition in these couples is extremely limited, and genuine giving is nonexistent. The other is not viewed as a separate person with his or her own wants and feelings; instead each is treated as an object and seen as an enemy to fight against. Unlike the symbiotic-enmeshed couple, boundaries for the hostile-dependent couple are often rigidly defended to avoid merging and engulfment. Note these characteristics in the following example:

Florence: I want it.

Michael: It's fundamentally more important to me than it is to you.

Florence: No it's not. I'm taking it. *(She grabs the paper.)*

Michael: I'm pissed *(said in an angry voice).*

Florence: Well, you had your chance.

Michael: Yes, to be rude and insensitive!

Florence: You just have to take care of yourself. I did! I guess we just see things differently.

In this Paper Exercise, Florence and Michael replayed exactly how their relationship evolved to the hostile-dependent position. After one year of marriage, Florence became pregnant. She was 19 and did not want to have the child. Michael said he would leave her if she had an abortion. So she made a decision to stay and have the child and establish a tight symbiosis with her son from which Michael was continually excluded.

In another example, we are back with Edna and Steve (see Chapter 1, p. 1), who vividly demonstrate how their aggression is immediately engaged. Ellyn gives directions for the Paper Exercise to Edna and Steve. Without saying anything, Steve yanks the paper from Edna.

Edna: I didn't have a good hold on it!

Steve: (laughs) I had a good grasp. It's mine now, but I'll give you another chance *(hands back the paper).*

Edna: You'll probably get it again. I'm a giver. I give, give, give because that's what my mother taught me *(said in an angry tone)*. What I really want to do is rip it out of your hands and stuff it down your throat! *(Both pull and the paper rips.)*

Steve: How dare you take it from me!

Edna: I don't think either of us was going to give up. If I give like my mother, I get nothing. Part of this seems better than nothing.

Steve: With us, somebody has to win and somebody has to lose.

Ellyn: Is this symbolic of how you interact?

Steve: This is just about how it always is.

Edna: Yes, we pull at each other. We're never a team grouping together. Somebody always gets the last word, but we're both usually angry!

Why, then, is the hostile-dependent couple considered *symbiotic?* The clear lack of self-differentiation in both partners, together with an extreme emotional dependency that is reciprocally demanded of individuals who cannot possibly provide what is needed or wanted, creates a volatile, hermetic symbiosis. Constant pressure is placed on partners to meet unrealistic needs. Fights often center on, "You're not meeting my needs!" Also, it is rare for either partner to have separate friends with whom time alone is spent. Dependency is so intense that each partner is likely to get angry when asked to put into words what is desired from the other. Each partner is presumed to be so similar to the other that any verbal expression of wants should be unnecessary. Mind reading is expected: "If he really loved me, he would know what I wanted!"

Maintaining a boundary around one's own emotions is almost impossible in a hostile-dependent relationship; each is unable to stay out of the "orbit" of the other's feelings. As soon as one partner expresses a feeling, the other feels blamed for it and conflict is ignited. Feelings are so diffuse that often the partners both will feel the same feeling at the same time. One client explained to Pete that she could not be empathic when her husband was sad, because she too would feel sad. It was easier for her to try to cut off his sadness than to have her own sadness elicited. When one partner competes to get his desires realized by acting childlike, usually the other joins in by acting even younger and more demanding and soon both are squabbling like two two-year-olds in a sandbox.

The lack of self-differentiation in a hostile-dependent relationship makes it extremely difficult for partners to identify and articulate what each wants, thinks, and feels. As a result, they are unable to represent themselves in a whole, assertive way. This, along with the ease of regression, leads to tremendous fear of both abandonment and engulfment by one another. Conflict and aggression are then used to maintain distance, while clinging and dependency actually increase.

THERAPEUTIC TREATMENT OF THE SYMBIOTIC HOSTILE-DEPENDENT COUPLE

Partners in a hostile-dependent relationship *hope* for a great deal but actually *expect* very little. They will talk about making changes in themselves or in the relationship that require enormous leaps in their maturity level. Yet inwardly they despair of ever reaching such lofty goals. Often, as a therapist working with these couples, you may feel overwhelmed by how and where to intervene. If you discuss the *content* of the problems the partners bring in, then you feel as if you are continually running behind; the couple can generate more problems than can possibly be handled, even if they were seen three times a week! Yet each problem appears to be critical and important. If as the therapist, you step back, away from the content, and help the couple look at their own system by giving them penetrating insights and brilliant observations about their process, your efforts are frequently met with apathy or a "So what?" attitude. The common response is, "All we do is talk about our problems, but we don't seem to make any actual progress." Is couples therapy relevant then for these couples? How does a therapist conceptualize realistic goals?

In doing couples therapy with hostile-dependent couples, our major goal is to develop self-awareness and to create the capacity in each individual to accept and support the emerging self of the partner. This is no easy task! To describe our approach, we will examine interventions that support this goal. Initially, we intervene actively to contain the primary defenses of distancing and hostility that are used by the couple. These interventions enable the therapist to take charge, to provide necessary limits for therapy to proceed, and to control the interaction in the room. Then, in order to lead the couple out of the hostile-dependent quagmire, we help the couple come to understand that an intimate relationship provides a profound opportunity to know oneself and to heal some of the wounds of childhood. This can only occur when empathy is developed and each can rely on the other in times of distress. As therapy proceeds, each learns to be more authentic with himself or herself and to support the authenticity that emerges in the other.

Containing the hostility: The ups and downs of Edna and Steve

We now return to Edna and Steve to illustrate the various interventions that can be used to solidify the beginning stages of therapy. If you will recall from Chapter 1 on the developmental model, Edna and Steve presented for therapy two years into their relationship. By that point, their interaction had deteriorated to childlike, hostile-aggressive behavior, epitomized by spitting and throwing things at one another.

After the two initial sessions in which we took the developmental history and did the Paper Exercise, we moved on to establishing the treatment contract with Edna and Steve. We began the third session by describing to them how their relationship was characterized by hostility and overdependence. We expressed our belief that as long as these characteristics continued, the relationship would be hurtful and debilitating. We then suggested the following three goals:

1. Replacing the hostility with more support for one another.
2. Changing the view of one another as "bad" to a more integrated view in which they were no longer expecting unconditional love from the other.
3. Developing outside friendships and activities.

They agreed with this contract and set up 12 weekly sessions with us, with an agreement to evaluate at the end of the three months.

Because of the primitive behavior evidenced in this couple, we actively structured the therapy during the beginning stages. We established limits on their behavior that would be necessary for us to conduct the therapy. We required that each of them agree to come on time to all of the sessions, and that they would not leave the room or throw things at each other while in the room. We also established an agreement that neither of them threaten to end therapy before the end of the 12 weeks.

Next we moved on to looking at how they could establish some limits on their aggression at home. We used our Limits exercise. In this exercise, partners are asked to go home and complete the following four statements:

1. The following behaviors are acceptable for me to use during a fight:
2. The following behaviors are acceptable for you to use during a fight:
3. The following behaviors are unacceptable for me to use during a fight:
4. The following behaviors are unacceptable for you to use during a fight:

After each partner fills out this questionnaire carefully and thoughtfully, we then negotiate agreements in the following session. Of course, partners are asked to make only agreements they believe they will be able to keep. If they are unable to agree to a particular point asked for by the spouse, then we look for alternatives that can be substituted so that the contract remains viable for both partners and has a higher probability of success. Although these agreements are not always successful, they do provide a safer and more predictable structure to the fighting that occurs when anger erupts at home. When Edna and Steve had completed this exercise, they had established the following agreements:

1. *Acceptable behaviors for Edna:*
   — Yelling
   — Stating what was wrong
   — Asking Steve to do something differently
   — Throwing any of her possessions against the wall in the backyard
   — Slamming doors

2. *Unacceptable behaviors for Edna:*
   —Driving away from the house in an angry rage
   —Hitting, scratching, spitting, biting Steve
   —Leaving suddenly during a fight without saying when she would return to finish it
   —Refusing to finish a fight
3. *Acceptable behaviors for Steve:*
   —Raising his voice
   —Demanding Edna listen to him: that now he has something important to say
   —Requesting a specific time for problem resolution
4. *Unacceptable behaviors for Steve:*
   —Leaving dirty dishes anywhere in the bedroom or living room
   —Spitting
   —Breaking any of Edna's possessions
   —Throwing things at Edna
   —Hitting or threatening physical violence
   —Leaving the house unexpectedly during a fight

During the following month of therapy, Edna and Steve were put in charge of choosing the topic for alternating sessions. One major limitation was placed on their freedom of choice: they were not permitted to discuss any of the fights from the previous week or any past unresolved disagreements. Instead, for this month, each would initiate discussions on what they *wanted* in order to make the relationship feel more positive. From these sessions they agreed to spend two nights a week together, Wednesdays and Saturdays, doing fun or special things as a couple. Saturday night was designated as Edna's night to choose what they would do, while Wednesday night became Steve's arena.

Steve and Edna later developed a plan for a camping trip with another couple. With our help in discussing the plans for this weekend, Edna was able to describe what it was she wanted Steve to contribute to make the weekend a success. Because of these efforts, they were able to go on the camping trip without leaving the house angry, and to spend an entire weekend together enjoying one another's company:

Edna: That was the best time we've had together in almost two years. I liked seeing you build the fire and cook the steaks and work together with Jack. I liked not having all the responsibility for everything connected to the trip.

Steve: It was great for me, too. The pressure was off. I wasn't looking over my shoulder for you to blame me or boss me around every other minute. I liked walking with you by the lake at sunset, and then going back and making dinner for the four of us. It was great that we could have a special time again.

At this point in the therapy, we continued to reinforce Edna and Steve's efforts to create and sustain positive interactions at home. We also continued to disallow any discussions in the office of specific fights. In addition, we moved on to examining how each of them perpetuated the view of the other as bad and withholding. We focused on Edna's projective blaming.

Pete: (to Edna) What would happen if you gave up your anger and stopped blaming Steve?

Edna: I don't know, I'm used to enduring a lot. It's easy.

Ellyn: And you are used to being angry—you even like it!

Edna: Yes, you're right. I don't know what it is like to be otherwise. Maybe if I did, I would like it. But if you've never known anything else, what is your incentive for change?

Ellyn: What do you get from blaming?

Edna: I get to invest everything in us. I can stay dependent on Steve changing. I don't have to feel threatened about me changing. I'd rather blame than get up and act.

Pete: So, a core question for you is what would happen if you stopped blaming Steve?

Edna: (smiles) I'd finally have to do something about me rather than lash out and blame him.

Edna then agreed to begin doing something for herself, although she voiced her fear that this would end in her discovering she no longer needed Steve.

With Steve, we focused on his fear that Edna would leave him, just as his mother had. In one session he said, "I give her lots of reasons to kick me out so that if she leaves me, I'll know I had some control over it and that it's not me that she hates." For the first time he was able to talk about how frightened he was when his mother left him at the age of three, and how he then became the target of his alcoholic father's rage and blame. By grieving the loss of his mother, he was able to see Edna in a different light. Here she was, coming with him to therapy, saying she wanted to stay with him, hoping to make their relationship warm and long-lasting.

As this initial phase of therapy drew to a close, we established agreements with each of them that they would participate separately in outside activities. Edna chose folkdancing, and Steve joined a bowling league.

In beginning the therapy with Edna and Steve, our emphasis was on containing the conflict that was generated so often between them. To succeed in helping them to gain control over their hostilities, we utilized many of the conflict–containment interventions described in the following summary. These interventions are specific and often highly structured. They involve the therapist being very active and establishing clear control over the session.

General Principles for Intervention

1. *Diffuse conflict as quickly as possible.* Hostile-dependent couples are expert fighters. They will continue fighting at home. In sessions, neither anger nor increased anxiety are useful. Moments of heightened intensity or emotionality are not helpful. The therapist must intervene rapidly to maintain calm. Since anger is easily expressed, it is important for the couple to learn how to respond differently to the anger that in the past has invariably escalated into fighting.

For example, Tim said, "Liz always exaggerates!" Before Liz could respond with her sarcastic rebuff, Pete said, "Well, then, every time Liz tells me you're changing in a positive way, I can expect to believe her *by half!*" Tim was able to laugh at himself when presented with this reframing of the exchange. Through this and other similar interventions, Tim began to develop a sense of humor about the ways in which he had instigated some of their fights. It is important that these interventions are communicated repetitiously with respect — and without the hint of sarcasm that can easily creep into humor. Liz, too, learned from these interactions and over time was able to ignore the bait.

2. *Establish limits and behavioral agreements about fights.* It is important early in therapy to help the couple set appropriate limits and ground rules on their fights at home (as we did with Edna and Steve), such as "no violence," "no threats of divorce," "no leaving the house in the middle of a fight," and "no suicide or homicide threats." As part of the initial treatment contract, have the couple agree to come for a specific number of sessions (8 to 10) without threatening divorce. In addition, the marriage becomes inadmissible as a subject to fight about during the initial phase of therapy. Serious discussion about separation or divorce may take place in a session, but not at a moment of reactivity to a daily fight. Define acceptable and unacceptable names to use during a fight, and define how to end a fight. For example, Tim agreed to stop calling Liz by his mother's name during a fight. Specify that ending a fight with a power play is never regarded as a "successful" fight. The most common of these power plays, of course, is simply walking out. Instead, encourage couples to take a "time-out" if it appears that emotions are escalating out of control. The person who calls for the time-out then must be responsible for specifying a time to reinitiate the "discussion." Help couples understand that if either partner refuses to be responsible for restarting a discussion (on which he or she had requested a time-out), this partner is sabotaging the future success of the relationship and setting up the other partner to nag.

The Limits Questionnaire used (see Appendix B) with Edna and Steve is useful in making the couple's agreements explicit. After filling out the questionnaire, the couple must negotiate agreements that reflect their particular capacities. Again, credibility, attainability, and consistency are crucial. Discourage agreements that partners will be unable to keep or, conversely, that redefine the goals on an overly simplistic level.

Finally, explain that it is difficult for any couple to forge new behavior patterns that are unfamiliar; as a result, it is natural that they will fall back upon old patterns from time to time simply because that is what they know best. The example of a man newly released from prison after serving 15 years can be useful. When he gets to the prison gates, he decides to return to the prison because he knows what to expect there; he knows the rules of the game in that environment.

Part of therapy is concerned with developing new, reliable patterns of communicating which allow each partner to experience the benefits of "leaving the prison" of their old ways of relating.

3. *Keep both partners thinking when angry and channel their anger through yourself.* When one partner is angry at the other, ask him or her to talk to you instead of to the partner. This helps the couple develop the capacity to listen to each other without escalating into conflict quite so rapidly.

In one session Steve began talking to Edna about a fight they had in his office in front of his employees. We asked him to think clearly and talk to us instead of to Edna until he figured out exactly what was angering him. Simultaneously, we asked Edna to change chairs and sit next to us rather than beside Steve. We also asked her to keep her thinking engaged. Anytime she felt like attacking Steve, she was to stand up and ask him to pause; once he had complied, she was to walk around the office while taking deep breaths and to let us know when she was ready to think and listen again.

By using this process Edna was able to understand that Steve felt ashamed and humiliated when his employees saw him fighting with her. His anger became understandable and Edna was able to respond empathically rather than having this fight degenerate into, "You said X—well, I said Y because you started it!" With the addition of this simple intervention, they were able to establish Steve's office as an off-limits place in which to fight.

4. *Respond to nonverbal cues by not following up on them.* Avoid asking the partners what they are thinking or feeling when they sit with pained expressions on their faces, giving long sighs or rolling their eyes. Although this technique may appear to contradict what many therapists are taught about bringing out feelings directly into the open, we have found that such inquiries only serve as "invitations" to hostile-dependent couples to escalate their feelings into full-scale arguments.

5. *Signal a confrontation.* When you are going to confront one or both partners, minimize the shock by giving them time to prepare

themselves for your confrontation. Help arouse their anticipation by letting them know that you know that your statement may create anxiety. In this way you begin to desensitize them to conflict by giving them more control. You can even increase the client's control by asking, "Are you ready to hear what I'm about to say?"

Edna, for example, would often nag Steve by complaining at the same time about his stinginess with money, the amount of time he worked, and his messiness around the house, which left no time remaining for activities with her. One day Pete intervened with her by saying, "I'm going to tell you something that may cause you to feel defensive, or may make you feel protective of yourself and want to fight with me. But, Edna, it seems as if whenever you get into an argument with Steve, you stack one issue upon the next, trying to bring all of them in at once, until pretty soon each of you feels frustrated, and nothing gets solved. You don't know how to get yourself out of the dilemma you've created. Let's pick one of your issues and focus on it." By carefully signaling the confrontation, Pete was able to help Edna hear calmly his feedback and choose the area of Steve's stinginess with his money. They then spent time negotiating some new arrangements about spending money.

6. *Predict future fights*. When communication begins to go more smoothly and the hostility between the partners is lessening, predict the inevitability of future fights. Tell them that they will experience peaks and valleys that are unavoidable; tell them to expect fights to arise in the weeks ahead. Paradoxically, by predicting the inevitability of future eruptions, you are decreasing their probability and minimizing their significance because, after all, there are fights in any relationship.

7. *Provide support and positive reinforcement for partners during the session*. Recognition is especially important when either partner takes responsibility for his or her own aggression. For example: "Steve, that was a clear observation you made about how you provoke Edna"; or, "Edna, it's good to see you noticing how you contribute to the escalations." Clear, strong gestures and comments to support any self-differentiation are useful at this stage.

8. *Help partners learn how to apologize to each other.* An interesting question to ask partners is how often they apologize to one another. The answer is usually, "Never." Hostile-dependent couples rarely know how to end a fight. If they do apologize, it is usually a "no-fault" apology (saying I'm sorry in an angry tone, with no inclusion of their own awareness of their mistake). You can help lessen the intensity associated with an apology by talking about how difficult it is to apologize and how the act of apologizing often activates fears of engulfment or leads to the apologizer feeling like a wimp. When the couple understand that an apology implies that the speaker is taking responsibility for his or her own behavior in a mature way, the apology often takes on a new, more positive significance. The apology "I'm sorry" is not sufficient if it does not include recognition and owning of one's own mistake. Learning to apologize leads to increased self-differentiation.

Tim had difficulty apologizing to Liz. He stated, "I feel like a little boy saying to my mother I am bad." After coming home late to a business dinner Liz cooked for his partners, he recognized that an apology was more mature than setting up Liz to stay angry at him. She had been generous in planning the dinner party at his request. Since he had made a mistake, he could be generous with his apology rather than making her look like a complaining, nagging wife. Saying "I'm sorry I made you angry" would be an undifferentiated apology. This implies that it is Liz's fault and if she had not gotten angry, there would be nothing for Tim to say, rather than a direct acknowledgment by him of his own irresponsible behavior. By making a direct apology such as "I'm sorry I put you in an uncomfortable position by being late for the dinner party," he can demonstrate maturity without putting himself into a little-boy position with his wife.

9. *Facilitate direct, positive interaction.* When one partner begins to make positive statements, encourage both partners to talk to one another. Let them know that they may experience some anxiety when hearing these positive statements because, even though positive interaction is what they both say they want, it nonetheless activates their fears of engulfment. During this time they can learn to recognize how they minimize or discount positive responses from their partner; they

also can learn to identify their own unique patterns of distancing. Progress is made when each recognizes what he or she does to actively discourage the partner from giving acknowledgment, compliments, or affection.

Edna came to a session reporting: "Last Sunday Steve was telling me how much he enjoyed going to the furniture store and choosing the chairs for our living room together; that it was wonderful seeing us cooperating again; and that only once was he tempted to criticize me. Right away I jumped on that one comment and asked him what he wanted to criticize. As soon as he told me, I was yelling at him. Later I realized how I had overlooked the good things he had said." We then asked Edna to tell Steve that she had heard his support and what she appreciated about that day with him.

10. *Develop consistent, caring behaviors.* If possible, choose one or two consistent, caring behaviors that partners are willing to do for each other. They need to develop new behavior patterns that are not self-centered in nature and that they can count on from one another. Check each week to see that they followed through in a positive way. It is essential to look for ways to acknowledge the positive changes, so that the focus does not remain centered in problems and pathology.

For example, Steve agreed to make the bed in the morning and not to leave dirty dishes in the bedroom or on the living room floor. Edna agreed to give Steve verbal recognition each day for doing this. She also agreed to take his shirts to the cleaners weekly and, in turn, he would acknowledge her efforts. Each time they arrived for their session, we asked them if they were continuing the agreed-upon caring behaviors.

Not every hostile-dependent couple will respond positively and cooperatively to this type of assignment. Some will act as if you are requesting superficial changes: that these small behaviors can't possibly make a difference. Part of the key to the successful execution of this assignment is how it is presented by the therapist. The couple who claim it is superficial are simply attempting to mislead the therapist by indirectly rejecting accountability for their own behavior. It is essential, therefore, that the therapist communicate firm belief and expectancy in the couple's ability to create a positive change in their lives, and to follow up by expecting accountability.

To preclude resentment by each partner for "having to make these changes," it is best to frame the requested behavior change in a larger context. For example, "This will be your beginning effort to work as a team." Some couples respond well to framing the assignment as a challenge, such as, "This will give us an opportunity to discover your capacity for change—we will discover just how hard or easy change is going to be!"

11. *Encourage cooperation by having partners do things together.* An example might be that of planning a special meal together for which the partners must decide what they will cook, who will do the shopping, the cooking, the cleanup, and so forth. The rule of thumb is to explore activities partners can do together that will decrease the fighting. Such assignments will only be successful, however, if both partners are simultaneously learning to understand and diminish their angry, competitive behaviors.

Sometimes we use a story that may put cooperation into a different perspective:

A man died and had the misfortune of ending up in Hell. But the first thing he saw there surprised him. It was row after row of banquet tables groaning with the most succulent dishes he could imagine. He thought, "This is Hell?" The next sight he saw also surprised him—emaciated people who were starving in this land of plenty. He then noticed their funny-looking arms. Their arms had turned into very long forks, so long that they could only put food on the forks but could not get the forks into their mouths. They were doomed forever to starve in the midst of this bounty.

Another man died and found himself in Heaven. He was not surprised to see row after row of giant banquet tables groaning with the most succulent food. He was surprised to see the people with long, funny arms with forks at the ends. However, these people were robust, happy, and contented. They were feeding each other!

This story may be referred to intermittently in the therapy when the focus is on cooperative activities.

12. *Develop outside friendships and activities.* Often, partners have no outside friends or very few outside relationships of any kind. As

one man said, "Why should we go out with other people? We just fight whether we're alone or we're with others, so we may as well be by ourselves and fight alone!" A major shift in this couple's pattern of interaction occurred after they both agreed to attend a square dancing class where, literally, they had to learn how to keep in step with each other and with other people.

13. *Use humor.* When there is no humor in a relationship, all issues are viewed grimly and therapeutic work progresses at a slower and more difficult pace. Indeed, a key diagnostic indicator of how rapidly couples are changing is their ability to have a sense of humor about themselves and about the predicaments they create. The use of humor can be modeled by the therapist's employment of it to diffuse conflict as described in # 1. Using humor also helps partners develop an observing ego that objectifies the other's behavior rather than taking it personally and internalizing it.

All of the above methods serve to help the therapist contain or diffuse the conflict and create a safe environment for therapy to proceed. However, these methods are not sufficient. A major difficulty of narcissistic and borderline individuals in hostile-dependent couples is their inability to override the emotional intensity of their present desires to see a larger picture. Developing and maintaining a vision of a better future is difficult. Each person has diminished empathic capacity and is caught up in an egocentric dilemma. These couples are so immediately driven by their own wants—feeling important, secure, reassured or bolstered, and safe from abandonment—that it is difficult for them to appreciate emotionally the desires of their partner.

Once the conflict has been contained, the work at hand is to help them see a larger picture and, in doing so, to see and begin to accept the emerging self of the other. Helping the couple accomplish this rests on the building block of empathy.

We describe to the couple the importance of building empathy into the relationship and how marriages will flourish when empathy is an integral part of them. A mutually agreeable goal is established that empathic responses will be a focus for changing their relationship. Some specific structured techniques to facilitate each partner responding to the other will be described more fully in the differentiating-

differentiating chapter. Also, with hostile-dependent couples, a larger context is created by helping each person look at his or her family of origin and explore the role or lack thereof that empathy played.

An important breakthrough in the development of empathy in Edna and Steve came when Edna understood how frightened Steve was that she would leave him. In the course of therapy she recognized the significance to him of his mother's abandonment. She came to recognize a pattern that he would use when he felt afraid of her rejection. The pattern often involved him doing something particularly annoying so that she would come down on him. As Edna developed more total empathy for Steve, she began to be able to ask him about his fears rather than responding to his invitations for rejection.

Hostile-dependent couples are among those most frequently seen for couples therapy and are those least likely to elicit empathy from the therapist. In fact, it is typical for therapists to feel an increasing sense of dread or anxiety as a session with a hostile-dependent couple approaches. What makes treating these couples particularly anxiety-provoking is the extent of the problems they hope to solve, the limited amount of time to solve them, and their expectation that the therapist will be a savior/magician. Effective treatment of these couples necessitates the therapist not getting involved in the frantic desperation or responding specifically to the content of the couple's problem. Instead, as we have described in this chapter, it is important to contain the conflict. After the conflict is contained, then the role of the therapist is to help the individuals interact with some positive, supportive behaviors directed toward one another and then to support the development of empathy in each partner. Clearly, this is a very different approach than trying to solve the specific content of their everyday problems. Once a therapist learns not to be so reactive to the crisis that is presented each week, his or her own anxiety will diminish, and it becomes possible to enjoy working with these couples and to bring a sense of humor to the process.

CHAPTER 6

The Symbiotic-Differentiating Couple

"Don't betray me"

When Dee and Roger arrived for their first couples therapy session, Dee was tense and apprehensive. After one year of individual therapy, she had come to realize that the emerging problems in her 16-year-long marriage were not all located in her. Now, as she sat facing her bewildered husband, she gave expression to the basic conflict she was experiencing.

Dee: There is a distance between us now, and I'm making it.

Roger: I don't understand how the distance helps you.

Dee: I feel more adult, but I'm also losing something and I'm afraid I'll lose more.

Roger: What?

Dee: Our perfect love.

Roger: I'll love you always. I'm the only one who will love you always.

Dee: I'm afraid the distance will get bigger. I'm afraid I'll be abandoned. I'm afraid I'll hurt you. I want you to show an interest in my life but not demand that I tell you everything. I don't want to tell you everything anymore.

Roger: You sound very critical, like you don't like me.

Dee: I think I've opened a can of worms I might regret.

This brief transcript poignantly highlights some of the issues and conflicts characteristic of a couple at the symbiotic-differentiating

98

stage. In the dialogue Dee demonstrates how she has begun to pull away from her husband and is simultaneously contemplating the consequences of her actions with some feelings of doubt and fear. However, from time spent in individual therapy, she now clearly knows what she wants: "I want you to show an interest in my life, but not demand that I tell you everything. I don't want to tell you everything anymore." In defining more privacy, Dee is strengthening her boundaries and establishing greater separation between herself and her husband. Roger is resistant to Dee's movement into this stage. He appears threatened and seems to prefer maintaining the current symbiosis. He further demonstrates his enmeshment by experiencing her expression of her wants as tantamount to criticism of him.

DESCRIPTION AND DIAGNOSIS OF
THE SYMBIOTIC-DIFFERENTIATING COUPLE

A couple's relationship evolves to the symbiotic-differentiating stage when one partner moves beyond the adaptation of the symbiotic stage and begins to self-reflect. Here, independent thinking begins and there is a shift toward looking internally for a sense of self. No longer is the partner seen as the source of self-awareness. As a result, differences become highlighted. The intensity of this stage varies in relation to whether it occurs early in the relationship, or if it occurs after a long-term symbiotic relationship has been established, as in the case of Roger and Dee.

In either case, this is the first time the system becomes unbalanced. The unbalance is created by one individual making a developmental shift before the other one is ready for the shift to take place. One partner, like Dee, moves out of the earlier established symbiosis. Often this movement is accompanied by feelings of guilt. The communication of both the independence and the guilt induces threat in the other partner, who usually interprets the differentiating partner's desires as being the first steps toward ending the relationship. This negative expectation often activates even more intense, dependent clinging.

When, how, and why does differentiation occur? If the symbiotic stage is often so blissful and emotionally rewarding, the question arises: Why do one or both partners move beyond this pleasant state of affairs? Why don't most people remain in this stage forever with their true love? The evidence is overwhelming that most couples do not and cannot maintain the high intensity of the initial stage.

The reasons why differentiation occurs in adult couples are similar to those described by Mahler in relation to children. Mahler highlighted three factors: the developing aggressive drive, including the need to experience developing functions and abilities; the increasing interest in the external world, with the father acting as a bridge into that world and stimulating the child's interest in it; and the mother's ability to allow separation and to become supportive of the separation-individuation process at a phase-appropriate time.

In couples, the aggression begins to surface as differences are recognized and adaptation begins to seem smothering. After a time spent in intense symbiotic gratification, other people and outside activities hold new interest, and often it can even be exciting to explore from the base of a successfully developing partnership. Finally, each partner may want the other to support his or her own unique process of separation-individuation. Since the partner is not a parent and will have desires of his or her own, the process is fraught with difficulties that we will highlight throughout this book. However, when each partner is able to support the separation process in one another, the couple's relationship can provide a true healing of earlier, negative object representations.

Usually differentiation begins after one or both people feel secure that they have established themselves as a couple. Adaptation will occur early in the relationship to ensure that the relationship is lasting and that indeed the love will continue even when the partners are physically apart. It is this sense of safety that permits the couple to risk entering into the differentiation process. With this security comes the desire to test the relationship to be sure it can withstand containing two different individuals, and that it will not suffocate either party. Sometimes it is the recognition of differences or the first disillusionment with the relationship that serves as the spark igniting the process of differentiation. When the cloud of romantic fantasy is no longer sufficient to obscure the differences between the two partners, reality emerges, and anger and disappointment become feelings with which the couple must reckon.

It may be something as basic as style differences in speech patterns that initiates the differentiation. One woman described this change: "When I first met my husband, he would talk very slowly. I would sit on the edge of the couch, hanging on to his every word. I thought he was so wise. Now, his slow talking drives me crazy with frustration." This is a classic example of how the virtues of the symbiotic-symbiotic stage turn into flaws as one partner begins to break out of what has become a restricting unity.

In the early phases of differentiation, it is common for the differentiating partner to "stick his toe in the water," so to speak, then get cold feet and back off for a period of time. However, anger at the differences may fuel and facilitate differentiation. The following brief exchange occurred between the therapist (Pete) and a wife who was tentatively initiating differentiation in her two-year-old marriage.

Melody: I can't express anger at Alan unless I have a procedure to solve the fights. Will you give me a procedure to use?

Pete: You'd like a procedure so that you won't have to feel the discomfort of your differences?

Melody: Yes, I guess that's so. Besides, I believe that if I fight with him, I'll drive him away and he won't come back. What happens if we have a fight and that is the end of our relationship?

Pete: You are so sure of the negative outcome that at this time it is difficult for you to even take a chance and raise a small disagreement.

As we will discuss later, when both partners are well into differentiation or early practicing, it is appropriate to help develop a procedure for solving fights. However, the first issue of differentiation is, Can the partners tolerate anger? Can they use the anger to recognize that they are different and that the differentness necessitates the confrontation of the fading symbiotic fantasy?

One couple had spent many years as political activists in the nonviolent peace movement. They had come together in their commitment to peace and to living a subsistence lifestyle. In their house, the wife made the weekly grocery list and the husband diligently did the shopping. For years he faithfully bought only what was on her list. As she began differentiating, she started including an expensive brand of ice cream on the list. Two weeks passed, and he neglected to buy it. Her anger surfaced. She confronted him:

Martha: Why didn't you buy the ice cream that I put on the list?

Sam: Well, it's very expensive, and I didn't think it fit within our budget.

Martha: It costs 40 cents more than the ice cream we usually buy. I'm tired of everything being bland and inexpensive. I don't always want to buy the cheapest variety of my favorite products. We've lived this way for a long time, and I've never said anything, but now I'm ready for a change!

Another example of how anger sparks differentiation occurred in the couple, Paul and Jenna, described in Chapter 1 (p. 12). After two years of an intense dating relationship, Paul decided to date other women. Jenna tried many different emotionally manipulative scenes to draw him back into their symbiotic involvement. When he refused and continued going off on his own, she used her anger in another way. She decided to get some individual therapy, and in the process of therapy developed a clearer and stronger identity. Specifically, she came to recognize that her identity as a woman was not based on her involvement with Paul. She decided to further develop her career and, in doing so, received a significant promotion. Altogether she spent two years in individual therapy, first detaching herself from the symbiosis, then defining her own goals in life, and finally coming to decide that she did want to be married and in a committed relationship with a man, without the old symbiotic patterns.

In Jenna's case it was anger that first pushed her toward the differentiation stage. Perhaps she was fortunate that the manipulative ploys through which she channeled her anger were unsuccessful. As she recognized that these methods were unsuccessful, she also found her own behavior repugnant (she had thrown herself down in the driveway in front of his car and ordered Paul to drive over her when she did not want him to leave). Through psychotherapy, she was able to redirect her anger into a challenging and constructive differentiation phase.

Often, recognition of emerging differences creates disillusionment in partners. This leads to feelings of loss, grief, or despair. Indeed, movement into the differentiation stage often involves a grief process. There is loss, sorrow, and anger at letting go of the wonder of those first times together. It is the death of a fantasy—the fantasy that it is possible to return to the euphoria of being "the one and only" or "the apple of his eye." The symbiotic gratification of being only in the world for each other is replaced with a harsher reality. Sometimes we call this "de-pedestaling." The therapist's task during this phase is to elicit the feelings connected to this loss and to be able to tolerate their intensity during the working-through process. Once the couple are able to resolve their grief openly and consciously together, they can enter the differentiation stage with a firmer foundation.

The following excerpt from a session with Jack and Nina captures the sense of "jumping off" into unknown territory that often characterizes a couple's conscious decision to look at one another openly and honestly during the first stirrings of differentiation.

Pete: Is it fair to say you might be taking your wife off a pedestal?

Jack: Yes.

Pete: And getting acquainted with Nina rather than an image of Nina?

Jack: Reality is difficult.

Pete: Is it hard to talk about feeling disillusioned?

Jack: Yes, I'm afraid if I really say what I think, she'll get angry and hurt or leave me.

Pete: Many people are afraid to stay through the disillusionment phase to discover what happens when they get underneath the masks. You might also be afraid about what will happen if she de-pedestals you.

Jack: You bet! I didn't even know I was on a pedestal.

Nina: Wait a minute. I've had you elevated for my own reasons and I've been going through some agonizing reappraisal, too—looking at how we relate, seeing how some of the patterns I used to want now make me sick. I don't want these anymore, and that is part of me de-pedestaling you and saying, "Hey, Jack isn't perfect."

Pete: So it's not easy to look behind those masks.

Ellyn: What would help each of you look and talk even when it isn't easy?

Nina: I'm probably going to be angry and hurt at times, but that's no reason not to go ahead.

Ellyn: Are you telling him you'll listen and hear him, even if you do feel angry?

Nina: Yes, and I won't run away and I hope he won't.

Jack: I won't either. Well, here goes.

Departure from the symbiotic stage can occur as dramatically as it started—"See you later, baby"—or it can occur with glacier-like slowness. At times, the disillusionment and beginning differentiation lead couples to recognize that indeed they are not meant for one another; that while the romance was exciting, they are not compatible to live an ongoing life together. When this situation is handled effectively, it can lead to a positive ending of the relationship, in which both people recognize their incompatibility and neither leaves with his or her self-esteem impaired. In other cases, the ending of the relationship may be more wrenching.

In the movie *Kramer vs. Kramer,* Ted Kramer poignantly expresses his pain about not being able to respond to his wife's differentiation: "For a long time I kept trying to make her be a certain kind of person . . . a certain kind of wife that I thought she was supposed to be. She just wasn't like that. And now that I think about it, she tried for so long to make me happy, and then when she couldn't, she tried to talk to me about it, but I wouldn't listen. I was too busy just thinking about myself, and I thought anytime I was happy, she was happy."

The most extreme form of differences triggering disillusionment occurs in the "Don Juan" or "Peter Pan" syndrome. Here, men move rapidly from one woman to the next the moment they sense a breakdown of the symbiosis as the current woman ceases to provide adoration and mirroring. As soon as the woman becomes a person with desires and thoughts of her own, it is time for these men to move on to another angel/virgin who will worship them. Rather than experience any of their shortcomings or the grief characteristic of the differentiation stage, they move on quickly to reestablish another symbiosis with a different woman who hopefully will bolster their image and be more "perfect" than the previous one.

When differentiation emerges after long periods of symbiosis, usually an external event serves as the catalyst. In the United States it is now common to find couples who have maintained symbiotic relationships for many years until their children leave home, or until the wife is influenced by the women's liberation movement. Many of these women attend support groups or go into individual therapy. From these experiences they learn to identify their own thoughts, feelings, and behaviors more clearly, and they begin to function in a more differentiated way in their marriages. Often when the husband is not involved in therapy, the marriage will end in divorce. Or, like Roger and Dee, the wife will initiate therapy, which will be very threatening to the husband, who would prefer to maintain the status quo.

Case example: Amanda and Jane

In the case example that follows, Amanda felt increased impetus to differentiate when Jane moved and began living in the same town.

Jane and Amanda, a lesbian couple in their early thirties, were seen in therapy by Maggie Phillips, Ph.D.* Four months before their initial therapy session, Jane moved to live in the same town as Amanda. Since theirs had been a commuting relationship for almost two years, they decided not to live together until they had successfully adjusted to greater proximity.

During the diagnostic interview, Jane described the problem from her perspective: "Amanda isn't spending enough time with me, and we've stopped having sex since I moved here." She also expressed difficulty in communicating with Amanda, stating that Amanda was often too busy or too tired from her job and other activities to talk about issues between them. Their therapist observed at this time that Jane appeared quite depressed, as she had not been able to find a job, missed her friends and the life she had left behind, and now was fearful that the relationship with Amanda might end.

Amanda acknowledged her recent withdrawal from the relationship,

---

*Dr. Phillips is a psychotherapist who trained with us and who practices in Oakland/Piedmont, California.

explaining that she had told Jane this would be a busy time for her and that she resented being made to feel responsible for so many things, especially Jane's adjustment to a new town and their sexual problems. She stated, "I want to support Jane's move, but Jane is getting increasingly clingy. Instead of beginning to get established on her own, she's getting more dependent on me. Simultaneously, I've begun to want more independence."

This couple reached a crisis point when Amanda was offered a new job requiring more responsibility at the same time that she was preparing to chair a local fundraising event. Jane feared that she would have even less contact with Amanda and was threatening to move back to her old hometown.

Diagnosis for this couple was based on their response to the Paper Exercise, the diagnostic and personal history interviews, and other clinical process information. During the Paper Exercise, Amanda began to discuss what the paper might mean to her; Jane immediately encouraged Amanda to take the paper since it was obviously more important to her, making no effort to explore its meaning for herself.

Amanda: I think the paper might be really special to me—like a new life direction.

Jane: If it's that important to you, then you take it *(gives Amanda the paper).*

Amanda: Are you sure?

Jane: Yes, it really doesn't matter to me. I can't think of anything just now. What is your new direction?

Amanda: Maybe something that has to do with writing. I've always wanted to write fiction—maybe now's my chance.

Other dialogue with the couple indicated that although Amanda had begun differentiating before Jane's move, such a tangible expression of Jane's desire to be closer and her rising dependency on Amanda resulted in Amanda's increasing her efforts to define her identity and insist upon her privacy. Thus, this couple was diagnosed as symbiotic-differentiating, with Jane fighting to maintain their earlier enmeshment when time together was idyllic and when each partner seemed equally committed to maintaining a close relationship.

THERAPEUTIC TREATMENT OF THE
SYMBIOTIC–DIFFERENTIATING COUPLE

The primary focus for therapy with symbiotic-differentiating couples is to facilitate differentiation in both individuals at the same time. The necessary step here is for *both* individuals to be actively looking for self inside of themselves, rather than looking for themselves in each other. In order to accomplish this, the couple must be able to resolve the loss of the symbiotic stage, to identify and express individual thoughts, feelings, wants, and desires, and to tolerate the anxiety created by handling the conflicts inherent in recognizing their individual wants and desires. Often there is tremendous anxiety experienced by an individual who stops adapting to the other and begins responding to his or her own thoughts and feelings.

Case example: Amanda and Jane (continued)

In doing therapy with the lesbian couple described above, the therapist's basic treatment plan was to find ways of moving both partners firmly into the differentiation stage, while at the same time encouraging them to maintain close emotional contact with one another. The therapist supported Amanda's attempts to differentiate, while simultaneously confronting Jane's symbiotic transactions and helping her develop more independent ways of thinking and behaving.

Early in therapy, individual contracts for change were established, in addition to the identification of mutual goals for the couple. When asked how each of them wanted their relationship to be different, they indicated a mutual desire for better communication, more effective ways of resolving conflicts, a more satisfying sex life, and more consistent feelings of closeness to each other.

The therapist explored the contribution each had made to the current difficulties and asked what each was willing to change about herself. Amanda easily recognized her patterns of withdrawal. She selected goals that involved being direct with her feelings when there was a conflict between them. Of central importance to her was facing her anxiety and handling the conflict, as well as being open with vulnerable feelings of sadness and fear, rather than using withdrawal to escape.

Jane, on the other hand, had difficulty defining goals for herself;

instead, she focused on ways in which she wanted Amanda to be different. With much encouragement, redirection, and confrontation, she was finally able to acknowledge her dependence on Amanda in defining herself and in stimulating good feelings about herself. After this breakthrough, she agreed to focus on defining her own wants in the relationship rather than expecting Amanda to know magically what she wanted and then getting upset when Amanda did not respond to her indirect cues.

A related intervention involved establishing clear lines of responsibility in therapy sessions by designating one or the other of the partners as the initiator of each issue that was raised. (The use of this technique to heighten the level of object relations will be discussed in the next chapter.) The therapist then focused on the initiator, making sure that her feelings and wants were clearly expressed before the issue was explored further. When issues were completed in a session and assignments or agreements made, they were followed up consistently at the beginning of subsequent sessions.

This approach was especially helpful in resolving the couple's sexual issues. Like many couples with sexual problems, Jane and Amanda had developed a wall of resentment regarding past disappointments which made difficult even a discussion of their feelings about sex. As noted, they had discontinued having any sexual contact, as is typical of many lesbian couples at this stage of their relationship.* Jane and Amanda were well aware of this phenomenon and expressed a sense of futility and hopelessness that a lack of sex must be part of their fate as lesbians, with the only alternatives being adjusting to the end of their sexual relationship or finding new sexual partners.

Because of these barriers to change, it seemed particularly effective to "chunk" the assignments related to sexual experience; that is, Jane and Amanda were helped to break down the issues related to their sexual dissatisfaction into easily manageable behavioral segments. For example, both partners had difficulty making time to be intimate together. Several therapy sessions were devoted to helping Jane and Amanda take turns in initiating and planning occasions for emotional and physical intimacy.

In addition, each had difficulty initiating lovemaking: Amanda, for fear of being reengulfed in the symbiosis from which she was still tenta-

---

*This concept is widely explored in the feminist press (Lindenbaum, 1985, p. 88).

tively emerging; and Jane, out of fear of rejection. Several sessions were devoted to assisting each partner find comfortable ways of making the transition from emotional/physical closeness to sexual closeness. By termination, regular experiences of sexual and emotional intimacy had become a part of this couple's daily life.

Another intervention that was particularly helpful was identifying how previous, unresolved impasses from their families of origin were influencing their current relationship. The therapist pointed out that Jane was recreating part of her family script with Amanda by responding to Amanda's independence with the same kind of intense anger and fear that she had experienced when her mother withdrew from her as a child. This led Jane to identify events during her late childhood and adolescence when her own attempts to attain greater independence were met with her mother's disapproval and emotional withdrawal. Her difficulties in allowing Amanda more independence, and in taking her own steps, were linked to Jane's childhood decision that being independent from a loved one leads to pain and abandonment. Through discussions in therapy and experiences at home, Jane began to see that Amanda welcomed her flowering, individuated growth. She then "redecided" to support growth in herself and in Amanda, and began to experience directly how this led to greater intimacy.

Similarly, Amanda was helped to see that her tendency to withdraw from emotional contact with Jane rather than remaining present to discuss their differences was related to her family role as a parental child, made responsible by her parents for the physical and emotional well-being of her younger sister who was severely handicapped. Amanda's withdrawal from Jane was traced to her early decision, "When I grow up, I won't take responsibility for anyone else." Because she felt that her role as her sister's caretaker had seriously restricted her own growth and development, she would withdraw whenever she felt that Jane's desires were beginning to intrude on her own developing identity. Thus, she often overreacted to Jane's desire for support, feeling that she was being made responsible for Jane's happiness and the welfare of their relationship. By using a Gestalt two-chair technique, she was able to talk to her sister and then to Jane, and to recognize that while some responsibility exists in any ongoing, intimate relationship, it is a very different kind of responsibility than she had previously carried in relation to her sister.

The importance of this strategy of exploring interlocking early decisions with lesbian couples may be particularly noteworthy. Much has been written about the tendency of lesbian couples to "merge" so that differences are obscured and boundaries blurred (Krieger, 1983). Many feminist clinicians and theoreticians have suggested strategies to interrupt this pattern of merging, including prescriptions of nonmonogamy and competition (Lindenbaum, 1985, p. 86). Another alternative is to focus therapeutically on how the unresolved personal issues of each partner interlock and contribute to the difficulties encountered in surmounting the developmental tasks of particular stages of couplehood. Using this intervention with Amanda and Jane proved very effective because it helped them to clarify their own issues and provided information that they could use in preventing and resolving subsequent difficulties.

A final intervention that was helpful in this particular case involved facilitating greater differentiation from the families of origin. Like many individuals, neither Amanda nor Jane had separated in a healthy way from her parents. Amanda had achieved an external level of differentiation from her parents by having little contact with them since "coming out" as a lesbian 10 years previously. During therapy, she was helped to maintain her identity around them while reestablishing emotional contact. This included encouraging her to tolerate their feelings about her being a lesbian. After several letters and phone calls, Amanda visited her parents and talked openly about her relationship with Jane for the first time. She asked for their acceptance. Shortly before termination, Amanda's parents came to visit this couple and expressed support for their union.

Unsurprisingly, Jane was less differentiated from her family of origin. Her father had died some years before, and Jane's contacts with her mother were marked by anger. Her mother refused to acknowledge her relationship with Amanda in the same way as her siblings' marriages. Through therapy, Jane developed the security that her own identity and satisfaction with the relationship were not dependent on her mother's "blessing." In subsequent contacts, Jane began initiating and stating her position on various issues rather than merely reacting to her mother's responses. By termination, Jane had made satisfactory progress in establishing a more adult relationship with her mother, one in which she could easily acknowledge differences between them without always expecting resolution of conflicts or synchronicity of opinions.

At a six-month follow-up, most of the couple's therapeutic gains had been maintained. They had begun living together shortly before the end of therapy; both had active work lives, and each was involved in separate leisure activities. In addition, they made regular time for intimacy and sex, recognizing that periods without sex were usually precipitated by external stresses. In general, they have enjoyed increased satisfaction with their lives together as a couple, and consider that their main difficulties are behind them.

Generating Motivation in the Passive Spouse

Typically, symbiotic-differentiating couples are experiencing a great deal of strain due to their discrepant goals. In short-term symbiotic-differentiating couples like Jane and Amanda, the conflict is often overt, whereas in longer-term symbiotic-differentiating couples the tension may be more covert. This tension becomes especially acute when the symbiotic individual is characterologically passive. The passive spouse says with his behavior that "my needs for comfort, security, and caretaking are greater than your needs for independence, support, and individuation."

It is difficult for the passive individual to "get outside of his own skin" and develop empathy for his partner's discomfort and desire for changes. He does not respond well to his own needs, so it is even more difficult for him to respond constructively to his partner's desires.

Fear and lack of self-awareness maintain the passive individual in his symbiotic position. His pull for symbiosis is greater than his discomfort from remaining in that position. He is reluctant to begin the complex process of differentiating himself from his partner. He intuitively or unconsciously knows the Herculean effort that will be required of him if he is to identify actively his thoughts, feelings, and behavior. Thus, for any movement to occur, the incentives and motivations for leaving the symbiotic position and beginning to differentiate must be greater than the comfort of remaining emotionally symbiotic.

It can be rare for psychotherapists to focus on enhancing a person's motivation for change. However, in the long-term symbiotic-differentiating couple, generating motivation for change is a must for creating change in this system. (In Chapter 9, we give an example of how Richard, a passive partner, was motivated to change by creating a future focus.) When doing therapy with short-term symbiotic-differentiating couples, like the lesbian couple described earlier, motivation may come from fear of the relationship ending, or may be mobilized by careful work on the part of the therapist to establish the initial treatment contracts.

With longer-lasting symbiotic-differentiating relationships, the question remains, What will motivate the passive, symbiotic individual to begin his search for self *inside* of himself rather than continuing to look for global caretaking from his spouse? Indeed, there must be powerful personal reasons for him to begin and sustain this journey of differentiation. The therapist must help this individual find a way to generate enthusiasm, desire, and energy. The desire for change does not come from awareness about why one is the way one is, nor does it come from "understanding." A strong desire for change will come from a person being able to say, "Yes! I can see how I'm going to benefit if I accomplish these changes!"

The dynamic of the passive-symbiotic individual presents a dilemma. How does the therapist help provide a mechanism for this individual to begin to differentiate either without interfering with the client's autonomy, or without encountering the same passive resistance as the spouse? Individual psychodynamic therapy which emphasizes insight, interpretation, and working through is often painfully slow with passive clients. Review or even encouragement of how the passive individual will prosper by moving beyond the symbiotic stage is rarely sufficient to crack his protective walls. Behavior therapy, which attempts to bypass these difficulties by focusing on successive approximations in behavior patterns, usually also meets with resistance as the passive individual halfheartedly carries out his homework assignment. We have found that in order to build the symbiotic partner's motivation for change, we must stress a future focus. When the individual gets clear and precise about what it is he wants to create and begins to develop very personal (even *self*-centered) reasons for changing on an emotional level, then he will become more creative in developing his own strategies to accomplish his purpose.

Case example: Jana and Luke

Jana and Luke were a married couple living apart when they entered therapy. Their goal was to explore the potential of reconciliation and resume living together. A major complaint that Jana had was Luke's passivity around the house and his lack of emotional responsiveness to her. Luke approached his job with a great deal of vigor which was not matched in his involvement with Jana. They both agreed that his passivity was a major obstacle to reconstructing their relationship in addition to being a major cause of the breakup.

Luke's initial contract was to focus on changing his passivity so that he would take more initiative with Jana. However, the agreements that he would make in the sessions were not kept during the week. Additionally, he would arrive at the sessions 10-15 minutes late on a consistent basis. Insight into the reasons for his behavior yielded no additional positive change. Luke said the sessions were uncomfortable for him because he felt as though he were being picked on even though he realized there was justification for Jana being quite annoyed with him.

After about three months of frustration building within Jana, the therapist (Pete) said to her that it was beginning to appear that she had three major choices: 1) to stay frustrated about Luke's promises to be different and his subsequent lack of follow-through with the agreements; 2) to become indifferent to her wants in the relationship and hence attempt to reduce her frustration; or, 3) to make the final decision to end their marriage. Jana said that she was ready for option # 3 and was running out of patience. She went on to say that her concern was that when she made her last proclamation to Luke (that this time she was leaving for good), he would reply with increased pleas for one more chance. At that point, she said it would be too late to change and this time she would be gone for good.

Luke looked at Jana and said he hoped she was not out of patience, because he was going to try harder to follow through with his agreements. Pete told Luke that individuals like him basically responded from two motivations: fear and pain. In this case the fear would come from the loss of the relationship; the pain would be the result of violating his own standards of integrity and the discomfort of being confronted with his behavior. If he were to make changes from his position of fear and/or pain, then these changes would not likely be sustained over a long period of time.

It was also explained to Luke that there was a third possibility for creating a different relationship with Jana. This possibility would involve four steps, and if he were not willing to do all four steps, then he might as well not even start. The sequence of steps was as follows:

1. Identify the specifics of what he wanted to create in his marriage.

2. Stay conscious of the outcomes that he wanted to create in his relationship. He would need to stay conscious of these changes during the week as well as in the sessions, plus reflect on our sessions during the week.
3. Generate a plan to implement the desires, and take some action toward following through with his plan.
4. Persist in following through with his plan.

Luke said that he wanted to think about this methodology but he did not feel criticized with the problem defined this way. Jana reinforced the idea that both time and her patience were running short.

We could not meet for two weeks, but when we resumed, Luke was there promptly at 9:00 A.M. Luke said that he had set aside about 15-20 minutes a day to reflect on the relationship. He thought about where they had been, where they were currently, and how he would like them to be together. He said he wasn't sure that his "meditations" were doing much good, but Jana quickly jumped in and said that she was beginning to notice small changes in his behavior. He had even bought a Snickers for her, remembering that it was one of her favorite candy bars. Additionally, he had called her on the phone and had initiated two "spontaneous" hugs. Jana said it helped her morale seeing Luke make these efforts.

Luke was somewhat perplexed by this turn of events. He said that in his heart of hearts, he really didn't believe that meditating on his desired future relationship would have much impact. However, there seemed to be evidence that these meditations did have an impact on his behavior. He liked getting the positive feedback from Jana but often felt that the recognition from her was condescending. That led us into a discussion about how she could more effectively show her appreciation for the changes he was making. For the next three weeks, Luke continued his meditations and also continued to make both behavioral and attitudinal changes. At the time this book went to press, the couple were still in therapy, had decided to live together again, and both were much more optimistic about the relationship they were beginning to create.

Individuals such as Luke typically have a very difficult time emerging from the past symbiotic position they have developed in a relationship. It is not easy for them to identify their desires, stay conscious of them, and then follow through with action to generate what they want to create. As with Luke, helping these individuals shift into developing their own motivation will lead to their leaving their emotional "fort" and venturing forth into uncharted territory.

Using the Couple's Process to Uncover Intrapsychic Impasses

The following transcript from one session with a symbiotic-differentiating couple illustrates how a mundane issue that is typical of the trivial fights in most relationships can be used as an entry point to uncover some of the deeper issues of this stage. This session occurred early in the couple's therapy. The partners were each 50 years old and had been married for eight years. The session began with both partners hassling about a problem they had coming to the session in the car. Brad was driving, they were late, there was a lot of traffic, he was tense, and Alice kept talking.

Ellyn: Would the two of you have a discussion about where you want to focus today?

Alice: *(disregarding the therapist's question)* What's interesting to me is that in the car you could have said, "I'm tense. Don't bother me right now."

Brad: But you knew that, you could see that.

Alice: It never occurred to me that you didn't want me to talk to you.

Brad: But, of course, I want you to talk to me, but not to burden me when I'm tense.

Alice: I didn't know that was so important to you. I didn't know you were having so much trouble. You assume that I'll intuit what's important to you. You assume I'm like you. That kind of thing doesn't make me upset; other things make me upset.

(Brad moves on to discuss an incident surrounding a telephone call in which he unsuccessfully tried to get through to Alice several times. After the third attempt he felt anger, which he defined as not permissible.)

Brad: I guess the problem for me is anger and then anxiety that my anger is not permissible.

Alice: How does that work in our relationship? When we left here last time, you were distressed about that. I think that's what the problem is and I'd like to know how it works in our relationship.

Ellyn: Why is anger not permissible?

Brad: I think until recently our relationship has involved you joining me in my anxiety. As you've gotten more independent, you don't join in my complaints and I keep wanting to pull you back in. I want you to be there when I want you to be there. I want you to go where I want you to go. I want you to speak up when I want you to speak up. I want you to do this and that when I want you to do it!

Ellyn: So, you feel angry when she's independent. Your anger is not permissible to you on its own, so you try to engage Alice in it or get her to parent you.

Brad: Yes.

Ellyn: So, when she withdraws or establishes any independence, you feel anxious and won't say what you want?

Brad: Yes, that's it.

(There follows a discussion of how Alice perceives the situation, which includes her description of the ways in which she believes Brad attempts to get her to be his mother and how she likes the power but not the responsibility.)

Alice: Well, I think he tries to get me to be his mother. I get caught. I enjoy the power, but another part doesn't feel free. I get impatient if I have to be positive all the time. Because of my therapy, I've learned to be a lot more independent, and that makes incidents like this very illuminating.

(More discussion takes place about the phone call. Brad had come home moody and Alice had tried to be the good mother by encouraging him to talk about it. Instead, he got angry at some

other trivial matter and tried to get her involved in his anger. This
part of the discussion ends with the mutual recognition of how
their pattern requires that each get involved with the other's
problems.)

Ellyn: I see a pattern where you get involved in each other's
problems and, in essence, you pass the anxiety back and forth.
Brad, you're anxious if the symbiosis gets very disrupted and
Alice takes too much independence. It's also especially threatening
for you to be too independent. If you move too far out of what's
acceptable, then you feel anxious, and that starts a pattern in
motion in which you put your anger on something external and
ask Alice to commiserate with you. You do something indirectly
to reestablish the symbiosis rather than say what you want or
express that you're angry. I'm wondering what makes your own
independence so threatening to you?

Brad: A way that I'm *not* independent is that I'm *super*responsible,
and I think I associate *independence* with *irresponsibility*. You
know, "Fuck you all, I'll just do what I want to do."

Ellyn: A very negative connotation to independence! What happened
when you were independent as a child?

Brad: Given the mother I had, all independence was considered rebellion.
She saw all assertive behavior as hostile.

Ellyn: So, you're scared that if you do what you want to do, you'll just
be a hostile, rebellious little boy. What did your mother do when
you tried to be independent from her?

Brad: She would cry that I was being inconsiderate of her or disloyal.

Ellyn: Ouch! I could feel that in my stomach.

Brad: But she herself was totally inconsiderate! She was one of the
most inconsiderate people anyone would ever want to meet!

Pete: (drawing sketches on the blackboard) So, here's you and here's
your mother, and there's a very narrow circle of acceptable
behavior. As long as you tiptoe around in that circle, you're okay
with her. But if you move outside of it, then you've been disloyal
to her.

Brad: Yes! If you didn't stay inside of her camp, she would draw a line and you would be totally rejected and outside. That's probably why I still get scared about Alice rejecting me if I disagree.

Pete: And it feels like there's no middle ground in which to have your own separate identity and still maintain a relationship.

Brad: Yes, and when I think about it now, I feel angry. Then I was mostly scared.

In this session Brad was able to use current interactions and feelings as a springboard to make contact with earlier feelings in his life experience. Recognizing the source of his anger helped Brad to give up his tendency to displace it or use it indirectly to attempt to reestablish the symbiosis. This led him to being more aware of his own feelings and assertive about his own wants, as well as more accepting of his wife's independence. He began taking weekend camping trips. He was able to allow his wife greater privacy and he stopped nagging and intruding upon her when she wanted quiet, uninterrupted time in her sewing room.

In treating symbiotic-differentiating couples, the primary goal is to facilitate active differentiation in both partners. Toward this end, both partners must be looking inside themselves to discover self. Until this basic shift has occurred, a pull toward symbiosis will always exist. Once the shift has taken place, the tasks of the differentiating-differentiating stage will emerge. These will involve developing the capacity to integrate difficult feelings, different thoughts, and conflicting wants into the ongoing fabric of the relationship, as well as learning to accept and support the emerging self of the other. We will describe in the next chapter how to help the couple do this.

CHAPTER 7

The Differentiating-Differentiating Couple

"I'll change if you change"

Craig: We're hassling so much lately. Every time I open my mouth it seems like you disagree.

Tam: Every time I want to do something or go somewhere, *you* say no.

Craig: (*turns and speaks to therapist*) Only lately did I realize I married such an active woman. She wants to go camping, to movies, to square dancing, and to spend Friday nights at bridge tournaments. I'm a home body and she thinks I'm a square because I don't want to go out more. Can we ever be happy together?

Differences now exist. Since both partners know more about what they want, think, and feel and are expressing these feelings, the differences become open and visible. In the differentiating-differentiating relationship, this invariably leads to conflict. Indeed, no two people are the same! Their wants will not always coincide and the differences inherent in their personality styles, values, and beliefs will come sharply into focus.

As one man said after about three months of couples therapy, "I guess I was a little slow in coming to the conclusion that Janet is really different than I am." After five years of marriage he was now recognizing that he and his wife were different beyond the appetite level. He had been aware of how her likes were different than his in the areas of food and drink, temperature, and sex. But it was hard for him to understand that what made her feel loved, appreciated, supported, and recognized

119

was quite different from what satisfied him. In fact, differentiation within a relationship requires the identification of what supports both the self and the partner in feeling loved and appreciated.

DESCRIPTION AND DIAGNOSIS OF THE DIFFERENTIATING—DIFFERENTIATING COUPLE

In this stage conflict exists without being obscured by denial or intensified into destructive behavior. In fact, arguing back and forth with each other begins to predominate as this stage develops. The process of solving the basic egocentric dilemma of "How do I become aware of *my* wants, and how do I become aware of *your* wants, and how do we strike a *balance* between our different wants?" is a fundamental element of differentiation. Rather than pushing their conflicting desires under the rug, as in the symbiotic stage, the partners now begin to recognize that they really are different people who need to get to know one another and to find out whether these differences can be effectively managed to promote growth in themselves and each other. To do this necessitates recognizing, discussing, and planning how to accommodate the many problems that arise.

While both partners are beginning the process of differentiation, they will continue to use symbiotic methods such as projection and manipulation as attempts to push the other to change. The thinking is, "If I can use my feelings or my behavior in some way to get you to be less different from me, then we won't have so many conflicts to work out." The arguing and fighting during this stage can feel particularly intense. All of a sudden there are many differences that are apparent: "If only I can just get rid of a few of them, then I'd have only one or two things to handle at once"; or, "If you'd just shape up in this one area, then we wouldn't have so much to handle all at once." One man described how he had previously inhibited differentiation in his marriage:

> I used to work everything out in my head. As soon as Leslie expressed an idea, I either agreed with her or frantically thought of a reason why she must not think that way. At all times I needed to be in control of keeping us calm. Any disruption was too frightening and meant I was unlovable.

This is also the period in which fantasy is shattered and reality sets in! Feelings of grief, loss, and betrayal must be resolved. While these feelings are in the process of being resolved, the couple may experience rapid mood swings from elation to despair. Satisfactory resolution of these feelings is often emotionally gratifying and helps to build a solid base for the relationship. How well the couple are able to navigate this aspect of the differentiation process together will set the backdrop for future stages.

Once partners recognize how they are indeed different, they then enter the process of learning to risk expressing these differences, while developing trust that the differences will be responded to noncritically, and will even be resolved eventually. The risk may seem so great to a couple that they have difficulty doing it in a straightforward way. Instead, they will ask for emotional support from one another in extraordinarily complex and convoluted ways and then become hurt and angry when the other does not respond. To express one's self straightforwardly requires a great deal of inner clarity and a strong sense of self-esteem. This is so because saying succinctly and directly "what I want" in essence gives the partner the power to either deny or gratify the desire. And, paradoxically, even when the desire is granted, gratification anxiety is not uncommon. Many individuals feel uncomfortable about getting what they want. As one woman said, "If my husband gives me what I want, then I'm obligated to him and I'm no longer entitled to say no." For other individuals, getting what they want brings up unresolved, painful feelings from the past when they were not responded to effectively. The following steps delineate the evolution of differentiation:

1. Developing the ability to self-reflect and *identify* what one thinks, feels, and desires.
2. Developing an increasing ability to *express* congruently what one thinks, feels, and desires.
3. Developing an understanding and acceptance of the partner as separate and different.
4. Developing an increased ability to respond effectively to these differences.
5. Developing the ability to respond effectively to one another's feelings in a way that supports increasing differentiation in each other.

6. Developing the willingness to enhance the environment or provide support for the partner in facilitating the creation of what is desired.

As well as being involved in these steps, a couple diagnosed as both being in the differentiation stage will have evolved beyond mastering their first disillusionment with one another. As long as the first disillusionment remains as a primary source of pain, effective differentiation is not occurring. To determine the extent of the resolution, the therapist can refer to the couple's response to question #6 on the Diagnostic Questionnaire (see Appendix A).

Paper Exercise

To diagnose a differentiating couple on the basis of the Paper Exercise, the couple must no longer emphasize merging or winning; instead, the effort is spent on examining the process of how to decide. The couple in the following example who did this exercise after one year of marriage are typical of highly educated, intellectually oriented individuals. Although their verbal acuity makes it tempting to ascribe an advanced level of development to them, their working level of interaction may be significantly lower than it appears during the initial therapeutic encounter.

Matthew: Do you want to tell me what it is, or do you want to talk about the process of how we will decide?

Fran: Let's talk about the process. How are we going to decide? Maybe if I find out something about why it is important to you, that will help me make an objective evaluation.

Matthew: Okay.

Fran: *(She proceeds by asking her husband many questions, such as, How will it affect you to have it? Will it hurt our relationship if you don't have it? Is it so important to you that you will be angry at me if I get it?)*

Matthew: *(gives short answers, then says)* You seem to be focusing more on what it is than on the process.

Fran: No. I want to understand how important it is to you to have it. I already know how important it is to me. I thought if I knew how much it meant to you, it would make it easier to decide. Will you tell me what it means to you?

Matthew: I was focusing more on the process of how we would decide to share something important to each of us. There are very few important things I wouldn't give you. I thought, Is there anything I could give you that would so negatively impact me that I wouldn't give it to you? Or, How could we decide in such a way that we would not be establishing a precedent so that when something was important to each of us, the same person would not get it every time?

Fran: That's why I was asking questions—I was trying to determine to whom it really means more.

(one minute remaining)

Matthew: Oh, my god! We might not make it. What was it to you?

Fran: To me, this paper was purely me. It was very individual to me and not something we were going to share. It has a lot to do with my identity as a person. It would mean a lot to me to give it up.

Matthew: How are we going to decide?

Fran: I don't think we will yet. *(Time is up.)*

Clearly the attention of this couple is on the *process* of decision making. Each defined the paper as something having individual meaning and value. They are not fearful of defining themselves, but they are unsure of how to respond in a way that accommodates both sets of self-definition. The wife believes that by understanding what it means to her husband, she will be able to decide objectively who gets the paper. Her husband focuses on developing a method for deciding issues of control. He seems anxious that one of them will always have power over the other, based on this one, current decision. Their discussion breaks down at the point when negotiation or being able to give to one another would help them tackle their impasse. Although they know what they are pursuing in the interaction, they are not yet able to arrive at a joint, completed decision.

"Fight Style"

A style for managing conflict must be developed in the differentiating-differentiating couple. A way of diagnosing how far into this stage the couple has progressed is to enquire about their style of managing conflict in their marriage. Using question #9 in the Diagnostic Questionnaire (see Appendix A) will begin to identify how conflict is viewed and how differences are managed. Well-differentiated individuals develop a "fight style" that is effective in their relationship. Although this style is never identical for different couples, it must be functional for both people involved. Since each individual learned different methods for handling conflict in the family of origin, it takes some time and willingness to grapple with the issues underlying the creation of a fight style that works. A successful fight style leaves each individual feeling understood, even if not agreed with; it is carried out without power plays and ends with a solution or an option with which to experiment.

Boundaries

Still another characteristic that indicates the emergence of differentiation in a couple is the reestablishment of boundaries that were merged during the symbiotic stage. This reestablishment may be expressed through separate activities, separate friendships, separate handling of money, and privacy (both emotionally and with physical space). One wife began setting boundaries in the differentiation phase as is shown in the following discussion:

Maxine: I want my food to be my food. I'd like you to stop taking food off my plate.

Rick: I don't like to waste money. I only eat food off your plate in restaurants. You never eat all you order. I can order a less expensive meal and then finish yours. That way we save money!

Maxine: I hate it! It feels to me like I'm out for dinner with a vulture who is watching every bite I eat. Every bite seems like I'm taking food out of your mouth.

Rick: How about if I stop sneaking it off your plate without asking?

Maxine: I don't even want you to ask for it or to expect it. Order enough for yourself.

Rick: How about if you offer it when you are finished? Only offer it when it's okay with you.

Maxine: All right. We'll try that and I'll let you know if it's working. Are you angry at me for bringing this up?

Rick: No. I just think it's silly. I don't care if you take food off my plate, but I'll respect your wishes.

It is both the capacity to identify one's own thoughts and feelings and the act of bringing these actively into the relationship that launches the differentiation phase. Without an awareness of self, the individuals will return to the symbiotic stage.

Successful differentiation also comes about when areas of responsibility and authority are clearly defined. Couples who define "who is in charge of what" remove the potential for nagging daily conflicts. Stress is greatly reduced, for example, when couples have an agreement about cooking, cleanup, laundry, and household maintenance.

Table 1 provides an overview of some of the inner- and outer-oriented processes involved in the kaleidoscopic unfolding of differentiation in a couple.

THERAPEUTIC TREATMENT OF THE
DIFFERENTIATING-DIFFERENTIATING COUPLE

How therapy is structured with a differentiating-differentiating couple will be highly dependent upon the capacity for self-awareness that has developed in each individual prior to forming the relationship. Even when both partners are well defined, with strongly developed senses of their own identities and the capacity to experience themselves and each other distinctly, the differentiation stage is still a conflictual time. As current differences are identified, the couple is challenged by the need to discover ways of managing these differences. Conflict inevitably accompanies such a process.

If minimal differentiation has occurred previously in the partners, therapy will need to proceed more slowly. Some individual therapy

Table 1

Differentiating of the Self
- Knowing one's own thoughts, feelings, and desires
- Expressing one's thoughts, feelings, and desires
- Diminishing emotional "contagion"—not getting pulled into having to feel the same feelings as the partner at the same time
- Developing awareness of what works for oneself in solving conflicts
- Handling "alone time," including private thoughts and private physical spaces
- Developing individual goals

Differentiating from Others
- Developing more balanced perceptions of the partner and being able to give empathic responses even at times of disagreement
- Handling discrepancies in desires for closeness
- Developing mechanisms for resolving conflicts with the partner
- Developing mechanisms for "how we do things as a couple"
- Recognizing and handling different value systems

Establishing Boundaries
- Developing separate friendships
- Delineating separate areas of family and household responsibilities
- Planning for separate activities
- Delineating separate areas of financial responsibility
- Developing the capacity to handle privacy within the relationship

---

sessions may serve as a useful adjunct. In these types of couples, the goal at home and in the therapy office is identical: to help each individual allow the "self" to emerge, and to come to know the feelings that reside in the real self. Simultaneously each partner must learn to tolerate and support the emerging self of the other. Arriving at this point requires progressing through the steps we listed earlier in this chapter. Like learning to walk, these steps are first done in a halting, awkward manner. However, with experience and help they will become more fluid.

As a therapist, it is important to create the environment in the office that will allow these steps to unfold. In this stage, the use of many structured techniques will often be counterproductive because they impose a structure that is more suitable for the therapist than for the client. This perspective of nonstructured involvement on the part of the therapist is in direct contradiction to the amount of activity we described earlier as being required in working with couples in hostile-dependent relationships. Most facilitative at this stage are questions that help each individual come to identify, understand, and articulate his or her own feelings. Too high a level of therapist activity will interfere with the client's growth process of "stretching" himself or herself to learn to focus on his or her own internal process. The client may instead begin to adapt to the structure created by the therapist.

Case example: Sylvia and Bruce

One indication for therapists that differentiation is beginning to occur successfully is when partners are able to interact with each other in a straightforward manner, free of the projection and/or manipulative attempts to get one another to change that typically characterize undifferentiated individuals. We witnessed a couple successfully differentiating with one another in the case of Bruce and Sylvia, who had been married for 10 years. Sylvia came to a session upset because she had tried to talk to Bruce about her uncertainty regarding whether or not to return to work, and if so, what type of work she would like to pursue. (She had worked prior to their marriage in several child-care jobs and also as a psychiatric technician.) As Sylvia began expressing her confusion to Bruce, he became impatient and irritated, urging her to "just make up her mind once and for all." Sylvia cried as she described his impatience with her. The following conversation ensued:

Ellyn: What is it that you want from Bruce when you talk to him about your career dilemma?

Sylvia: I want him to ask me questions but not expect me to come up with a quick answer. I want to sit in a quiet place and be uninterrupted by the telephone or our kids.

Initially, Bruce felt unable and unwilling to respond in this way. He stated, "I'm impatient! This has been going on for 10 years! Will it go on for another 10 years? I'm tired of her indecision."

Sylvia was then asked to talk more about what made choosing a career so difficult for her.

Sylvia: I hear my mother saying how good I am with children, and then I think I should either be a teacher or do child-care work. I hear you saying I have a good logical mind, and then I think I should go into accounting. I get confused and I think that both of you know me better than I know myself. All I know so far is the things that I like best are the things that I do around the house.

Ellyn: Sylvia, how did your parents respond to your activities as a child?

Sylvia: I could never do things fast enough for my father, and my mother always carefully prescribed things she wanted me to excel in. She was always pushing me to be the best, but it was always in areas of her choosing. That's why I wish Bruce would stop hurrying me.

Bruce was then asked to express his feelings and any lingering impatience so that he would be able to ask Sylvia questions and help her begin to identify more clearly the things that brought her satisfaction. After hearing about Sylvia's childhood and talking more about his impatience, Bruce recognized that he felt helpless to solve her problem. He was relieved to understand that it was not his job to provide solutions. Once he could separate her inner issue of learning to identify and evaluate her talents and desires from his supportive role as her husband and friend, he was able to view Sylvia as a separate person and to help her. He no longer accused himself of failing to help her solve her dilemma. At this point, Bruce was able to begin actively to facilitate Sylvia's process of inner searching:

Bruce: Sylvia, tell me more about the things that you like to do.

Sylvia: I like the remodeling work that I've helped do on our house. I like baking for and with the kids. I really most enjoy being a homemaker, but I don't want to stay home forever.

Bruce: What do you like about being at home?

Sylvia: I like being in control of my time. I like being home when the kids get home from school. I like the feeling that I have when the house is clean and I've added things to a room to make it look especially pretty. I like making new curtains and choosing the colors.

When the session ended, Bruce and Sylvia had agreed to have

several more discussions like this one in the coming weeks. Over time Sylvia was able to identify that her truest form of pleasure came through decorating and remodeling work. She began to take a series of design courses at the local junior college and eventually started a small interior decorating business which she ran out of her own home.

This example demonstrates how Sylvia's differentiation process had been impeded in her early life by her parents, and how the same pattern was being recreated in her marriage. In response to both her parents and her husband, Sylvia had typically been angry and rebellious yet unable to identify enough about what she wanted to be able to create change for herself. By bringing Sylvia's unresolved issues into the couple's awareness, Ellyn was able to help Bruce alter his pattern of interaction with Sylvia, and Sylvia was able to become more in tune with her most genuine feelings. In this way, the couple's relationship became mutually healing and facilitative of further development for each partner.

Conflict Management

Since the process of differentiation is a time of emotional turmoil and conflict, both within the couple relationship and also within each individual person, a means for resolving conflicts in *wants*, *goals*, *values*, *personality styles*, and *philosophy of life* must be developed. As we can see from Sylvia and Bruce's case, how each individual approaches these difficult feelings will depend on two major factors: 1) the individual's prior history of managing conflictual and ambiguous feelings; and 2) the response of the partner to newly emerging differences and disagreements. If the differences in the couple are masked for the sake of peace and harmony, there will be unnecessary restraints on the growth of the individuals and the relationship. Neither will evolve fully into the differentiation stage and symbiotic interaction will prevail.

Much has been written in the psychological literature about managing anger and conflict in couples. Both Richard Stuart (1980) and George Bach (1969) have described very specific techniques for managing conflict, and we will not review the many effective approaches that have been presented elsewhere. However, we will highlight a method we have developed to teach couples to manage a large variety of conflictual situations that occur at home and in the therapist's office. For this method to be effective the therapist must be emotionally comfortable, allowing the couple's conflict to surface in the differentiation stage. Otherwise, the therapist might steer the couple away from addressing their problems directly. However, since raising differences can rapidly degenerate into a squabbling, blaming interaction, the therapist must be prepared to manage this as well.

The therapist's dilemma when working with a bickering couple is that often both partners seem to be right and justified in what they are describing about the other. In an attempt to be fair and not align with either partner, the therapist typically will let one person ventilate anger to the other, and then let the partner respond. The response is often one of justification or a cross-complaint which will detract from the problem at hand. It is easy for a therapist to feel bewildered by the apparent fact that both partners are justified in the emotional upset they are experiencing. Attending to one partner's problem to the exclusion of that of the other partner leads to one partner feeling "ganged up on."

The screaming and blaming or muted anger that often accompany disagreements between partners in the process of differentiating is an emotional cry to be heard and responded to. During these times, each person will find it difficult to take into consideration the emotional resources and availability of the partner. Generally, there is a global demand for a symbiotic solution: "My partner must be totally available and all-giving." Usually, such a demand is met with defense.

We begin to structure this chaos by teaching the partners a technique in which one partner is the *initiator* and the other is the *responder*. Each of these positions has prescribed roles. The role of the *initiator* is to:

— bring up the problem;
— describe his or her feelings about the problem;
— describe what he or she wants to happen or would like to feel or accomplish by the end of the discussion.

The role of the *responder* is to:

— listen;
— ask questions until she or he understands why the partner feels the way he or she feels;

—respond with empathic statements before moving into any problem solving or decision making that will be focused on helping the initiator;

—stay with this position until a soothing moment has occurred and been experienced.

At the beginning of each session, we ask partners, "Whose issue will we address today?" The couple must negotiate and decide. We build in an expectation of only attending to one partner in each session. This helps the other learn to delay gratification and develop more frustration tolerance.

It is important to understand that both of these roles require complex maturational skills. The initiator must rely on self in order to express clearly the issue and the feelings of concern. For relatively undifferentiated individuals, this request by the therapist creates an optimal push and leads to the building of new self-awareness and further ego development. It also prevents symbiotic interaction and/or "mind reading," and requires the initiator to think and feel at the same time. Often, the relatively undifferentiated individual will become impatient or angry with the therapist at the expectation that he or she label feelings or make direct requests. The therapist must then exert extra effort to help the initiator articulate and resolve the anger felt toward the therapist for pushing in this direction. In doing this, the therapist provides a positive role model for the partner to internalize and, over time, will come to be experienced as caring by the initiator.

The responder, by virtue of being in this role, is required to focus in a concentrated way on the other as a distinct, separate person. By prescribing this role, the therapist helps to inhibit an escalation of feelings or competitive needs. The prescribed goal for this individual is to be empathic, nurturing, and soothing. Usually, in very undifferentiated individuals it is best to begin focusing on feelings that are not directly connected with the partner, and then move gradually to those that are.

Often, the initiator is unable to begin with a clear statement about his or her concern but instead will "unload" cathartically. Many individuals believe that ventilating their feelings is all that is necessary; they then sit back and wait for the responder to reply. We interrupt this behavior by refocusing on the initiator and asking him to think about the feelings he has just expressed. We ask questions such as: What is the core issue that is upsetting you right now? What is the main problem you want your partner to respond to? Will you tell your partner in one sentence what you are feeling and what you want her to do? Often, after the catharsis and questioning sequence, the initiator is able to clarify the issue he or she wants to resolve.

For example, Rebecca angrily complained about her husband's incessant sexual demands: "I feel like I'm living with an animal; you are treating me like an object." After Rebecca ventilated more of her upset, we asked her to say more about what she was feeling.

Rebecca: I'm scared. I'll never live up to Ian's demands. I'll never perform to his standards. I'm getting frightened to go to bed each night.

Ellyn: Do you know what you want Ian to do?

Rebecca: I'm not sure. What I want is a lot to ask for. It will make him mad.

Pete: Will you say, for you, what you want.

Rebecca: I want you to stop pushing for sex. I'd like a month of no sex without you being angry — and I'd like to keep coming here to talk about it.

Now we ask the responder to respond in the role we described above. In doing so, we are structuring the responder's activity in a way that directly facilitates his or her ability to pay attention to the *other* rather than to himself or herself. We want the responder to move out of a self-centered, defensive position and into one that expresses a caring interest in the partner.

In the above example, Ian, as responder, first said, "If you would initiate once in a while, I wouldn't push you so hard."

Ellyn: Ian, it would be easy to feel combative in your position. See if you can put your anger aside and respond to Rebecca's feelings.

Ian: I never realized before that you were frightened. I thought you were being stubborn and trying to thwart me. I'm sorry you've been afraid of me. I can see where I've been tough on you.

In a later session, after Rebecca had talked more about her perform-ance fears, Ian said, "I love you—all of you, just the way you are. I didn't marry you for sex or for your body. I married you because of you."

As partners alternate back and forth between each role in different sessions, a situation is created that enhances the development of object relations: both individuals are gaining real-life experience in learning how to shift between a self focus and a focus on the other. Although this appears to be a structured technique, it is one that allows for freedom and autonomy of expression in both partners. The initiator-responder roles remove competitive, escalating transactions and pro-vide an environment in which it becomes possible for both partners to have their own issue resolved.

Problem Solving Versus Developmental Change

The types of solutions we help couples pursue are dependent upon whether the central issue is one requiring straightforward problem solving or whether it is an issue involving developmental changes. Less differentiated couples try to take a developmental conflict and treat it as a problem-solving process. Problem-solving situations are easier and can be handled with *quid pro quo* agreements. These agreements are most successful when the items to be negotiated are discrete and identifiable, such as, "I will go to the movie you want to see tonight if you will go to the hockey game with me next week." In these negotia-tions, each person gives a little and is willing to make a trade-off to solve the problem.

Most conflicts, however, are not solved so easily because there is a developmental issue at their base. For example, often the partner in the role of initiator is searching for a soothing, nurturing response from the other partner that will indicate the partner's ability to be empathi-cally differentiated rather than responding from a demanding self-centered position. We think of these exchanges as soothing moments— moments in which the initiator has communicated clearly and the responder has returned a communication that is effectively empathic. What is communicated is caring, understanding, appreciation, and the message that the responder knows what it is like for a brief moment to live in the initiator's shoes. For these moments to occur, the initiator must be able to express feelings without blame, and the responder must be able to put aside a defense or need to counterattack and respond in a giving way that supports developmental growth. Such special moments need time and closure: time is needed for the initiator to absorb the impact of the partner's response; closure is needed for both parties to recognize on an emotional level that they have related to one another in an effective way. The initiator has communicated a well-differentiated request that enables the partner to understand the self of the initiator; and the responder also has been able to give in a well-differentiated way. Moving too quickly to problem solving is, therefore, counterproductive and contraindicated, for it diminishes the poignancy of the moment and minimizes the success of significant communication between the partners.

Another way in which developmental problems require a different emphasis occurs when the initiator is asking for a change from the partner that is not a simple behavioral change but one that actually requires developmental leaps. The initiator may act as if he is requesting a very small change when, in fact, what he is asking for would require major changes in personality structure. For example, "I'd like you to be more affectionate" or "I'd like you to be more open and expressive" or "I'd like you to be neat and organized." Such changes cannot be negotiated in a *quid pro quo* fashion. In fact, the therapist who supports a *quid pro quo* response will be predisposing both himself and the couple for failure. Instead, both the initiator and the responder can be informed that the requested change is not small but, on the contrary, quite large and significant. As discussed in Chapter 3, the initiator is then asked to participate in creating the change he or she is requesting. The more extensive the change that is being requested, the more the initiator will need to help in creating the circumstances that will facilitate the desired change in the responder. Of course, this is only possible if the responder is willing to make the change.

Case example: Eva and Charles

Eva and Charles came to therapy with the problem of poor communication. Eva was most upset about the lack of communication and complained, "Charles never talks to me. He's withdrawn. I get so frustrated I could just shake him!" To make matters worse, Charles had become less involved in household responsibilities, leaving more and more of it to fall on Eva's shoulders. In the evenings when both would return from demanding jobs, Charles would retire after dinner to his woodshop and Eva would clean the kitchen, do the laundry, or pay bills. Charles's desire in therapy was for Eva to stop nagging him; Eva's desire was for increased attention and communication.

In one session in which Eva was the initiator, she said to Charles: "I'm angry, I'm sad, and I'm lonely. I want you to talk to me more. You withdraw more and more often, and we can't even sit down and talk to each other. I'd like for us to spend some time in the evenings talking to one another."

Charles responded that these "emotional summit conferences" made him feel anxious and uncomfortable. Although it was common for Eva to talk to her friends or to get together over a cup of coffee, Charles said he had never seen his parents have emotional discussions and he had never done this as an adult with his buddies. It was an extremely uncomfortable process for him to sit down and talk about feelings. He admitted that talking to Eva might be enjoyable but he could not imagine just sitting down and talking.

At this point, Eva began to express her frustration in a way that belittled Charles's difficulty. Here, the therapist (Pete) intervened and pointed out that Charles was not Eva, and that what came easily to her was indeed quite threatening for him. Pete then asked Charles how Eva might help him.

Charles: It might be easier if I had a screwdriver in my hand and could work in my woodshop. Perhaps, in the garage. Maybe we could talk in the garage.

Eva: But if we're out in the woodshop talking, I won't have your full attention. You probably won't even listen to what I say, you'll be so involved in making those end tables.

Pete: Charles has just opened the door for you. Would you be willing to go through that door to join him—perhaps bring a pot of tea or a comfortable chair, and experiment? Would you do that a few times to see what happens?

Eva agreed and a few weeks later reported that although the discussions were not earth-shattering, they were leading toward a greater ease in talking to one another. They were beginning to discuss their own individual interests and some activities they could possibly do together as a couple. From this, Eva recognized that as long as she was fixated on having the conversation take place at the table or on the couch, she was locking herself into a rigid position rather than focusing on what she wanted, which was increased communication. Charles was willing to develop more communication with her once she was able to acknowledge and respond to his anxiety about talking in a close, intense, one-to-one situation. When Eva was able to give to Charles, by meeting him at a level that fit what he requested, Charles, in turn, was able to respond by giving Eva what she desired.

It is important to initiate this process of helping to create a facilitative environment with small, manageable steps. This allows partners to have the experience of mutually creating a solution to a specific problem. By beginning with problems having a lower emotional charge, partners have a higher probability of being successful. Then, as they develop more of a spirit of trust and cooperation, the more difficult problems can be tackled.

When both members of the couple are actively involved in working toward the solution of a problem, we shift the focus of their work into a larger context. We do this by reminding them that they are building a stronger foundation for the relationship by increasing their mutual trust and cooperation. Even if the problem seems small, it is the process of supporting one another in building a solution that leads to a stronger foundation for the relationship. This creates a momentum for making changes that will give partners the ability to redesign their relationship in the future.

To summarize, some of the important principles are listed below:

1. Attend to only one issue at a time by having one individual be the initiator while the other is the responder.
2. Have the initiator identify her feelings and what she wants to end up solving rather than having her describe what the responder needs to do and how he needs to do it.
3. Involve the initiator in creating an environment that is conducive to change when he is requesting an extensive personality or characterological change from the partner.

4. Help the responder understand and empathize with the initiator.
5. Help the responder connect emotionally with strong personal reasons for making and incorporating the change that is being requested.
6. Find realistic steps that further the individual's development rather than looking for perfect solutions.
7. Use straightforward *quid pro quo* agreements only with discrete, noncharacterological changes.
8. Place the patterns the couple are working to develop into a broader context—that of increasing trust and mutual support so they can build a flourishing relationship together.

Facilitating an Internal Focus

Many individuals have difficulty in making the shift to looking to themselves for a sense of satisfaction. Instead they look to their partners and believe that by adapting to their partners, they will be happy because they are sharing in the partner's happiness. Until each individual is committed to his or her own growth, differentiation will not unfold successfully.

Case example: Edna and Steve

This was true for Edna in the case we described in Chapter 5. As they moved into the differentiation stage of their relationship, Edna still wanted Steve to generate all the excitement and good feelings in their relationship. She would anxiously await his homecoming each evening to find out what he had in store for their evening. The following dialogue demonstrates how we used a gestalt technique to facilitate Edna's movement into further differentiation. Prior to this session, she had been blaming Steve for her unhappiness while simultaneously being unaware of her own desires. This excerpt occurred at a point in the session when Edna had again become angry at Steve, blaming him for another miserable evening.

Pete: *(speaking to Edna)* Turn to Steve, hold your happiness in your hands and say to him, "Here is my happiness; I'm turning it all over to you."

Edna: (laughs) I've been doing that. I don't know if I want to keep doing that!

Pete: Do it. See how you feel.

Edna: (turns to Steve, holding her future happiness in her hands) Here's my future well-being. I'm entrusting my life to you. Treat me gently, because I'm all in your hands.

Steve: (takes what she's holding in her hands)

Pete: What do you feel as you turn your future happiness over to Steve?

Edna: Scared.

Pete: That's what you've been doing. Is that what you want to continue doing?

Ellyn: (to Edna) Will you say one other thing to him? Will you say, "I'm giving you total responsibility for my future so that I can stay a dependent little girl"?

Edna: (begins to cry) I'm giving you my future so that I can stay a dependent little girl.

Ellyn: What do you feel?

Edna: Like a little girl.

Pete: That's what you've been doing.

Edna: That's right. This is where I've been for a long time. I feel stuck here. I don't want to be here, but I feel like this is where I'm meant to be.

Ellyn: Take it back slowly and see what you feel as you take it back.

Edna: (takes back her handful of happiness from Steve) Like I want to protect it.

Ellyn: Now do it again very slowly, and see what you experience when you hold your happiness in your own hands.

Edna: (does it again, first asking Steve to hold it again so that she can take it back very slowly) Part of me feels elated and part of me feels scared. I'm excited by the possibilities, but I'm also scared. I might goof it up, and then I'd have only me to blame.

Ellyn: *(to Edna)* Do something else. Now hold your happiness in your own hands and talk to it and get to know it. Take your time, go slowly.

Edna: *(looking down at the happiness she's holding in her hands)* I'm going to have to get to know you. I don't know what you're all about. I might make some mistakes along the way, but I'm determined. *(said more strongly)* I'm determined, I'm determined to get to know you and to stop blaming.

In a later session, we asked Edna to sit in a second chair and be her own happiness. To do this, she needed to get in touch with what would bring happiness to her rather than looking to Steve to provide happiness for her.

Edna: *(being her own happiness)* I'd like you to take some time for me. *(long pause)* There are two ways I'd like you to take that time. I'd like you to take some quiet time alone in the house, either in the morning or at night, and I'd also like you to make some friends and spend some time with them. In the quiet times, I want you to think about what it is that makes you feel good—what it is you want in the future from your life.

Ellyn: Now change chairs and ask Edna if she's willing to help you do that.

Edna: *(switches from happiness chair to Edna chair)* Yes, I'm willing to do that, and I know the quiet time will be especially important to me, too. If I take more time for myself, then I can get to know myself. I have to stop being so afraid of getting to know me. The quiet will help, and I will get to know myself in a way that I never have before.

Pete: *(speaking to Steve)* How are you feeling right now about what Edna has done?

Steve: Deeply moved. I was impressed to see her defining the obstacles to her happiness and deciding she was willing to do something about it.

After these two sessions, Edna continued becoming more self-defined. She developed a few close friendships and overcame her previous fear of traveling alone. A high point for her came when she traveled alone to Alaska for two weeks.

Steve's movement into the differentiation stage was less dramatic than Edna's, but his progress was no less important or substantial. Behaviorally, he gave up much of his passive behavior (such as leaving dirty dishes on the living room floor and coming home late in the evening) and began to express verbally what he would and would not do, rather than saying yes verbally and no behaviorally.

Differentiating from the Family of Origin

While the process of differentiation occurs throughout life, differentiating from the family of origin is crucial during the differentiating-differentiating stage. Much of the family therapy literature written during the past 15 years addresses techniques to facilitate greater differentiation from the family of origin. Unless both partners differentiate from their families, they will not be able to establish themselves as a couple with a boundary around themselves. Instead, they remain under the amorphous but potent influence of dysfunctional family patterns. For couples for whom this is a new concept, we sometimes introduce the following exercise. We give them a graph and ask that they plot their perceptions of their parents' marriages. After the line representing their parents' marriages is put onto the graph, we then ask them to plot their perceptions of their own marriages. (Note the example on the following pages of the graphs done by Edna and Steve. Particularly note the similarities of unresolved conflicts in all three couples.) Often this exercise identifies ways in which the current marriage is identical or parallel to the marriage established by the parents in the family of origin, such as with Edna and Steve.

Although the description of this technique appears to be cognitive in nature, the application of it seems particularly helpful with clients who are unsophisticated in the therapy process. In order to access the vast amount of information needed to produce one graph, fairly deep levels of experiential memories, images, associations, and past experiences in relation to the primary family experience are activated.

Edna's Graphs

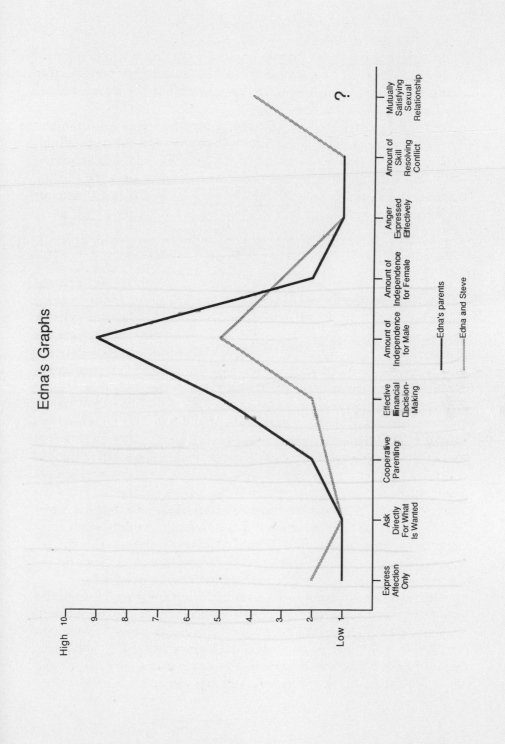

High 10
9
8
7
6
5
4
3
2
Low 1

Express Affection Only
Ask Directly For What Is Wanted
Cooperative Parenting
Effective Financial Decision-Making
Amount of Independence for Male
Amount of Independence for Female
Anger Expressed Effectively
Amount of Skill Resolving Conflict
Mutually Satisfying Sexual Relationship

——— Edna's parents
········· Edna and Steve

?

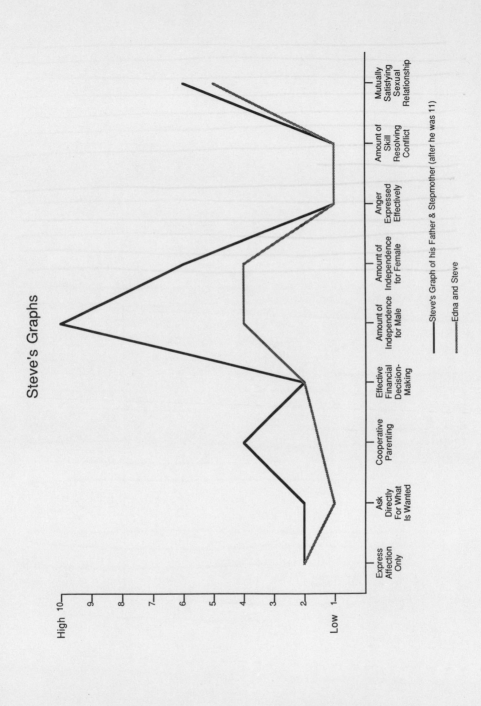

Steve's Graphs

Express Affection Only
Ask Directly For What Is Wanted
Cooperative Parenting
Effective Financial Decision-Making
Amount of Independence for Male
Amount of Independence for Female
Anger Expressed Effectively
Amount of Skill Resolving Conflict
Mutually Satisfying Sexual Relationship

High 10
9
8
7
6
5
4
3
2
Low 1

——— Steve's Graph of his Father & Stepmother (after he was 11)

━━━ Edna and Steve

Since it is common for couples to come to therapy early in their relationship, feeling very frightened because conflict is emerging, it is reassuring for them to understand that differentiation is a healthy growth process. Rather than fearing that something is drastically wrong, they recognize they are involved in a process that is exactly appropriate for the amount of time they have been together. It is a relief to discover that conflict is not necessarily a sign that this relationship was not meant to be!

Ironically, as differentiation increases and partners recognize the depth of their differences in terms of what they want and desire from one another, a greater sense of cooperation and closeness will emerge. In leaving behind the symbiotic solutions of mind reading and automatic need gratification, couples will develop a stronger base of commitment that provides the backbone for the upcoming practicing stage.

CHAPTER 8

The Symbiotic-Practicing Couple

"Don't leave me/Leave me alone!"

Michiko (age 23), a Japanese American, and Peter (age 24) were hometown high school sweethearts who rekindled their relationship in the summer of Peter's junior year of college. They maintained a long-distance, intense relationship while Peter finished college and Michiko worked and lived with her parents. After their wedding, they traveled for the summer and then moved to an apartment. Peter enrolled in a doctoral program in economics.

Michiko had never been without someone to take care of her. She had lived with her parents until her marriage to Peter. Her expectations were that Peter would provide totally for them financially, as well as providing them with an active social life. Peter initially enjoyed the paternal role he played for Michiko. She was pretty, and he was proud to have her looking up to him and depending on him. However, soon after their marriage, he recognized her lethargy and her increasing dependence on him. This frightened him, and he began to move away from her.

Peter found his program intellectually stimulating and he had made friends quickly, finding the new companionship rewarding. Early in the year he had also begun participating in T-groups at the Business School. It seemed that all the stimuli in his environment were pushing him toward greater individuation.

Michiko, on the other hand, was uncertain about what she wanted to do. She had spent the first months of their marriage decorating their apartment and looking for work. Jobs were scarcer than she had anticipated, so she took a job teaching English to young Japanese children who had newly arrived in the United States.

As time went by Michiko began to feel lonely and isolated. She missed spending time with Peter but did not know how to tell him or how to ask for his help directly. She became depressed and moody, and would closet herself in the bedroom without speaking to Peter for several days. As she became more desperate for Peter's love and support, her manipulative behavior escalated into extreme proportions. Although she hoped he would take pity on her and give her more attention and affection, her behavior only resulted in his spending more time away. Their current state-of-affairs did not fit the view either of them held of a happy marriage. Their problems came to a head late one night when Peter returned from the library to discover that Michiko had torn two of his notebooks containing important class notes for his final exams into millions of tiny pieces and scattered them around the bedroom.

Although the details of this case vignette may make it appear that the destructive patterns developed primarily as a result of the external stresses, it became clear in diagnosing and treating this couple that their problems would continue regardless of specific changes in the sources of stress. This was because Michiko desperately wanted to remain at the symbiotic stage and wanted Peter to join her there. Peter, however, was committed to his own development, but was having difficulty initiating differentiation with Michiko. Later in this chapter, we will look at some of the significant aspects involved in treating this couple.

DESCRIPTION AND DIAGNOSIS OF THE SYMBIOTIC-PRACTICING COUPLE

The symbiotic-practicing stage occurs when one partner shifts energy away from the relationship into independent activities and relationships. Identity development becomes primary. This represents a significant change from the beginning stages of the relationship in which the primary source of excitement and fulfillment was found in joint activities, and in the assurance that each partner centered his or her life more exclusively on the other. As a result of this shift, strong tensions develop in the relationship.

The partner who has not yet moved into individual development will often feel betrayed and abandoned. The premise of the relationship had been, "If we are very similar, then we will never part," or "Our major source of satisfaction comes from one another." Now as the shift occurs, the symbiotic partner begins to feel threatened by the possible loss of the relationship and, as a consequence, "holds on" even more tightly than in the initial stage. It is common for this person to make statements such as, "It's just not the same as it used to be," or "My partner isn't there for me like before." The accused partner typically responds with, "I'm going to be smothered if things continue this way!" or "This relationship is making me feel claustrophobic!"

Although the differentiating and practicing stages appear to be shades of the same behavioral continuum, a significant diagnostic difference exists between them. In the differentiating individual, the energy is still directed toward the relationship: emphasis shifts away from purely symbiotic exchanges to the gradual awareness of differences that may be expressed either through an earnest desire to reconcile them effectively, or through manipulative attempts to change the partner. In either case, the context is *relating*. By contrast, in the practicing partner energy is withdrawn from the relationship and refocused into newly coveted, self-directed pursuits.

The symbiotic-practicing stage for couples is virtually equivalent to the practicing stage of the young toddler who jumps down and runs away from his mother whenever she tries to hold him. When she runs after him and scoops him up in her arms, he wiggles to get away. The harder she holds, the more he struggles!

Constant tension exists during this stage, and for some people the struggle takes on a life-or-death quality. Stubbornness and selfishness become new factors with which to reckon. The individual who has moved into the practicing stage is fiercely protective of her independence, and her own future development seems critically dependent on continuing the momentum. Independent activity and personal growth become more highly valued than intimacy or time spent in nurturing the relationship. The practicing partner wants her own way and will show little consideration for the desires or requests of her partner. Whereas during earlier stages of the relationship a strong nonverbal connection existed between the partners, this stage is noted for its lack of emotional contact. The practicing person becomes oblivious to why her behavior is having such a painful impact on the spouse. The more the practicing partner pulls away, the more the other will attempt to return the relationship to the safe and comfortable gratifications of the symbiotic stage. A dynamic struggle is the inevitable result. It may be blatantly verbal and conflict-laden, or it may occur on a more behavioral level where the conflict is acted out via an affair rather than via open and direct verbal communication. As the practicing person begins to feel smothered and engulfed, he seeks a relationship that is free of the constraints and high emotional involvement of the primary relationship. In turn, the affair is likewise terminated as soon as any emotional demands are made because there is such fear of sliding back into the symbiotic stage and losing the individuation that has begun.

For many couples, there is little understanding or awareness of what this struggle is about or why it is happening at this particular time. Each blames the other for the betrayal. Accusations of "Why are you doing this to me?" become common. The symbiotic partner, in particular, seems to feel unloved and demands explanations about the other's behavior. Usually the practicing partner has difficulty explaining clearly why he suddenly wants more independence and more distance from the relationship. Both partners begin to label this time as a *falling out of love*. What began as a potentially healthy movement for the relationship now becomes interpreted as a beacon of disruption or destruction.

The symbiotic partner is the one who is attempting to maintain the emotional connectedness of the relationship. As the practicing partner becomes invested in activities and involvements away from home, the more difficult it becomes for the symbiotic partner to maintain the emotional connection. Over time, the symbiotic partner finds it increasingly hard to ask directly for what is desired, particularly in emotional areas. Instead, he feels progressively threatened about the possibility of the relationship ending, so that his fear and confusion escalate into angry, demanding behavior.

Simultaneously, the practicing partner becomes increasingly withdrawn. Behaviors that were once enjoyed by both are now experienced as smothering and demanding, and attempts to maintain emotional closeness are repelled and resented. Together, partners become locked in a negative feedback system in which they continue to reinforce destructive feelings and projections about one another. Ironically, the practicing partner usually does not encourage the symbiotic partner to move into equally independent behaviors, as would be expected.

Rather, the very human and vulnerable side of the practicing individual continues to want a safe and loving base at home.

Many times, the symbiotic-practicing impasse ends in divorce, separation, or at the very least, severely impaired self-esteem for both partners.

Why does one partner shift into a more independent phase of the relationship while the other does not? Several factors may contribute to this common type of disequilibrium. First, the needs and current life circumstances of each of the individuals may differ markedly. As in the example of Peter and Michiko, or when one partner is working at a challenging job while the other is caring for a home and/or newborn infant, the life circumstances alone can nudge the couple into relational imbalance. In addition, cultural supports and prohibitions often encourage identity development for one partner while discouraging it for the other. Most sociocultural groups support different behaviors in men than in women. Traditionally (even archetypally), men have received more support for independence and self-development than have women. They have been trained to go out into the world and act as providers and protectors, while the women have functioned as the homemakers and caretakers for both spouse and children. The "hunter mentality" developed in men has not been totally eradicated with the veneer of civilization, and it leads men to avoid the emotionality of the differentiation stage and frequently supports them entering the practicing stage first. The advances of the women's liberation movement in the last 20 years, however, have led to major shifts in roles between men and women. In the United States it is now common for women to venture first beyond the safe, secure boundaries of the relationship. This confronts men with previously unknown feelings of insecurity and inadequacy, and often leads them to desperately attempt to reestablish the symbiosis.

Also, individuals' expectations about marriage may differ markedly based on experiences from their own families of origin. The partners' levels of ego development may have been different from the beginning, but not obvious during the circumstances surrounding their falling in love. This occurs more commonly in marriages that happen quickly. Finally, there is the natural human evolutionary drive toward growth and development, which is an idiosyncratic process within each individual and therefore not likely to emerge in synchrony with another's.

Unresolved childhood developmental issues will also help to determine who moves first and how threatening the change is for the partner. This was the case for Tiny, a 35-year old contractor, who was desperately attempting to maintain a symbiotic relationship with his wife. Although he blamed his lack of success on her, he nonetheless used his failure to become financially and emotionally dependent on her.

Tiny had grown up as the younger and smaller in a set of boy twins. Even though he was 6'4" tall and weighed 225 pounds, his father still called him "Tiny." During his childhood, Tiny's father had been threatened by any success on Tiny's part. When Tiny would begin to beat his father on the golf course, his father refused to play golf any longer with him. Simultaneously, Tiny's mother babied him by picking him up each day after school, telling him how sorry she was that he didn't like to play with friends or participate in sports, and then bringing him home to keep her company while she did the cooking and cleaning. The combined messages from his parents led Tiny to conclude that both adulthood and success were dangerous goals, since either threatened the loss of love from one parent.

Tiny played out this view of reality in his current marriage to Anita by depending on her financially and by getting drunk on occasion and not showing up to sign contracts when he was offered new job possibilities. He blamed his lack of success and symbiotic behavior on Anita by saying that she would undercut him when he did have a potential job, by making demands on him that he care for their children.

Another way that Tiny learned to expect a symbiotic relationship in his own marriage was through the scenario his father and mother repeatedly portrayed at the dinner table. His father expected his mother to be able to read his mind and pass the bread or gravy to him without his having to ask. If he needed to ask for seconds—or, indeed, for anything on the table—he would become enraged and yell at Tiny's mother. She did not protest.

With the valence of these early unresolved issues pulling Tiny toward a symbiotic relationship, he had tremendous difficulty coping with his wife's move toward differentiation, and even more difficulty when she began practicing.

Couples such as Tiny and Anita who have never differentiated together will have tremendous difficulty when one member of the couple moves into the practicing stage. Without the base provided by differentiating together, the independence and exploration of the practicing stage become extremely threatening.

The symbiotic-practicing relationship develops from the intersection of three major factors:

1. The couple has enjoyed an initial positive and mutually satisfying symbiosis.
2. Minimal differentiation has occurred between the partners so that they have not yet developed mechanisms within the relationship to handle conflicting desires, anger, or ambiguity.
3. A developmental shift occurs unexpectedly in one partner resulting in increased demands for independence.

Diagnostic interview: Margo and Bob

Following is an initial diagnostic interview and added commentary with a couple, Margo and Bob, who had been married for three years. We chose this case material to illustrate how the use of our diagnostic interview can help elicit and identify both the overt responses and the subtle indicators from each partner that coalesce into a diagnosis of the symbiotic-practicing couple. Also, the interview follows a predictable developmental sequence that enables these issues to unfold.

Pete: Will the two of you tell me why you're here and what it is you want to get out of being in therapy?

Bob: (to Margo) Why don't you go first?

> *Bob begins by deferring to his wife. Perhaps he has difficulty actively asserting what he wants or defining himself.*

Margo: Okay. It seems like we're not able to see things eye to eye. We just want different things. We're fighting a lot more. It seems as if Bob is, well, as if he's just clinging to me. I'm doing some different things. I have some new friends at work. We like to go out and dance and Bob doesn't like to do what I want to do. It's frustrating, and I'm not sure I want to be in the relationship anymore.

> *Margo begins by noting the rising conflicts between her and Bob, which constitute a major change in the relationship. She succinctly*

describes her growing independent behavior and Bob's recipro-
cal sense of threat.

Pete: (to Margo) It sounds like you're wanting more distance in the relationship, and that you're also questioning whether you want to stay in the relationship. What about you, Bob, what is it you want?

Bob: Well, I think we have a good relationship. I think when people are in a relationship, they ought to want to spend a lot of time together. Margo seems to want to spend a lot of time by herself. I think when you're in a relationship, you ought to find things both of you enjoy and do those things together.

Here Bob attempts to reaffirm their "good relationship" and his need for the continued symbiotic involvement.

Pete: What do you feel, Bob, when Margo wants to spend more time away from you?

Bob: She spends enough time away from me. She goes to work, she has a lot of girlfriends. I feel like there's a lot of time apart as it is, and I want to spend more time with her.

Early in the interview, Margo revealed that she is spending more time away from Bob. She wants to continue socializing with other people. This is important enough to her that she is consider-ing divorce to escape from her husband's clinging. Bob, on the other hand, using an almost whiney voice, describes how he is wanting more time together. He seems fearful.

Pete: I hear you say you'd like to spend more time with Margo, and I'm still wondering what it is you feel when she doesn't want to spend time with you.

Bob: I feel a loss. I just don't feel complete by myself. When she goes to work, it's okay. I'm glad that she has a career. But I feel like I should come first most of the time.

Bob wants Margo to complete him.

Pete: It sounds like you feel scared or angry.

Bob: Maybe angry. I just can't understand why she wants to be in a relationship with me and spend so much time away.

Margo: We spend a lot of time together. We're together evenings, weekends; we're together seven days a week except when I'm at work.

> *Bob is fearful; it seems that having time together is calming for him, just as it is for the infant to be held in his mother's arms. Of course, at this stage in the relationship, the more time he demands, the more threatened his wife becomes that she will need to give up her newfound independence. Her voice sounds panicky when she says, "We spend a lot of time together. We're together evenings, weekends, seven days a week except when I'm at work."*

Pete: I'd like to back up a minute and get some history on your relationship. How long have the two of you been together?

> *Instead of intensifying the conflict as Pete might do in a therapeutic interview, he explores the early history of the relationship to get a more complete diagnostic picture.*

Margo: We've been married for three years and we were together for a year-and-a-half before that.

Pete: What was the very beginning of your relationship like? Will you think back to when the two of you first got together four-and-a-half years ago? What did you experience then? *(Both give big smiles and look warmly at each other.)*

Bob: We spent all our time together then. We worked together and lived together. We went to school together. I thought it was great. *(Margo laughs.)*

Margo: Yeah, we lived in a one-room apartment, and we got along great!

> *Laughter and warm smiles reveal that the earlier closeness was not a problem for Margo.*

Pete: At that stage of the relationship, the closeness wasn't a problem for either of you. Then something happened. Margo, what do you think changed?

Margo: I finished school and got a job. People at work started planning all kinds of social activities. At first I'd just go out during work, but then I started wanting to be included in doing things with them after work, or going out for a drink, or going out to dance. Bob doesn't like to do those kinds of things. We'd go places, and Bob would just hide in the corner and not do anything. After a while, I just started going by myself. It was a lot easier. He wouldn't be part of the group, so it made sense for me to go by myself. I started doing more and more things by myself and enjoying them. Before, it used to be just the two of us doing things that we really enjoyed. We didn't have all these outside influences then.

Pete: (turning to Bob) Is that how you see the change?

Bob: Yes. It was when we finished school that things seemed to change.

Both identify the same historical turning point.

Pete: Bob, is it hard for you to develop yourself and your own social network away from Margo?

Pete explores Bob's self-perceptions to determine more about what is preventing him from developing his independence.

Bob: I just don't have the same social needs as she has. She now seems to want to be with other people all the time.

Pete: You don't have the desire to develop in any of your own directions, like Margo is? If you did, would that be easy or difficult for you?

Pete sidesteps Bob's resistance and questions him again.

Bob: I don't think that would be hard at all.

Margo: To do what?

Pete: For him to go out and develop friends of his own and independent activities away from you.

Margo: I don't think he could.

Margo undermines Bob's self-assertion.

Pete: You don't think he could? There seems to be a disagreement between the two of you about what Bob can do.

Pete emphasizes the conflict to arouse Bob's energy, to determine how he will respond.

Bob: Before I met Margo, I had a lot of friends but I picked her over my friends, and now maybe I'm a little bit angry that she's not doing the same thing. I gave up my friends for her, and now she's going out and making her own friends, and I feel like I lost out somewhere.

Bob responds to the challenge with a mild expression of anger and another indication of his immaturity. His view of marriage is quite primitive in that he considers it a contest that he has lost and has an either/or choice of wife or friends. Pete notes this pattern for a later time and continues with the diagnostic interview.

Pete: Margo, did you know he'd done that?

Margo: It never seemed to me that he liked his friends either.

Again, Margo undermines rather than supports Bob.

Pete: I'd like to shift and ask the two of you a question: In your relationship now, what is it that you find most rewarding or pleasurable?

Margo: We play together really well. We have a lot of fun when we're in a good place. I like how creative Bob is.

Bob: I definitely agree with all of that.

Bob returns to an earlier position of deferral and passivity rather than expressing an independent opinion.

Margo: Bob has a really good image of himself. I feel very supported by him, and I feel a lot of comfort from his support of what I'm doing. I try to be supportive of him, too.

Bob: I don't need much support. I enjoy supporting her. I think that I have a lot more self-confidence than she has.

> *Pete begins to ask another question, but Margo interrupts to point out that Bob did not say what it is that he enjoys about the relationship.*

Bob: I agree with everything you said.

> *Another deferral from Bob, even when Margo solicits his own thoughts.*

Pete: I'd like to ask one more question. We need to clarify what it is that each of you individually wants to get out of being in therapy, and what it is each of you as a couple wants to get out of therapy?

> *Pete goes on to establish a treatment contract.*

The therapist begins the diagnostic interview with Margo and Bob wanting to understand each individual's view of the current problem. Throughout, he checks both people's perceptions. Never does he accept one view as the whole story, thereby entering into an early coalition with either member of the couple. He also wants to uncover and understand the feelings that are created within each individual by the current problem. The interview then progresses to determining what the early stages of the relationship were like for each partner, and to uncovering whatever current developmental block is preventing the relationship from unfolding naturally.

In this diagnostic interview, Pete establishes that both Margo and Bob identify the same historical turning point for difficulty emerging in the relationship. That point occurred after graduation when Margo betrayed the original "nonverbal marital contract." As her self-esteem was enhanced by her accomplishments in the larger social world, she began to move outside the exclusive circle which she and Bob had created. Conflict surfaced and the homeostasis established earlier in the relationship no longer worked. Margo became increasingly active in pursuing friendships and activities away from home, insisting that she would never let Bob stop her, even if this resulted in divorce. Bob felt threatened and became increasingly demanding. Together, they were unable to resolve this impasse. Because the relationship had not evolved through the differentiation stage in which they would have worked out mechanisms for handling their differences, they were unprepared for the abrupt changes and stresses of the practicing stage.

They also had developed a covert agreement in which Bob was to appear strong and self-confident by supporting Margo. Both agreed that Bob had a positive self-image and that he didn't need much support. By participating in this agreement, Margo was able to enjoy the comfort of Bob's support while expanding her own development in the outer world. At the same time, she covertly undermined his independence and thus did not need to feel threatened herself by losing the comfort of her home-based support system.

This particular feedback process is significant in the dynamics of the symbiotic-practicing couple. Many beginning therapists tend to view the individual who is practicing as the healthy partner. The other is often labelled as "dependent," or is seen as stifling the relationship. In making the diagnosis, it is important for the therapist to recognize that the practicing partner benefits enormously from the support of the partner who remains committed to the symbiotic position. *The problem in the relationship, then, continues due to the feedback process of overt and covert agreements between both partners.*

THERAPEUTIC TREATMENT OF
THE SYMBIOTIC-PRACTICING COUPLE

After the symbiotic-practicing diagnosis is made, the therapist and couple develop a plan. The overall contract for the therapy should be defined by the couple in their own language. The goals will involve helping the couple manage the differentiation process together and then learn how to support greater independence in one another. This therapeutic focus requires a delicate balancing act, because couples often come for therapy when one wants more closeness while the other wants more distance. Indeed, what the symbiotic partner wants is not new and better insights into the problem, but proof that the therapist understands and will help undo the betrayal of the spouse. For the symbiotic partner the major goal is, "How am I going to get my spouse to shape up and go back to the way he was, and how can I gain the therapist as an ally in this mission?" At the same time, the practicing partner has his own agenda: he wants to have his cake and eat it too! He wants to continue expanding his newfound freedom while maintaining a secure anchor point at home. This polarization in partners' goals may even necessitate initial establishment of discrepant treatment contracts.

Such was the case for Bob and Margo. They established the following contracts for themselves.

Bob: I think basically we have a good relationship with just a couple of kinks in it. I'd like us to work these out. I don't think it's the right move for us to split up right now.

Pete: When you say you'd like to make the relationship work better, what is it that you're thinking you will be doing to help make the relationship work better?

Bob: I'm not sure. Our problem seems to be that we can't balance our time. I'd like to have more closeness. I'd like to have Margo put more energy toward me.

Pete: So your goal would be to have more closeness?

Bob: Yes, that's right.

Pete: And you will do what it takes on your end to create more closeness in this relationship?

Bob: You bet.

Pete: Margo, what about you?

Margo: My goal is to have more variety of things in our lives and not spend so much time together. I feel like I've put Bob as a priority for long enough. I'd like to see and do other things. I'd like to be able to do more things independently—and bring more richness into the relationship from other sources so that we're not the only source of enrichment for one another.

Pete: So you'd like less togetherness and more diversity?

Margo: That's right.

Pete: And you will do what it takes from your end to bring that about?

Margo: For sure!

In describing our therapeutic approach with symbiotic-practicing couples, we want to convey a sense of plurality and creativity. There are many ways to intervene: first are the *process interventions* designed to change the patterns by which the partners interact; second are *behavioral interventions* intended to develop skills that promote differentiation within each individual; and last are *intrapsychic interventions* focused on identifying the historical influences operating within each individual and then understanding how the shadows of the past are helping to maintain the impasse in the present. After clear structuring has occurred at the beginning to provide safety for the couple to work on their own issues, the therapy process involves intervening in a way that will promote a mutual process of differentiation.

In structuring the initial phase of treatment for the symbiotic-practicing couple, it is important to help them arrange some predictable time together each week. This condition diminishes the anxiety on the part of the symbiotic partner and helps the practicing partner realize that he will not need to spend constant time at home. It is also essential for the couple to agree on having no affairs, or, if there is an ongoing affair, to wait until the affair has been terminated or put on hold before committing to couples therapy. As long as the affair continues, it will serve as a magnet like "alcoholism." All the focus in the room will be on the betrayal (the alcoholic) and this often prevents the couple from straightforwardly addressing their own issues. Frequently, the partner having an affair will not wish to terminate it until he or she is sure the marriage will change. In this case, we may hold several sessions to explain what happens in couples therapy and to help each partner give voice to their fears. Then couples therapy is stopped until the commitment to "no affairs" during therapy can be made. When we were working with one couple, the husband balked at the requirement that he discontinue his affair, so after three sessions couples therapy was stopped. Only two months later when he had seen his wife begin to move out of her symbiotic position and begin dating did he make the decision to give up his affair and commit himself to working on his marriage. At that point, couples therapy was resumed.

Case example: Lisa and Aaron

In the following verbatim transcription, we demonstrate some important aspects of the early phase of therapy with the symbiotic-practicing couple. This interview highlights how, even when desires seem so diametrically opposed, there are ways to facilitate emotional understanding and mutual compromises that provide a foundation of support for more active differentiation. Usually, this therapeutic movement involves exposing the pain and common grief that underlie the partners' respective anger. Once the angry betrayal is understood to be each person's reaction to losing the intensity of the symbiotic stage, partners become freer to give to each other as well as to continue their own differentiation process.

Aaron and Lisa came to therapy after one year of marriage. After experiencing a close and satisfying symbiotic period, Lisa had begun to demand independence and separation from Aaron, who felt no such need. The following interview occurred during the second session, which took place after the diagnosis had been made and a 10-week plan established. Both partners had committed to working on the relationship without threatening separation or divorce. In this interview, they reveal a feeling of mutual unresolved loss in leaving the symbiosis, and a mutual unresolved process of differentiation. They also demonstrate the cybernetic manner in which the independent activity of one partner activates the clinging behavior of the other.

Ellyn: What do you want today?

Aaron: I don't know.

Lisa: I'd like to get to the point where we quit coming up against the wall time after time, so we don't have to keep coming here.

Aaron: (with back turned toward Lisa) I'm for that.

Ellyn: Aaron, will you look at Lisa when she's talking to you?

Lisa: Whenever I want to discuss this, you don't want to face up to it.

Aaron: What?

Lisa: We can't talk anymore.

Aaron: There's no time to talk. You are always off on some adventure, running off doing some new thing.

Lisa: I can't get you out of the house.

Aaron: I can't get you to stay home.

Very early in the interview, their mutual anger and feelings of betrayal become evident. Lisa's anger is most apparent in her voice; Aaron's in his body language.

Ellyn: Aaron, are you angry at Lisa?

Aaron: I'm getting there.

Ellyn: You seem angry. Tell Lisa what you are angry about.

Aaron: That my wanting to spend time with you is somehow wrong. It seems like that should be positive, not negative.

Ellyn: Lisa, are you angry at Aaron?

Lisa: You bet! I'm angry that getting you to do anything outside our cozy little home is like pulling teeth. You don't want to grow anymore. That frustration makes me angry. I feel like you are holding me back. That I am holding myself back.

Aaron: You exaggerate. That's not the situation. You're unfair!

Ellyn: Stop! Will each of you tell the other what you heard. What is the other angry about?

They have not yet heard each other. Each blames the other without hearing the loss or betrayal. Ellyn decides to follow the anger a little longer before focusing on their mutual loss.

Lisa: It sounds to me like he's angry at me because I like to go out and do things. Is that why you're angry?

Aaron: No. It's just that you always have to be doing something, making some plan or other. There's no communication.

Lisa: I feel compelled to do other things. Our time alone is not what it used to be. We've grown in such different directions, we don't have any common ground.

Aaron: I agree with you. You're too busy doing your own thing to keep the common ground intact. We don't have time to talk about what matters and what we care about. We are growing apart.

Ellyn: Aaron, instead of blaming Lisa, tell her what you want.

Aaron: Yes, I want to relax with you. I want to talk and enjoy you and not be pushed all the time.

Lisa: Have you ever come up to me and said, "Let's just sit down and talk?" I've never said no.

Aaron: Well, you said earlier that we're not communicating. Obviously, the need to talk is there. I don't think I have to make it so obvious by putting it in words.

Aaron expresses his assumption that it should be unnecessary for him to define his wants. He'd prefer they were intuited by Lisa and that she would respond without him having to ask directly.

Lisa: Give me a break! I can't read your mind. If you have a problem and want to talk about it, speak up!

Ellyn: You both have a problem.

Instead of siding with either partner by fixing blame, Ellyn intervenes by stating clearly the mutual nature of their problem.

Lisa: (long pause) Maybe the reason I'm so reluctant to talk is that I don't know what to say anymore.

Ellyn: How do you feel about that?

> *Now it is time to expose their loss and help them understand that they are both experiencing pain.*

Lisa: To be honest, I think I'm avoiding the issue, not wanting to face up to it.

Ellyn: Not wanting to face what, Lisa? You sound sad.

Lisa: (begins to cry softly) I guess I am. When I think about what we used to have together, how special it used to be. Maybe that's why I keep trying to fill that emptiness with activity. I don't want to face the fact that we are not the way we used to be.

Ellyn: Will you tell Aaron more about what you miss?

Lisa: Yes. We were beautiful! It was so exciting. Things weren't predictable. I felt like we were constantly growing and changing. You were the best thing that ever happened to me. Now I feel like you are holding me back, you're such a big part of my growth. If you're not going to grow, at least I will. Because you don't indicate any interest in new things, I feel like you're stopping me.

Lisa has difficulty allowing her grief, without switching back to anger and blaming. She insists on taking her independence, while blaming Aaron for stopping her.

Ellyn: You switched from your own sadness into blaming Aaron.

Lisa: I guess I just miss the way we were. *(cries)* What about you *(looking at Aaron)*?

Aaron: (long silent pause)

Lisa: (to Ellyn) See, I can't get any . . .

Aaron: (angry) Give me a chance! What's your hurry? I have a lot to say. I miss the past. I don't understand the hurry that something new needs to happen every day. You just said you missed the past. Well, you're right. We're leaving that behind and I don't like feeling like I'm the one dragging it or trying to hold onto the past while you're running on ahead. That's what I feel like.

Aaron is still angry. He does not like his desire for emotional connection being misinterpreted. Ellyn decides to see if he can touch his own loss.

Ellyn: Both of you miss the closeness you had.

Aaron: I miss the way we were. I find a lot of excitement and pleasure in just being together, talking and sharing. I'm afraid the future you want is less and less of something that matters to me. That what's in my heart doesn't matter, that all the future has in store for us is that we are activity partners, like partners in doubles tennis. I want to be sharing. Do you know what I mean?

Lisa: Well, yes and no. I understand, but I don't agree that doing things together is only empty activity. How else are you going to grow and change if you don't do new things and have new experiences?

Aaron: There are a lot of things you can find inside, too. Don't just pass me off like I'm nothing. By sharing ourselves, the outside activities will be better. The emptiness comes from the fact that there is nothing here *(pointing to his heart).*

Ellyn: Does it sound to each of you as if you want the same thing, or two different things?

Both Lisa and Aaron have been angry and polarized for the past few months. Ellyn wants to see if they can recognize their common loss and be willing to move toward each other.

Aaron: Ultimately, I think they're the same.

Lisa: Me, too.

Aaron: I think we want to be close and growing.

Lisa: We are each taking a different approach and having trouble understanding, accepting, and supporting the other's approach. I don't know what to do.

Lisa has softened considerably. However, she does not know how to begin meeting Aaron half way.

Ellyn: Lisa, is there anything you see you could give to Aaron to support him with his approach?

Lisa: Maybe we could spend a certain amount of time each week, when it's just you and I doing nothing, or going to dinner, or being by ourselves.

Aaron: That's something. That's a good place to start. It seems like scheduling time is so . . . I guess I just want it to happen. Let's do it!

Lisa: What's wrong?

Aaron: I'm just being a romantic.

Ellyn: So, Lisa, you'll do that?

Lisa: Oh, sure *(said very warmly)*.

Ellyn: Lisa, what are you feeling just now?

Lisa: Touched. I'm glad to do it because I miss the closeness. I don't like the emptiness. I'll do what I can to be close again.

Aaron: Sounds great.

Ellyn: Now, Aaron, is there something you can do to support Lisa?

Aaron: I knew we'd get to that eventually. Well, I suppose I could take a more active role in planning what we do and not be passive and end up resenting you. *(looking at Lisa)* Will you let me have a more active role?

Ellyn: Are you asking Lisa's permission? You can do it without her permission. Will you do it?

Ellyn confronts Aaron's symbiotic transaction so that he will not leave the session still making Lisa responsible for his actions.

Aaron: Yes. I know there are things we can do together that will give you what you want and give me what I want. So, I'll be making some first moves. I'll do it.

Aaron and Lisa fit the three diagnostic characteristics described earlier for the symbiotic-practicing couple. Their prognosis is good. They came for therapy quickly after the problem surfaced, and the love they have for each other shines through their anger. In the second session they were able to move through some of their anger to their loss and respond effectively to the interventions. Another aspect that evolved in this interview that is important in the early phase of treatment with symbiotic-practicing couples is the commitment to spend some time together each week. By establishing that agreement in a therapist's office, it moves the partner in the symbiotic position out of needing to beg for time together.

Symbiotic-Practicing Questionnaire

We have also developed a questionnaire that we use with symbiotic-practicing couples to help partners define more explicitly what they want from the other. The questions read as follows:

For the partner in the symbiotic position:

1. What I want from my partner when I'm scared is
2. What I expect from myself when I'm scared is
3. What I want to do to become more independent is
4. What I want from my partner to help me become more independent is
5. What I expect myself to do to be able to support his independence is

For the partner in the practicing position:

1. What I want from my partner when I'm independent is
2. What I expect from myself when I'm taking my independence is
3. What I want to do for my partner when she/he is scared is
4. What I expect myself to do to support my partner's independence is

These questions not only ask partners to be explicit about their own wants, but also communicate by implication the expectation of accountability. This is particularly important for the partner in the practicing position. Often, this person believes that it should be acceptable for him to take his independence without any regard for the impact of his actions on the partner. Often, the independence is seized in passive-aggressive, acting-out, or hurtful ways. By asking the practicing partner to be clear about what he expects of himself as he moves into independent activity requires that he manifest these changes in a more direct and straightforward manner.

Linda (age 30) and George (age 32) came to therapy after one year of marriage. Linda was frightened because George had begun to spend so much time away from home. When she tried to address this directly with him, he only stayed out later at night or became angry at her for making demands that impinged upon his freedom. Early in therapy they completed the preceding questionnaire at home and then further clarified their answers in a therapy session with Ellyn's help. Their responses were as follows.

(George)

1. *What I want from Linda when I'm taking my independence is:*
   a. Listen to me talk about the things I'm doing away from home without crying.
   b. Be flexible about our shared responsibilities such as chores and errands.
   c. Give me a hug when I leave the house.

2. *What I expect from myself when I'm taking my independence is:*
   a. Be clear about what I'm doing and where I'm going—being active rather than reactive.
   b. Pay attention to my feelings, stand up for myself, and stand my ground without attacking Linda.
   c. Be aware when I'm doing something that feels crucial to me in terms of my independence and then letting Linda know that this is an area in which I would like her support.

3. *What I want to do for Linda when she is scared is:*
   a. Listen to her, talk to her, without giving her static, sarcasm, or anger.
   b. Be willing to spend some time together.

4. *What I want to do to support Linda's independence is:*
   a. Give her encouragement to spend time with other people and get involved in new activities.
   b. Don't leave the house a mess for her to come home to extra chores.
   c. Give her a hug when she leaves the house.

(Linda)

1. *What I want from George when I'm scared is:*
   a. Emotional support, listening to me, a few words of encouragement.
   b. If he's leaving home, tell me where he's going and when he will come back.

2. *What I expect from myself when I'm scared is:*
   a. To tell George I'm scared rather than to start nagging him.
   b. Ask him for a hug.
   c. Do something separate like going outside and gardening.

3. *What I want to do to become more independent:*
   a. Begin spending time again with women friends.
   b. Go to San Francisco alone for a weekend.

4. *What I want from George to help me become more independent:*
   a. Support and suggestions.
   b. That he not push me into it or push me away.

5. *What I expect myself to do to support George's independence:*
   a. Listen to him tell me about the things he enjoys when he's away from home.
   b. Discuss the plays that he's acting in and stop becoming frightened when he goes to cast parties.

In working with the practicing partner, limit setting will be an ongoing issue. In the above example, George did not want to inform his wife ahead of time when he had play practice and what time he would be home after cast parties. Helping the practicing partner define clearly what he wants and then setting clear limits around what he will and will not do is crucial. The limits must not be externally imposed by the spouse or therapist; as with George, they must be self-directed. In completing this exercise, Linda and George were able to provide a framework for themselves in which they could support one another and begin their own differentiation.

An extreme example of how one man indulged in the practicing position was by having his wife brush his hair whenever he wanted to go out to work or socialize. Although she knew he was quite capable of grooming himself, she felt that this was one way he depended on her. He said she did such a better job than he, so each morning she would let out a sigh as she began her ritual of combing his curly locks. For her, it was an act of intimacy, however meager and demeaning.

The husband also kept secret bank accounts, private income tax returns, and refused to let his wife socialize with any of her friends during times he was at home. His initial declaration to his therapist was, "I've come to make it clear that this relationship does not need fixing!" To say the least, he wanted to maintain the status quo; and he wanted his partner to "stand still" and provide a safe base from which he could venture out into the world of his choice. He only wanted the therapist to cure his partner's depression while he continued to enjoy himself.

Often, the symbiotic partner is afraid that the spouse will have an affair. One couple came in with a presenting problem of the husband wanting more independence. His desire was to spend one weekend day playing sports with the guys and then to have a few beers after the game. Cheryl, his wife, could not understand why Malcolm did not want to spend weekends with her. After three-and-a-half years of marriage, Malcolm's desire to have one day for himself was growing more intense, and their arguments over this issue were becoming increasingly heated.

In the first session, with gentle questioning and support, Cheryl was able to express clearly her fear that Malcolm would get high in the bar, start dancing or flirting with some other woman, and then fall into a full-blown affair. For Cheryl, the only solution to this seemingly inevitable outcome was to nip the process in the bud; that is, stop Malcolm from playing ball in the first place.

Instead of communicating her fearful line of thinking directly and clearly, however, she would nag, "Why don't you want to spend time with me like you used to?" "Why can't we spend more time together on weekends?" To Malcolm, this felt as though the walls were closing in, and with each confrontation, it was getting harder for him to breathe. The familiar cycle of the symbiotic-practicing couple was in full motion: the more he wanted space, the more desperate she felt. When he heard Cheryl clearly articulate her concern, his body posture relaxed and his facial muscles took on a much softer contour. He was able to reaffirm his own desire for a monogamous relationship and tell Cheryl that he did want to spend time with her. They then agreed to set aside one weekend day for themselves as individuals, and one scheduled weekend day for them as a couple.

Often, differentiation is skipped in the symbiotic-practicing relationship because the practicing partner is fearful of conflict and has difficulty being assertive or remaining assertive when anger surfaces in the partner. During childhood, this individual may have learned or decided that anger is unsafe or unacceptable, or he may have learned how to convert his anger into passivity, rebellion, or sadness. In any case, he clearly has not learned how to express it in a direct, assertive, problem-solving way. A pattern unfolds whereby the person goes through life avoiding confrontation so as not to re-evoke unresolved feelings from childhood.

Case example of treatment of symbiotic-practicing couple: Michiko and Peter

We now return to Peter and Michiko (see beginning of this chapter) who clearly demonstrated the evolution of their relationship into the symbiotic-practicing stage without successful differentiation. Peter was indeed fearful of anger. Instead of facing any of the conflict with Michiko, he spent more and more time at the library or in activities with new friends he was making in his graduate program. Michiko, too, was fearful of anger and had no role model in the direct expression of assertive feelings. Her reasons were both familial and cultural. Like any obedient Japanese daughter, she had been taught to respect her elders, specifically her father, and not to ever "cross" him. She was also the youngest of three girls and most of her thinking had been done for her by her parents and her older sisters. She had come to believe that she would leave home and be securely taken care of by another man.

Peter's reason for withdrawing from any angry feelings was much more dramatic in origin. When he was 15 years old, his father committed suicide. His father, previously highly successful as president of a major university, was suddenly terminated from this position by the university's board. Unable to cope with the loss, he ended his life. Prior to his father's death, Peter had never seen his father angry. Peter then saw his anger when he was terminated, and the next thing Peter experienced was his father's death. Peter decided that anger led to destruction and death. As an adult, he was terrified of facing any of his conflicts with Michiko because he could only imagine it leading to anger and loss of the relationship or something even more destructive. Michiko, without recognizing how she was reinforcing Peter's fears, exacerbated his expectation by destroying his school notes when she was angry, and on occasion, alluding to possible suicidal feelings when she was moody and upset.

Therapy with this couple spanned a two-year period of time and combined both individual and couples work. Several changes occurred before they were able to manage actively differentiating together.

During the initial phase of couples therapy, Michiko and Peter solidified an agreement to work out an effective relationship together as their long-term goal. They also committed to spending time together twice a week. After they each identified their own major issues from childhood, Michiko requested individual sessions. In these sessions she expressed her desire to live separately from Peter for a period of time. She did not believe it would be possible for her to come to know herself while living with him; his presence, she felt, was too powerful and she feared she would resort to moodiness and pouting. Couples sessions were used to help Michiko separate physically from Peter, without her move being interpreted as desertion from the relationship. At first Peter was frightened that she was now going to leave him abruptly just like his father had. However, couples sessions were used to explore her motivation for the move and to allay Peter's fears.

In one session Michiko described her move: "I feel very frightened leaving you but I have never been on my own. I'll never know I can do it unless I actually do it. I'll always doubt myself. I want to feel proud of myself, to know that I can hold my head up high, that I won't have always been a Daddy's girl. I hope you'll understand and not think that I am leaving you." Through this type of dialogue, Peter came to understand that her move was for the purpose of supporting her own development and not a betrayal of the relationship.

Michiko moved into her own apartment and continued in individual therapy for the next nine months. During this time she made a clear decision not to commit suicide. She also decided to return to school to get a Master's degree in history, and, most important, she began giving up her lifelong position as a dependent little girl, and began thinking and acting for herself.

At the same time, Peter came for individual therapy. He focused on resolving his rage surrounding his father's death and abandonment of the family and came to understand the importance of him not withholding negative feelings in his relationship with Michiko.

After one year of individual therapy, with intermittent couples sessions, they resumed couples therapy on a regular basis. These sessions were used to integrate their individual changes into a different foundation for their relationship. Specifically, they grappled with the extreme differences in each one's view about suicide (Peter's originating from his father's tragic death and Michiko's stemming from the Japanese culture's veneration of hari kari). Michiko told Peter about her decision not to commit suicide and together they arrived at an understanding that suicide would not be mentioned casually or manipulatively in times of conflict. Next they addressed some of their conflicts about living together and redistributed their responsibilities along less traditional lines. Peter decided to do the cooking and to learn how to prepare some Japanese specialties, while Michiko would grocery shop, pay the bills, and handle repairs and insurance. At this point they decided to live together again.

They continued their couples work for another six months and focused on managing conflict with one another in a direct way. Many of the techniques and methods discussed in the chapter on differentiation were used to facilitate this parallel unfolding of the couple and the individuals. At a six-year follow-up both Peter and Michiko had completed school and were expecting their first child.

In the symbiotic-practicing relationship, the practicing partner's narcissistic and often volatile shift of emotional energy away from enmeshment and onto individual development usually does not promote growth. In a sense, the practicing partner "skips a grade" by moving out of symbiosis and into practicing before the couple has laid the foundation for mutual change by actively differentiating together. Thus, the task of the therapist becomes one of enabling the couple to differentiate in a connected manner.

CHAPTER 9

The Practicing-Practicing Couple

"I want to be me!"

As an individual moves from the differentiation stage into the practicing stage, a shift occurs from focusing on "Who am I?" to focusing on "Who am I *in the world?*" The practicing stage in an adult is parallel to the same stage in children described by Mahler: the child experiences elation in exercising her autonomy as the unfolding individuation reveals her own unique capabilities. How successful the child becomes in traversing this stage will be determined partially by the parents' capacities to respond to and support the unfolding individuation in the child. The parent who is invested in having the child develop in a particular way (such as the classic "stage mother" or "super-jock father") will discourage the unique traits that are emerging in the child and encourage only those that please the parent. A child who consistently has the experience of receiving "Don't be you" messages from the parent will have difficulties individuating throughout life. In an adult, these difficulties may show up as: 1) lethargy or procrastination surrounding "doing"; 2) a lack of desire to develop one's talents due to fear of rejection; 3) sincere confusion over which parts of the self to focus on enhancing in a way that will be personally satisfying; or 4) turning to the partner for help and direction in figuring out which talents would be best expressed.

The adult equivalent of the early practicing stage in children occurs when partners turn away from the intensity of relating in order to creatively express themselves in the world. If the practicing adult was supported by her parents in her first individuation experiences, then she may enjoy discovering how to realize her own talents during this

173

stage without undue struggle and conflict. However, for the adult who was never responded to effectively as a child, the practicing stage will be fraught with difficulty.

When both partners are practicing, then the *practicing-practicing* relationship occurs in which the two individuals are primarily focused on actualizing themselves in the world. It is a time of creative self-development and identity formation. How successful partners are at navigating this stage, and how satisfying this type of relationship is for the two of them as a couple, will depend on whether they have evolved through the previous stages together and have arrived at the practicing-practicing stage with a solid foundation of differentiation underneath them.

During the preceding differentiation stage, both individuals went through their own unique growth processes by which they discovered their separate identities. As a result, both have a greater awareness of their own and their partner's thoughts, feelings, values, and beliefs. The differences that inevitably surfaced during the differentiation stage have been actively addressed and the individuals are choosing to remain in a relationship with one another. Functions and responsibilities turned over to the partner during the symbiotic and early differentiation stages have now been reclaimed by the self. As a result, autonomy has increased and the individual's focus has shifted outwardly: now the desire *to actualize the self in the world* blossoms and there is a new need to establish a strong, tangible identity away from the relationship. Couples who have evolved through symbiosis and differentiation together will have a strong foundation of affection, intimacy, and successful problem-solving mechanisms to support this period of independence. Even with these strengths, the practicing period is invariably unsettling. Couples with a rich relational history can use their prior experiences as an anchor point of comfort and familiarity to balance the stress and to keep each of them from moving so far away from the relationship that they never return.

Frequently, couples who are seen for therapy during the practicing-practicing stage have become involved with one another without establishing an initial foundation of closeness and connection during the symbiotic phase. Often these are two people experiencing periods of their lives in which self-expression is crucial. They wear "relationship blinders" in order to focus myopically on their own achievements.

With so much intensity focused on identity development, there is little energy left over for the relational intensity needed to establish a bonded connection of deep feeling and commitment. The merging that is so characteristic of the symbiotic stage poses too great a threat to the unfolding individuation of the practicing partner. These couples are easy to identify. They emphasize their personal growth, while viewing the relationship as secondary; they need to staunchly defend their boundaries, and separate living arrangements are frequently maintained. (They may even be unable to leave a robe or toothbrush at one another's houses.) These individuals remain as individuals and never establish a coupleness. While frantically investing their time and energy in their own activities and using the relationship only secondarily as a source of support, they are able to defend against their fear of too much closeness and thus prevent a premature loss of self.

Individuals who become involved with each other during periods in their lives when self-development is primary are frequently unable to weather the practicing stage and thereby maintain the relationship. Over time, they simply become emotionally disengaged, or they engage in power struggles. When disengaged, they are often both in career positions that afford a compelling source of satisfaction external to the relationship. The result is an attitude of "You do your own thing, I'll do mine, and if we happen to connect, that's lucky"—but there is not much energy or excitement put into the relationship itself.

When these types of couples become engaged in power struggles, they are characterized by an attitude of "*I* want what *I* want, and I *don't* want to compromise for the relationship." It should be noted that these power struggles are quite different from those that occur in the hostile-dependent relationship, where the demands are projected outwardly: "*You're* not meeting *my* needs well enough." In the practicing relationship, by contrast, the demands are most often *self-involved*. One woman described it: "I compromised for the sake of our relationship long enough. Now *I* want this vacation in Hawaii, and *I* won't give in!"

Practicing-practicing relationships established without a foundation of symbiosis or differentiation are usually characterized by projection, transference, and repetition of early script decisions. Even though both partners are focused outwardly, each tends to view the other as a devourer who will interfere with his or her developing autonomy. They are not yet confident enough in their own capacities to establish themselves in the world, and they have not experienced enough of the individuation process to believe in their inner abilities to discern what is right for them and to bring it to fruition. In this volatile context, the closeness of a relationship is an ongoing threat to the fragile, unfolding individuation.

By contrast, when a base of differentiation has been established, the practicing-practicing couple will look very different. Having navigated the differentiation stage together, they are able to define their own selves and to appreciate the emerging self of the other. Now, as the practicing stage unfolds, each develops greater self-esteem and no longer needs to look to the partner as the primary source for self-valuation. Thus, the practicing stage often results in diminished intimacy, as the emotional need for one another lessens and as the challenge and stimulation of individual growth beckons. The times of confusion and uncertainty that characterize this stage, while difficult, will usually be weathered, as a direction in life that best fits each partner's individuated talents is searched for and identified.

DIAGNOSIS AND TREATMENT OF THE PRACTICING-PRACTICING COUPLE

Case example: Edith and Kevin

In the following case example, partners in a practicing-practicing relationship were helped to infuse more closeness and emotionality into their relationship as they each continued to individuate. By being helped to establish a base of problem-solving skills and greater flexibility in their ability to respond to one another emotionally, they were able to continue building their relationship while undergoing an expected two-year separation. The couple was seen by a psychotherapist who trained with us.

Edith and Kevin had been involved for eight years, were not married, and had lived together for six years. Kevin was a financial consultant and Edith a doctoral student at a nearby university. When they entered therapy, Edith was feeling upset by the lack of closeness between them and complained that they were too busy going their own separate ways. Kevin agreed that they had become almost "strangers under the same roof" and had many bitter quarrels which often resulted in hurt feelings that lasted for weeks. Edith had threatened separation but agreed to a therapeutic contract of no separation and of not expressing threats of separation except during sessions.

In the initial therapy sessions, Edith and Kevin repeatedly presented issues that resulted in power struggles between them. A common example involved who would control the use of their living space and whether or not they would be able to share this space. For example, Edith complained that she was unable to study when Kevin was around and there was "tension in the air." Kevin insisted that since he was gone at work all day, he deserved to relax at home without worrying about encroaching on Edith's "territory."

The diagnostic Paper Exercise was used during this initial phase of therapy. This couple essentially reenacted the tug-of-war that had become characteristic of their relationship: after they defined what the paper was, each insisted that he/she knew best how the paper should be used. Typical of practicing-practicing couples, they did not resolve the conflict in the allotted time. Without any prompting, they were able to see the parallel between the exercise and their relationship, commenting that the "we" in their relationship had been replaced by "me first."

Additionally, their therapist conducted an interview to assess relevant intrapsychic issues. This interview was used to identify unresolved issues from their families of origin which might be contributing to their current difficulties.

Edith's answers revealed that she had grown up in a highly traditional family where anger was never displayed directly and displeasure was expressed through long periods of silent, icy "withdrawal." Her family was large and all the children were treated rigidly and uniformly. As a result, she learned not to trust that she would be responded to as an individual and that direct anger was disrespectful, according to the family rules. The only negotiating skills she learned from her parents' modeling were to express her needs in a vague, intellectual way or to withdraw into angry silence. She decided early to grow up and leave home as quickly as possible and to "make it on her own."

On the other hand, Kevin grew up in a family where active fighting was a familiar way of approaching conflict. He learned early to get his needs met by "steamrolling" his mother with his anger. During these interactions, his father would remain passive and uninvolved and usually Kevin would succeed in getting his way.

Kevin and Edith's patterns often clashed. Since Kevin did not understand Edith's intellectualizing or like her icy silences, he often escalated into an angry confrontation. Edith viewed his anger as disrespectful and without changing her position would withdraw, feeling hurt and deciding that she was unimportant to Kevin just as she had felt with her own parents. These unresolved early issues kept Edith and Kevin at "war" with one another and very separate emotionally.

On the basis of this diagnostic information and some very differentiated interaction between them, this couple was diagnosed as having an impasse at the practicing-practicing stage, without having developed a successful fight style. They also evidenced little or no movement forward toward the rapprochement-rapprochement stage.

Because of this diagnosis and because Edith and Kevin were so close to separating at the time they began therapy, initial therapeutic work involved helping them learn ways of maintaining their separate identities while developing a successful fight style. They completed the Anger Questionnaire (see Appendix C) and the Limits Questionnaire (see Appendix B) and were able to make the following agreements, which resulted in a gradual decrease in conflicts:

1. Neither of them would leave the house during a fight.
2. Each would express feelings to the other for five minutes of uninterrupted time, while the other listened.
3. Edith would listen to Kevin express his anger until she felt scared; then she would tell him that she was frightened and that he seemed out of control to her; Kevin would examine his anger and attempt to deescalate.
4. Conflicts would be negotiated until both felt resolved with the outcome.

Working with these agreements led Edith and Kevin to take greater control of their power struggles and to resolve more issues on their own. They were able to negotiate a schedule that ensured that both partners' needs were met for spending time alone in their apartment. While issues raised in initial therapy sessions were primarily about unresolved fights during the previous week, soon few conflicts were aired during meetings. Instead, sessions were devoted to developing ways of lessening the couple's disengagement and facilitating more closeness.

Throughout the middle phase of therapy, attention was focused on helping Edith and Kevin develop a greater capacity for intimacy. Because Kevin had difficulty expressing his feelings and often would withdraw, whereas Edith was analytical about her feelings and would upstage Kevin with verbose dialogue, several structured exercises were introduced during therapy sessions and then given for homework assignments. For example, they were asked to express feelings on a given issue, choosing among only four basic feeling words: *angry, sad, scared,* and *happy.* This process helped equalize their positions by requiring both to use the same structure for communication. From doing this, Kevin gradually gained confidence in his ability to express himself and was no longer intimidated by Edith's apparent superiority in this area.

The following dialogue illustrates how Kevin was helped to express his feelings and be vulnerable without losing himself.

Kevin: (speaking to Edith) Not much has really been happening at work that I can tell you about. You don't really seem that interested, anyway. Remember how you used to tell me that you were more interested in your feminist political activities and that I should expand my personal life so I had more interesting things to discuss with you?

Therapist: Kevin, how are you feeling right now? Use a feeling word to let Edith know how this has affected you.

Kevin: Well, I'm really angry. I know you said that you were interested a long time ago, but I'm still scared that you aren't really interested . . . that I'm not really important to you.

Therapist: Kevin, hearing your anger and your fear makes me know how you feel now. . . . How about you, Edith?

Edith: I'm glad he said how he was feeling, but I really don't know why you hold onto the past, Kevin. You know I'm interested in your work. Some of the business aspects of your work are fairly dull, but I know the people you work with now and I like to hear news of them. Remember last week when you told me about Bill's promotion?

Therapist: Edith, how do you feel about what Kevin said? I'm not sure from what you're saying.

Edith: I'm sad that you still don't trust me, Kevin. I do want to share more of your work life. You spend a lot of time at work and I know so little about that part of you.

Therapist: Now I can hear you, Edith. Kevin, how are you beginning to feel toward Edith? Are you still far away from her on this issue?

Kevin: No, I feel closer now. I'm sad, too, Edith, that I don't share more of my daily life with you. I guess I automatically shut myself off. I'd like your support in continuing to be more open with you.

The termination phase of therapy with Edith and Kevin focused on helping them prepare for an upcoming physical separation. Edith was accepted at a postdoctoral program in the mid-west and was planning to move there for two years to pursue her studies. Sessions were devoted to working through each of their feelings about the upcoming separation and anticipating difficulties that might arise. Both agreed to continue supporting each other's individual endeavors while planning frequent contact and continuing to build greater emotional closeness.

At a one-year follow-up, Edith and Kevin reported maintaining frequent contact and spending regular vacations and long weekends together. They both felt good about how they had been able to support each other's individual goals during this period of physical separation. Each reported satisfaction with the way their relationship was evolving and said they did not feel a need for further therapy.

This case illustrates how Edith's and Kevin's ability to incorporate their fighting agreements and quickly diminish their power struggles validated that a base of differentiation had preceded their current period of struggle. It also demonstrates the continuum of response possibilities that exist *within* the practicing-practicing stage. Indeed, the range and scope of practicing activities are as unique as the individual personalities of the people carrying them out.

Certainly not every couple in the practicing-practicing stage will choose a long period of separation. However, because Edith and Kevin had moved beyond their impasse and both had high thresholds for separation, they believed that they could indeed survive a lengthy one as a couple, and that this separation would benefit each as individuals.

The Thirty-Day Plan

In working with practicing-practicing couples, we wanted to develop an approach that would help them use the momentum from their own developmental growth processes to carry them into new dimensions of positive relatedness. This method would help partners relax their boundaries in a nonthreatening way and thereby shift their interactions from those of distancing and rigidity to actively positive exchanges. To facilitate this shift, we developed the "Thirty-Day Plan: Creating a Wish List." This plan serves the function of either supporting the movement of the couple toward more openness and looser boundaries, or of identifying the impasse that is preventing each individual from moving beyond the developmental "stuck point." The plan is most effective in constellating and focusing cooperative energies when it is used early in treatment with practicing-practicing couples with whom differentiation has already occurred.* The therapeutic implementation of the plan requires a high level of structure, activity, and firmness on the part of the therapist. When successful, the "Thirty-Day Plan" leads the couple out of the isolation and self-absorption of the practicing stage and back into a more mutually creative relational and developmental experience.

To participate in this process, a couple must make a minimum four-week commitment to spending 15–20 minutes each day at home carrying out specific instructions. Because the plan involves several steps, we will use two complete case examples to illustrate the way in which it unfolds. In the first example, Mia and Richard were a couple who had evolved to the practicing-practicing stage without sufficient differentiation. Here, the Thirty-Day Plan helped to elicit the unresolved intrapsychic issues that were impeding their differentiation. In the second example, Dana and Carl demonstrate how the practicing-

---

*It should be noted that hostile-dependent couples and practicing-practicing couples without differentiation have also profited from using this technique on a short-term basis. These types of couples, however, are usually unable to sustain for an extended period of time the level of commitment necessary to use the plan in a way that creates a growthful impact on the relationship. When used with such couples, the plan is effective in catalyzing previously unrecognized psychodynamic impasses.

practicing relationship had evolved throughout their seven-year marriage, and how using this particular intervention helped to interrupt their power struggles and provide a supportive milieu in which they could begin to resolve their specific issues.

Case example: Mia and Richard

Mia was a professional woman in her mid-thirties whose presenting problem in individual therapy was a public speaking phobia. After the third session, however, she made a casual, passing remark that she was going to leave her husband, Richard. Surprised by the unexpectedness of this information, the therapist (Pete) asked her if Richard knew she was ready to end the marriage. She said she wasn't really sure, but thought he probably had some awareness of her open dissatisfaction with their marriage. They had been married for 11 years, and his frequent absences and chronic passivity around the house when he was home were "driving her crazy." She acknowledged that they had had good times together and that there were very positive aspects to the marriage, but she could no longer tolerate these behaviors. She explained that although Richard was in individual therapy, little progress was occurring, in her opinion, relative to their marriage.

Pete asked Mia if she would like to go through an exercise that would last one month, adding that if she went through this exercise and still wanted to leave the marriage, at least she would feel that she had given her best effort to determine if anything could be salvaged from the relationship. She agreed that she could give it another 30 days, and said that she would ask Richard to come to the next session in order to participate in the plan.

In beginning this process, we ask the partners (in this case, Mia and Richard) to describe their *ideal relationship* by listing the aspects that currently are going well, and, in addition, by describing what they want "more of" in the future. In effect, the couple are requested to imagine a "Wish List" for their relationship that will include everything they would like it to be. We caution that these items are intended to reflect what they *want* rather than what they think they *should* have. We also suggest that they be general rather than overly detailed in formulating the items on the Wish List, because asking for details at this point often leads to arguments.

As much as possible, the partners are told to avoid using the words *don't* and *stop*. For example, we ask that they avoid listing the negative request to "stop nagging and criticizing," and instead list the positive desire for "more appreciation of my efforts at doing the household chores."

Mia and Richard created the following lists:

Mia	*Richard*
—Play more together	—Be supportive and understanding
—Be more loving	
—Be more of a team	—Have fun together
—Be more nurturing	—Support each other's goals
—Be able to trust Richard, so I could fall back and he'd catch me	—Work together in harmony
	—Be seen by Mia as competent and dependable
—More positive interaction	—More empathy and awareness of each other's feelings
—More energy sharing	

After this first list was completed, Pete asked Mia and Richard to describe the support they would most like to receive from one another in order to enhance their individual growth. Pete stressed that each of them should be explicit and specific about the kind of support wanted. Mia responded:

> Let me know that you are happy that I'm establishing my career so successfully. Don't get angry when I have to work on a Saturday.

Richard's request was equally clear and specific:

> Compliment me when you notice that I'm putting energy into getting organized at work and at home. Let me know when you see me being competent.

Next, we helped both partners identify the areas of needed change, explaining as follows:

> In order to change your relationship in a manner that reflects the above list, you will probably need to change something about

yourself. At this point, think of the personality trait or character-istic that you will have to give up, as well as the trait or character-istic that you will have to increase or acquire in order to assist you in creating the relationship described in your lists.

Mia: I need to give up being so critical of Richard and seeing him as incompetent, and I need to acquire more caring and patience.

Richard: I need to change my anger and withdrawal into active partici-pation in our relationship.

At this point, we ask partners if they believe it is possible to ac-complish the list. If there is any item that seems totally impossible, we remove it from the list.

Now we give the directions that the couple must follow at home. Pete explained to Mia and Richard:

Talk to each other twice a day about the items on your Wish List as if they were already occurring or already have occurred. Give acknowledgment to each other about these items in the present tense, even if you have not yet convincingly demonstrated them. For example, you might say to your partner: "I appreciate your keeping the house neater," or "I feel your support much more now," or "Thank you for listening to me without giving advice or trying to make me feel better."

At this point do not worry about the "truth" of your conversation. This is future talking. Keep in mind that the talk is about *who you want to be*, not who you are today.

These gentle reminders of how you want to be will act like a magnet in pulling you forward and taking the stress of blaming off your relationship. If you are struggling with a future decision about where to live or to buy a house, give yourselves a general reinforcement such as, "I'm glad we're making the decision about where to live."

We have found it easier for couples to solve difficult problems when they are approached from a position of trust and support. Doing this exercise builds in the expectation that the relationship is going to flourish.

These daily conversations may last anywhere from one to five minutes. The important thing is to do them twice a day.

The next part of the exercise has to do with the characteristics you have identified as the ones you are going to give up and those you are going to develop. For example, if you want to give up being jealous and develop more trust, then every day this week, as soon as you begin to feel jealous, create an opposing fantasy in which you imagine yourself being supported by your partner, and recall the trusting elements in your relationship.

In other words, every time you begin to think, feel, or act out the trait you want to give up, actively replace it with the trait you want to acquire.

In the final part of this exercise, you are to fantasize, reflect, and think about the future two times a day, for a few minutes. Imagine yourselves six months or three years from now—whatever time period you prefer—and create scenes in which you have made your list happen. Imagine what your relationship is like in great detail, when you have created all the elements on your lists.

After the couple have completed the assignment and we have answered any questions, we tell the couple that their next session will begin with talking about *their successes* in executing their Wish List exercise.

When the couple returns for subsequent sessions, it is important to follow through with the positive, forward-moving direction initiated in the plan. "What did each of you do to be effective with the Wish List?" is a good question to use to begin the next session. Often, the couple will exert pressure to return to negative patterns of complaining and blame, and to engage the therapist as referee. For the duration of the plan (four weeks), however, the therapist refuses to engage in this negative pattern and instead uses the time in the office to help the couple create what they want to have happening at home.

After giving this assignment, we commonly encounter two main results: either the partners will be successful and have an unusually good week, or a core problem (script issue) that remains from childhood will surface. The latter occurred with Mia and Richard. They returned to the next session with the following report:

Pete: How was your week? Did you carry out your Wish List?

Richard: As tumultuous as ever. I tried, but Mia wouldn't do it.

Mia: I'm having a major resistance. I can't get behind it. We took a walk this morning and Richard pressured me to verbalize why I wouldn't do it. I think I'm hating all men. All my business associates are women and, like me, they are going through major struggles with men. Since I was a little girl, I have tried to please my father but to no avail. He wouldn't love me no matter what I did. Now I'm angry and I'm done changing for men. I'm sick of men telling women what to do and how to do it in business. I'm on a soap box! I won't change for men. I'm probably overreacting to Richard, but he's a man.

(Later in the session, after Richard had described numerous examples of carrying out the plan.)

Pete: Is this new — your recognition that you're so angry at men and so resistant to giving to Richard?

Mia: I've known I was angry before, but this exercise made me realize how much I don't want to give.

Pete: You didn't realize how hard it would be for you to change. If I can be blunt, until now you have had Richard's passivity to say that the relationship would be fine without it. You couldn't have intimacy with a guy you identified as passive. Now, Richard puts the brake on his withdrawal, starts approaching you, and you pull back. Now you are confronted with your own fear of closeness and vulnerability.

Mia: I understand what you're saying, but I'm angry and it's not getting through to me emotionally.

It was clear that Mia's anger was propelling her independent thrust to leave the relationship and was making her unwilling to put any positive energy toward Richard. Instead of focusing directly on Mia's anger, Pete asked Richard if he would be willing to continue to carry out his part of the plan with Mia even though she was not going to participate in it. This approach served three purposes: first, it indirectly validated and respected Mia's anger; second, by focusing on Richard and asking him for an autonomous change, Pete removed himself from the bind of being one more man asking Mia to change; and third, it provided a circumscribed focus for change in Richard. It was explained to Richard that his independent follow-through would benefit him as an individual as well as the marriage. Both Richard and Mia had agreed that his passivity at home, as well as his involvements away from home, had created a continuing problem in their marriage. If Richard could give to Mia and expect absolutely nothing in return, then he would have altered his passive patterns of behavior in ways that would benefit all aspects of his life. Pete was careful to emphasize the importance of Richard clearly understanding that he could expect nothing in return for his reaching out to Mia. If he harbored secret expectations of getting some kind of positive recognition from her, the whole process (including his marriage) in all likelihood would collapse. Richard agreed that he would be willing to carry out the plan in this manner for the three weeks that remained.

Mia looked relieved. She agreed that she would give the marriage another three weeks, as long as there were absolutely no expectations on her to change. The agreement was solidified between Mia and Richard. The observant reader will note the transference implications of Mia's hating all men and not wanting to change for any man, while working with a male therapist.

The following week, both reported that they had lived up to their agreement. Mia was giving absolutely nothing to Richard, and Richard was expending energy toward Mia by expressing appreciation and recognition for what she had contributed to their relationship over the years, and by taking more initiative around the house. He added that all of this was particularly difficult to do because Mia was so unresponsive, and because he was unaccustomed to solving routine problems that came up around the house. Most of the session was spent giving support to Richard for his autonomous change and continuing to place it in the context of his larger life goal of becoming more active. Some of the hour was also spent in uncovering how his pattern of passivity developed in his family of origin.

In the next session Richard again talked about the difficulty of sustaining his unrewarded level of giving, but added that Mia was responding in a friendlier way to him and he appreciated this even though he was fighting his expectation that even this minimal level of recognition would continue. Mia said that it was hard for her to stay in a passive, nonresponsive position, and that she was beginning to believe that Richard was acting genuinely in his unrewarded efforts to make the marriage work. Because she believed Richard's sincerity in doing this "no-strings-attached process," she felt comfortable in giving back to him. Pete raised the possibility that she might be "moving too fast" toward Richard.

In the last session of the four weeks of the plan, Richard reported his continuing efforts. Not only was he significantly more active than he had been a month ago, but he was beginning to find it easier. Mia described feeling guilty that she had been forcing herself to withhold spontaneous, affectionate responses. She initiated changing the agreement and deciding that she would become slightly more interactive with him. Both decided to continue in couples therapy.

For the next three months, Richard contributed more than half the effort to solving household problems. This sustained level of responsibility taking served as a critical reminder to Mia that she could begin depending on her husband as a partner rather than having to continually adapt to his passivity. Mia also recognized that her anger was actually a defense against her fear of dependency. She came to understand that she was not actually angry at all men, or even specifically at Richard, but that as a child she had been unable to depend on her mother (who was constantly anxious) or on her father (who was both emotionally and physically unavailable). As she recognized more completely her fear of depending on Richard, she was also able to get in touch with her fear of exposing any vulnerability to him. She felt threatened that if she did so, she might lose control and become constantly anxious like her mother.

At the end of the third month, Mia and Richard decided to terminate couples therapy while continuing to interact more at home to build their Wish List relationship. Richard reported that an unexpected benefit for him of this process was feeling more comfortable with Mia's being two inches taller than him. He indeed was feeling much more "equal." Having resolved some of her dependency fears, Mia requested individual therapy in order to continue working on her individual issues. She focused on her speaking phobia, and periodically spent time talking about her relationship with Richard. About eight months later, both Richard and Mia asked us to run a couples group in which the focus would be on what couples wanted to build and create, not on problems or what was wrong with the marriage. Several months later we began such a group for couples who had moved to the practicing stage or beyond. It has been a deeply rewarding experience to work with this group in which the focus is on marital health rather than marital distress. (See Chapter 10 for further discussions of this group and advanced relationships.)

Case example: Dana and Carl

In this case example, Dana and Carl (first mentioned in Chapter 2) came to therapy locked into severe power struggles and on the verge of divorce. Initially, it appeared as if very little differentiation had taken place within their relationship. However, in exploring some of the history of their seven-year marriage, we discovered that they had indeed differentiated in many areas.

Both Dana (age 35) and Carl (age 45) were accountants who had married after meeting at work and dating exclusively for a year. Both worked in a large, prestigious accounting firm. This was Carl's second marriage and Dana's first. Carl had two boys, 11 and 14 years old, from his previous marriage, and together they had one daughter, three years old.

From the moment they entered the office, their physical appearance advertised their wealth and success. Both were vital-looking and very attractive. They described a marriage that had been very happy until two years ago, when several events occurred that caused stress and unhappiness for both of them. Carl had been offered a promotion to a job in a distant city and wanted badly to make the move. Dana, on the other hand, wanted to simplify her work life by moving to the country, scaling down her work commitments, and having more time for family. Carl's company was pressuring him for a decision within six weeks.

In addition, Carl had resumed a nonsexual friendship with a woman whom he had dated before he knew Dana. Although this was not an affair, Dana believed that the other woman was more his "emotional partner" than she. Dana felt excluded by Carl from important decisions, including some of the parenting decisions that he would make about his two sons.

When the couple called for therapy, they asked to see both of us "to be sure all perspectives were covered." They were threatened by the possibility that one therapist might side with the same-sexed partner; therefore, it was "safer" to have both sexes present. Carl began the first session by flatly stating, "This is probably useless. We've tried therapy before, a year ago, but we never solved our major problems." With Carl's clearly negative expectations hanging in the air, we used the first session diagnostically and included the Paper Exercise as part of this initial process. (Although the couple's response was presented in Chapter 2, we are including it here again for ease of reading.) The couple responded as follows:

Carl: What did you pick?

Dana: Moving to the country. What did you choose?

Carl: Funny, I picked moving to New York.

Dana: It seems like it is ourselves.

Carl: Ourselves in relation to each other.

Dana: So we're back to this again, either New York or the country!

Carl: When I started this exercise I said to myself, "This is just an exercise. It isn't very important how it comes out." Suddenly it's become very important, now that I hear what you want.

Dana: I want you to have what you want, but not if it means me giving up what I want.

Carl: I could give in, but I don't want to. I think this is what always happens.

Dana: Well, here is where we are stuck!
Carl: This is how we always end up!

Both reported feeling angry and stubborn at the end of this exercise. They agreed that, indeed, it had given us a graphic demonstration of how they repeatedly butted up against the same emotional impasse.

From this exercise and from their interactions during the session, we observed that their dialogue was self-defined and focused on solving specific problems, but also extremely competitive. Each needed to define his or her own stand with a vehemence characteristic of a debator or arbitrator rather than a marriage partner. They would barely wait for one another to finish speaking before jumping in to make a point. It was doubtful that they had heard more than a few words of what the other had said before beginning to formulate their own response. They seemed almost totally unable to receive support from each other.

Several hours prior to the second scheduled appointment, Dana called to cancel, saying Carl had decided not to return and that he thought the first session was a waste of money. After consulting with one another, we called Dana back and asked her to tell Carl that he was indeed quite correct. The first session would definitely be a waste of money unless they returned for the second. He had given us the information we needed, but he was closing the door on hearing our diagnosis and suggested plan for help. Two hours later, Dana called again to say that they would be in for their appointment.

We began the second diagnostic session by giving our diagnosis. We drew two dark, heavy circles on the blackboard; and inside one we wrote "Dana," and inside the other, "Carl." We described them as two strong-willed, independent personalities who, out of fear of losing their independence, were totally unwilling *to receive* affection and support from one another. We demonstrated how rigidly they defined and protected their independence and pointed out that the consequence of this behavior was an almost total absence of vulnerability or emotional intimacy. Put simply, their fierce independence left no room for love. In actual fact, the independence they so coveted was not as fragile as they believed and did not need their constant vigilance. On the contrary, it was responsible for their gaping lack of interdependent interactions.

Interestingly, they had opposite responses to our diagnosis. Dana was relieved that we could see what was going on and understand it. Carl, however, was extremely pessimistic about any possibility of changing the situation. He decided that he would be willing to come to therapy for four more weeks, but if he did not see any change by this time, he believed that he would file for divorce and move to another city.

The first session. Given the short time allotted to create significant change, we suggested that the initial therapeutic focus be on learning how to receive from one another rather than on the content of their specific problems. We also recommended the Thirty-Day Plan as the way to begin.

In describing their Wish List, both expressed a desire for more time together with greater closeness, for more time apart for individual pursuits, for cooperative parenting, and for freedom to maintain outside friendships. The traits that Dana wanted to give up and acquire were described as "changing my rebelliousness into cooperativeness," while Carl stated he wanted to change "my aloofness and stubbornness into initiating time together."

In requesting individual support, Carl asked Dana not to interfere or become upset with him when he wanted time alone, and Dana asked Carl to let her participate in some parenting decisions about his two boys; she also wanted him to let her know that he valued her opinion and her input.

After obtaining their answers to the three sections of the Thirty-Day Plan, we also elicited their commitment to spend the necessary amount of time each day thinking and fantasizing about the creation of their Wish List. They also agreed to make the changes they had described at least once during each week.

The second session. When Dana and Carl returned for the second session, they reported that they had had five "good days" before slipping into their old competitive, argumentative patterns of interacting. We spent time at the beginning of this session with Carl and Dana practicing talking to one another as if the items on their Wish List had already been actualized. We then moved on to explore why each of them was so insistent on maintaining their independence in such a way that barred them from any experiences of shared intimacy.

Carl described his childhood image of being shipwrecked on a desert island and his compelling desire always to be able to fend for himself. Robinson Crusoe was indeed his hero, and he had vowed to never allow himself to become dependent on anyone else. We used the following metaphor to gently but firmly confront Carl's entrenched attachment to what he viewed as independent behavior.

There was a ship in the ocean, and one night it encountered some blinking lights. The captain of the ship told his radio officer to send a message saying, "I am a captain in the U.S. Navy; we're coming through; move three degrees off course." The blinking lights returned a message saying, "You move three degrees off course." The captain of the ship became quite angry and told his officer to send back the message again, saying, "I am a captain of the U.S. Navy; you move three degrees off course." Again, the reply came back, "You move three degrees." The captain then became even angrier and decided to send the message himself. He went to the radio tower and sent the message: "We're coming through! I'm a captain in the U.S. Navy. You move three degrees off course." And the reply came back, "I am a lighthouse, *you* move three degrees off course!"

Carl was quite taken by this story and could acknowledge that perhaps, at times, his stubborn independence might be self-defeating.

Dana reported growing up in a family in which she believed she had to fight constantly with her brothers in order to get anything for herself. Because she was the only girl in the family, and her father valued boys, she believed that she needed to project a tough, strong, independent stance in life in order to make her way. She also had gone into a traditionally male profession to prove that she could compete successfully with men. We talked about how she would not be able to help create and participate in a fulfilling marriage in which she would give and receive on an emotional level as long as she continued to perceive Carl as being like one of her brothers.

The third session. After the second session, Carl and Dana went on vacation together and were gone for two weeks. Upon their return, they eagerly reported that they had spent the best time together in several years. Instead of doing a lot of activities separately (as they had in the past), they each had agreed to participate in things that were fun for the other. These included windsurfing, parasailing, visiting botanical gardens, and touring the city's cultural center. Both acknowledged that there was something to be gained from sharing in activities that created excitement for one another.

In this session, they broached the very difficult problem of each of them wanting to live in separate places. Carl again became very pessimistic, believing that it was an either-or, country-or-New York decision, and that this decision would inevitably lead to a divorce. Instead of discussing the content of this problem, we proposed a process that they could use actively over the next two weeks as a means of addressing the problem together. The process included the experience of both of them being on the same side of the issue at the same time. They agreed to spend one week in which they would both look at how to make living in the country a viable, fulfilling option. Then, during

the second week, they would both look at making life in New York successful. For these two weeks, they were not to have any arguments or
debates about the merits of one location versus the other. Instead, they
could only discuss the two locations in the proper weekly context of
putting their best efforts into taking the same position. We then agreed
that we would talk about the problem two weeks later.

The fourth session. When Dana and Carl arrived for their fourth
session, they reported that they had spent the weekend looking at
country houses together and that they had found the process extremely
rewarding. They also reported an incident during the week in which
Carl had included Dana in an important decision related to his older
son. Not only had he included her, but he had let her know that he
valued the way she thought about the schooling decision, and he even
ended up acting upon her suggestion. With the momentum of these
positive shared experiences, we continued to focus on how receiving
emotional input and support from one another does not necessarily
lead to a loss of self.

Dana also tackled the issue of Carl's relationship with the other
woman. She surprised herself by the resolution she discovered which
allowed her to be giving and yet maintain her sense of self. She told
Carl that she would no longer interfere with this relationship and that
she would even support him spending time with the other woman as long
as three agreements were made between the two of them. These were:

1. Carl would tell her the truth when he was seeing her, and not
   sneak off to do it.
2. Dana did not need to have a friendship with her also.
3. Carl would agree to make parenting decisions with Dana first.

Carl agreed with these provisions, and Dana felt as though she had successfully found a way to take the woman out of the middle of their
relationship.

The fifth session. Although this was the last agreed-upon session,
the couple decided to return until they had solved the problem of
where they would live. We agreed to tackle this thorny problem in the

next session, after they had spent another week looking at the option of living in the city.

When they returned for the fifth session, they surprised us with having already made the decision. Carl talked about the emotional impact he felt when Dana actively tried to make living in a big city a viable possibility. He described how, for the first time, he felt like he truly had a partner who would not interfere with his direction in life. The process was so meaningful to him that moving to New York no longer seemed essential. What he realized during the course of their interaction was that he did not want to give up city living. They negotiated a compromise in which they would sell their large home, move to a smaller home in a small city nearby, and also buy a country place. Dana agreed to this with an understanding that she would cut back on working one day a week so that she would be able to take frequent three-day weekends in their country home.

In this final session, we reviewed their accomplishments and their feelings of increased commitment to one another and to their future together. Because each of them felt somewhat tentative and scared that the changes would not hold, we set up a check-in session one month later. Two days prior to that session, Dana called to cancel: "We're doing great," she said excitedly. "We're doing even better than we thought we would be doing when we left that last session. We've had some difficult financial issues come up with Carl's ex-wife and his sons, and we've handled them together. We don't really need to come in. We'll call you in the future if we get stuck."

Very often couples such as Carl and Dana get into unresolvable arguments because they have polarized their positions. These polarities arise from rigid thinking and thoroughly inhibit the couple's ability to perceive possible solutions. The basic problem inherent in these "polarities" is that both partners define the problem in such a way that solving it will support only one person's egocentric desires. Polarity thinking therefore can be circumvented by asking both partners to think on the same side of the issue at the same time. When couples are able to do this, the strong amount of energy that is invested in one side of the polarity can be harnessed and applied to creating solutions with both people working in concert.

The case of Carl and Dana demonstrates how quickly it is possible to facilitate movement in a practicing-practicing couple by focusing on the process rather than on the content of their specific issues. If we had tackled the content of their problems initially, we probably would have encountered rigid boundaries and the necessity for each to defend self. By giving the couple a goal to strive for—the capacity to receive from one another—we allowed them to shift from being legalistic, perfectionistic arbiters to softening with one another and allowing their gentle, cooperative sides to emerge. In fact, Carl's shift from an extremely pessimistic position on the verge of a divorce to open negotiation and willingness to involve his wife in the parenting of his children was quite dramatic. As both were able to open themselves up to one another again, they began enjoying the warmth and closeness of shared experience.

Some of the positive feelings of excitement and adventure that can characterize the practicing stage were expressed clearly by a woman client as she and her husband were leaving one of our couples groups. During the time she spent in the group, she moved through a very active differentiation stage into practicing. At first, she was surprised by her desire to leave the safety of the group and even feared that this might be a self-destructive decision. However, she soon recognized that she was drawn by "the spirit of adventure" and "bored by the predictability" of some of the repetitive patterns presented by new group members. She said, "I no longer want to be involved in the fine intricacies of the working-through of others' problems. Although I am getting understanding, affection, and honesty, I'm not getting many new insights, and I no longer feel the need for the emotional support I've just described. I now see my desire to leave as a sign of real developmental progress. Not flight from pain, but flight toward adult freedom." Her freedom and private time became quite cherished as she went on to become a well-known writer.

When an individual is able to enjoy and flourish during the practicing stage, movement to the next stage may feel threatening. However, loss of one's highly coveted independence is not necessarily the outcome. The feelings of enhanced self-esteem that are developed during the practicing stage enable the individual to reinvest in the relationship with an increased capacity to appreciate his or her partner and experience deeper intimacy.

CHAPTER 10

Rapprochement . . . and Beyond

When partners move from the practicing stage into the rapprochement stage, it is clear that they have a commitment to themselves and their own independent identities as well as a commitment to being in the relationship. They return to the relationship with a stronger sense of self and a greater desire to experience vulnerability and intimacy with the partner. The skills from the earlier stages have been or are being mastered and utilized in an ongoing way (except, perhaps, when the couple is under excessive stress). The individual knows more fully his or her own thoughts, feelings, and wants and is taking an active role in expressing them. Time has been spent developing individual talents; individuation is flowering unencumbered by continual relationship sacrifices. Questions related to career have been clarified, and satisfying leisure activities have been established.

What is not yet fully established in the rapprochement partner is the ongoing capacity for deeper intimacy, or the ability to manage closeness and independent distance with ease. What is also not developed is the depth of commitment to the partner as a separate individual to whom one must give and respond. During this stage, partners will learn a great deal about themselves as giving individuals. Are they able to respond with increasing consistency and constancy? Are they able to give support to the partner, even when they disagree or it's not convenient? Are they able and willing to expose themselves with greater vulnerability? Because these couples are easy to recognize, we will not segment this chapter into diagnostic and treatment sections. Instead, we will describe some presenting problems and our work to resolve them.

THE PRACTICING-RAPPROCHEMENT COUPLE

"One foot in, one foot out"

When one partner moves into the rapprochement stage before the other, the rapprochement partner will struggle with the conflict of supporting the independence of the practicing spouse while at the same time experiencing his or her own deeply felt needs for increased closeness. Indeed, there is a common sense of frustration during this time as both partners recognize the validity of their individual needs yet continue to be exasperated by the simple lack of poor timing. The rapprochement partner generally recognizes and acknowledges the importance of the practicing spouse's continued involvement in areas of externalized creative development. Despite this fact, the rapprochement partner has a difficult time with the lack of gratification.

In the practicing-rapprochement combination, practicing partners are often fearful that they will sacrifice their own individuation process by "putting themselves second" when partners in the rapprochement position return and want more time together, more closeness, and more intimacy. For a newly practicing partner, the pressure of the other's desires and requests may communicate the misperception that intimacy means sacrificing self or, at the very least, reducing options and overcompromising. When practicing partners have previously developed an ability to be empathic, they experience a further dilemma if they say no to their rapprochement partners so that they can continue to experience the individuation they so desperately desire: on the one hand, their compassion pulls them toward responding to their partners' requests, and on the other hand, their emerging energy of self-development pulls them toward satisfying their own desire for continued personal growth.

Because the practicing-rapprochement couple have gone through differentiation together, they already have an inner template for handling and processing conflicting desires. Therefore, the therapist is able to keep a clear, strong focus on the circumscribed issues presented by these couples. One typical problem is the apparent incompatibility in the activities of their respective "stages." This incompatibility often can be resolved with an exploration of each partner's needs; and because practicing-rapprochement couples have a high degree of flexibility, there is more possibility for negotiation and creative problem solving.

Case example: Megan and Clay

Megan and Clay had been married for 20 years. Clay was at the height of his professional career in a management position with a drug company. Their children, raised primarily by Megan, were growing up and getting ready to leave home. As Clay planned to reduce the energy he devoted to his job, he wanted to spend more time with Megan, doing things they had postponed in the past. For the first time in their marriage, however, Megan wanted to focus attention on her own aspirations. Their newfound time together had become tumultuous, with clashing wills, and they sensed that their relationship was in jeopardy. They began couples therapy wondering if it would be possible to sort out their confusion, to regain their equilibrium as a couple, and yet to satisfy the disparate needs they each had at this time in their lives.

As Ellyn sought to diagnose the conflicts presented by Megan and Clay, she identified their fights to be an inevitable consequence of their stage of relationship: practicing-rapprochement. (See Appendix E for Megan's and Clay's answers to the Diagnostic Questionnaire.) Megan was frightened that she might give up her own dreams and be tempted by Clay's money to succumb to a life of leisure. Clay's identity was well established and it was difficult for him to understand how fragile Megan felt in establishing her individuating self. As he pushed her for more time together, she found herself engaged in a power struggle with him. The effect of the power struggle was threefold: 1) it created distance which allowed Megan more time for herself; 2) it helped her feel stronger and surer that she would not compromise or relinquish her own identity in order to please Clay; and 3) it left Clay sad and lonely in his desire for more intimacy.

To structure the therapy in a positive direction, Ellyn asked Megan and Clay if they would be willing to work together to find a solution that would enhance each of them as individuals. They agreed. Next, Ellyn asked each of them to fantasize an image of where their marriage would be after both children had left home. This exercise focused their attention onto the future and encouraged the two partners to search for points of intersection rather than divergence in their respective goals. After several weeks of focusing inwardly on this question, their individual images began to take shape. Megan envisioned turning her hobby of collecting antiques into a business, and she asked for Clay's help with the financial management. Clay agreed and said he would look forward to accompanying her on buying trips, as long as they could also include some travel and vacation stops that were meaningful to him.

For Megan to successfully resolve her fear of losing her identity, she needed to confront her image of her mother by using Gestalt two-chair dialogues (Goulding & Goulding, 1979, pp. 195–212). Her mother had remained passively in her father's shadow throughout her life. By talking to "her mother in the other chair," Megan recognized that she was fearful of losing her mother's love if she moved out into the business world. She cried and said, "I am a different person than you and I won't be happy unless I express me. I hope you will understand, but even if you don't, I'm not going to stop now." After doing this work, Megan quickly recognized how she had Clay in the same position as her mother, expecting his disapproval. She then told him how much it would mean to her to have his support with her antique business, rather than for him to undermine her and always try to keep her in his shadow. Clay agreed, and at age 45 Megan changed her script from "happy homemaker" to "businesswoman," even though it later came to light that this did displease her mother.

This brief vignette vividly illustrates the crucial role initial sessions play in determining the direction that couples therapy will take. Instead of focusing on fights and power struggles, the future focus enabled Megan and Clay to create a mutual image that combined both of their needs. Megan could pursue a personal goal that would enhance her sense of self, and in doing so she could move closer to Clay and share more intimate time together.

Case example: Rita and Jordan

Jordan was a 47-year-old executive whose doctor recommended that he join an ongoing men's group on "Type A" behavior. Taking seriously his physician's concern over his high blood pressure, Jordan attended the group regularly and after a few months of participation began to make significant changes in his lifestyle. Once hard-driving and success-oriented, he now turned some of that energy toward his wife, Rita, who worked afternoons and many evenings. Her schedule had fit Jordan's hectic hours quite well; they saw little of each other except on weekends, which Jordan frequently cluttered with take-home work.

When Jordan told Rita that he wanted her to quit her job so that she would have evenings available for time together, she was initially fearful that his new longing for togetherness would pass in a month or two. She would have given up a comfortable job that meant added income they both enjoyed, only to be left alone evenings as Jordan regained his working momentum.

As the therapist, Pete, began working with this couple, he explored Jordan's feelings and motivations at length in order to discern the authenticity of the important shift he was making in his life. Through discussions with both Jordan and Rita, and from Jordan's responses to the Diagnostic Questionnaire, Pete determined that Jordan was a well-differentiated partner who, though overly active in his career, was fairly developed in terms of his self-knowledge and his relationship skills. Since his career constituted a successful manifestation of the practicing stage, Pete believed that Jordan's shift in lifestyle was an indicator of his movement into the rapprochement stage. We should note that there is a perceptible difference between the individual who is suddenly scared by a medical diagnosis and is driven by fear to change his ways, and one who experiences a genuine desire for more closeness and a level of intimacy that he has not previously had in his life. Jordan's medical diagnosis was far from critical, but it had caused him to "stop and take stock." With two decades of successful career experience to his accomplishment, Jordan felt ready and willing to let go of it as a single-pointed focus.

Rita, meanwhile, had not had the positive self-connected work experience that had characterized Jordan's career. Although she enjoyed her job, she knew that it did not touch her deeper needs. She, too, was a well-differentiated partner; what she now realized she yearned for was an experience of individuation through which she would be able to actualize her creative aspects in the outer world. In essence, she was ready for greater exploration of her practicing stage.

Once it became clear to Rita that Jordan's proposed changes were more than whim or fancy, she came to a decision that would benefit both of them: she was willing to quit her job and be in a position of not bringing home any income, and she was willing to keep her evenings free. However, she was unwilling to spend her days in activities of little meaning. In high school and college she had studied painting and sculpture, and had always wanted to pursue her artistic talents. Now she realized she could devote her days to doing something that mattered far more to her than her current job.

In both case examples we see the relative ease with which practicing-rapprochement couples come to support each other once they resolve the fear underlying their struggle. Because partners in this stage usually have a well-developed sense of empathy, they will maintain a more balanced perspective on both sets of desires than is typically present in couples at the earlier stages. Once the practicing partner completes the work necessary not to sacrifice his or her own individuation in exchange for greater closeness, the couple will be able to work together as a team in solving their conflicts rather than being pitted against one another in a contest of wills.

THE RAPPROCHEMENT-RAPPROCHEMENT COUPLE

"Homeward bound"

In this combination, the commitment to the relationship is clear — "the dance partner has been chosen" — and it is now time to improve the "dance" together. The earlier skills that have been developed by both partners are implemented and practiced in an ongoing way. In reaching the rapprochement stage, both have made a commitment to themselves and to the marriage. They now can continue to learn to give genuinely as they reach for ever richer levels of commitment, intimacy, closeness, and vulnerability. In doing so, they deepen their capacity to express feelings to one another without the threat of permanent merging or loss of identity.

Since both partners have been through the practicing stage together, they have become aware of themselves and of each other as individuals. The power struggles have diminished and are manageable. Ways of solving problems have been built into the relationship. The differences between the partners are understood with much more depth; they recognize that these differences can be used either to create stress and crisis or to enrich the marriage. A clear choice has been made to work with the differences as a means of enhancing the relationship rather than as an excuse for creating distance, separation, or divorce. In doing so, partners no longer are trying to change each other's basic traits or personality styles. If they do begin to try to change one another, they are able to return to a self-directed focus more rapidly: "What is it that *I* can do differently?" Because of this well-developed focus on self-responsibility, the rapprochement stage facilitates a greater resolution of those intrapsychic issues that have interfered with the ongoing growth of a solid, committed relationship.

It is at this stage that learning to give even when it is not convenient will be most impactful. In therapy, partners are asked to search and identify what it is that most deeply touches them when they are feeling vulnerable. For example, one attorney in the rapprochement stage was fearful about going to court for a specific trial. He told his wife that what he would like most when he returned home after the trial was peeled pistachio nuts and watermelon hearts. Imagine his delight when he returned home and was greeted with pistachio nuts with the shells removed as well as chilled hearts of watermelon!

Couples rarely come for therapy when they have arrived at this stage. When they do, it usually is the result of an external stress such as a job promotion and potential move (as with the couple in the case that follows), or problems surrounding a sick or aging parent. In general, most couples view this stage as a time of growth and renewal.

These couples are not the type that motivate therapists to acquire additional knowledge about treatment. In fact, most therapists find these couples to be delightful clients. The efforts they have made toward knowing and responding to each other's desires are bearing fruit. Problems are more challenging than divisive for these couples. Indeed, depending on the therapist's own relationship, it is possible the therapist will feel a twinge of envy toward this solid and growing relationship.

Case example: Pauline and Curt

Pauline had grown up in a family with only her mother and younger brother. Her father had died when she was six. As a child, she played the dual roles of being husband to her mother, and mother to her younger brother. Her mother was so grief-stricken at the sudden death of the father that she had been unable to function fully.

When in therapy at the rapprochement stage, Pauline was able to ask Curt to give to her when she felt vulnerable. When asked what she meant, the dialogue went as follows:

Ellyn: Tell Curt how you'd like him to support you.

Pauline: I want more closeness, but I'm afraid if I'm vulnerable he'll forget how strong I am.

Ellyn: (to Curt) Tell Pauline what you think about what she said.

Curt: After 10 years, how could I possibly forget!

Pauline: When I'm getting ready for a press conference, sometimes I feel scared—more scared than I ever let on. At those times, I'd like you to take over, take me out to dinner, and talk to me about the interview. Listen to my presentation, hear my doubts, tell me any weaknesses you hear in my ideas, and don't patronize me. Tell me I'll do okay if you think so, or give me ideas about how to improve the presentation if you see loopholes. Help me think it through without seeing me as a dumb little girl, and don't expect me to cook and manage the house as usual.

Ellyn: What especially in what you said helps you feel supported?

Pauline: Having Curt say, "Tonight, I'll take over." Then I can relax and feel like he's doing the thinking and the organizing. *(with tears)* It makes me feel safe, like I never felt when I was little. It especially helps if I know that he doesn't resent it or feel put out by me.

Ellyn: Tell Pauline how you do feel.

Curt: (to Pauline) I love you. Giving to you is truly a pleasure—and don't worry, I know what a good mind you have.

The central issue for Pauline in this case was her fear of exposing her vulnerability and her dependency and allowing Curt to take over. Her doubts about her own adequacy were fleeting and her desire to have

Curt take over and do the thinking was explicit and not representative
of a symbiotic position.

Future Focus

As in doing therapy with practicing-rapprochement couples, using a
future focus when working with rapprochement couples is often impactful.
If the Thirty-Day Plan is used, rapprochement partners are often able
to identify clearly the different components of their Wish List and to
take an active part in carrying them out. Another effective way to use a
future focus is to help partners identify a purpose for their relationship
and then to define goals that will help them bring their purpose to
fruition. Often this identification of the purpose and goals allows any
unresolved intrapsychic issues to surface. These will be specific issues
that remain from the past and that have continued to inhibit the
relationship in one way or another.

Early in treatment, couples who have arrived at the rapprochement
stage are asked to take home the following questionnaire and work on
it together.

Planning Our Future

1. *What is the purpose of your relationship with your partner?*

2. *What goals do you have for the development of your relationship over the
   next _____ year(s)?*
   1 year _____   5 years _____   10 years _____

3. *What goals do you have for your own development as an individual over the
   next _____ year(s)?*
   1 year _____   5 years _____   10 years _____

Case example: Mary and Stan

Mary and Stan had been married nine years at the time they came
for therapy. Stan was being offered a higher management-level position if the two of them would move to another city. Since they had
moved to their present home only two years previously, they were
again confronted with the possibility of uprooting themselves and

starting over. Both of them knew that the higher salary and lower cost of living in the other city would help them reach some of their goals, but Mary especially was not looking forward to reintegrating herself into a new community.

~~Early in therapy, they were asked to complete the Planning Our Future questionnaire. When they returned for the following session, Stan and Mary reported having worked together on these questions for several hours. Their responses were as follows:~~

1. *What is the purpose of your relationship with your partner?*
To be effective parents to our children, raising them to have a healthy, trusting outlook on life; to share our love on an intimate level with one another, to create a home in which we may grow emotionally, spiritually, and professionally, both as individuals and as a couple.

2. *What goals do you have for the development of your relationship over the next ____ year(s)?*

1 year ____   5 years ____   10 years ____

One year: Have a child (Mary was pregnant at the time); continue communicating effectively and openly with each other about our wants and desires; buy a house; continue our community involvement at the JCC; decide on a mutual leisure activity that we can learn together; develop a more open sexual relationship.

Five years: Be established in a home we own and in a community that we enjoy; be active contributors to the community through volunteer activities; have had a second child and be involved in the children's preschool; continue improving our communication and our sexual relationship; begin reestablishing a relationship with Stan's family and improve the relationship with Mary's family.

Ten years: Live and participate in a dynamic social community; be financially well established in a home we like and in a settled lifestyle; have amicable involvement with our children by the grand-parents from both sides; have at least two activities that the family enjoy doing together and plan to do when we go on vacation or have a weekend together.

3. *What goals do you have for your own development as an individual over the next 1, 5, and 10 years?*

Mary

One year: Finish my pregnancy eating healthily and exercising; give birth to a healthy child; settle into motherhood with enjoyment; take night classes to finish my degree.

Five years: Be involved in satisfying part-time work; be active in the community and school; be enjoying our sexual relationship more and be contributing to making it more varied.

Ten years: Have a deep sense of intimacy and commitment in my marriage; have had a second child; be soundly established in a community that I feel committed to; be healthy—in good physical shape; be developing a career.

Stan

One year: Decide about my job; learn to parent; develop more effective interpersonal skills.

Five years: Be settled in a community where I want to stay; be actively involved in the temple; be earning at least $75,000.00; have improved the relationship with my family.

Ten years: Know that I am a loving husband and parent; be recognized for a contribution that I have made either in my career or through my community involvement.

In doing this work, Stan and Mary recognized that although there were some positive aspects to the proposed move, overall it would impede or obstruct some of their important goals. Specifically, they decided that the proposed new community was not one in which they would like to settle; for both of them, being settled in a community and having a strong sense of connection with that community was crucial. If they were to make this move, they would then need to move again in several years. This would mean that although they could pursue the goal of having children and a family, over that time they would not be moving forward on their goals to integrate themselves in a community, as they had already begun to do at a community center in their present town. Because of these considerations, Stan decided to forgo the immediate promotion but to look for a new job sometime after the birth of their first child. Both agreed that although the town in which they lived currently was expensive and would necessitate careful planning financially, it represented the type of community in which they would like to raise their children.

Looking ahead enabled Stan and Mary to solve the difficult problem of deciding whether or not to take the job promotion. It also enabled them to understand that although they would encounter some short-term, financial discomfort, in the long-term perspective they would be working more consistently toward their dreams of the life they wanted to create. By using a future focus, the problem of Stan's possible promotion did not become a competitive one in which Stan's professional advancement was pitted against Mary's desire not to uproot herself once again. Instead, it led to a reaffirmation of the mutuality of their goals and to collaborative planning during which they strengthened their commitment to their marriage and to their future dreams.

Group Work

Couples groups can be especially facilitative for couples at these later stages of development. Here, partners are able to use the group experience as a means of building and strengthening their relationship, rather than as a kind of courtroom to arbitrate disputes. We bring together couples who are unencumbered by major, ongoing, unresolved struggles. The purpose of these groups is to work in a *facilitative* rather than treatment modality. We ask these couples to identify what they want to create in their marriages, and then develop mechanisms together as a group to help each couple actualize their goals.

One such group consisted of seven couples who met once a month for four hours. We began by asking these couples to identify their individual strengths and then to consider how they could utilize these strengths in their marriages. Their levels of differentiation were consistently high, and we greatly enjoyed observing the unfolding and active utilization of the skills acquired from their previous developmental stages. In this process, we discovered that these couples in the later developmental stages were able to identify what they wanted from the other couples in terms of both support and ideas, and were eager to incorporate what they learned into their own relationships.

Our role as therapists in this type of advanced group differed considerably from other couples groups. In groups with couples in earlier stages, the participants' problems usually dominate the content and process of the group dynamics. In this group, by contrast, the group tended to structure itself. Because the couples were freely supportive of each other, there was an atmosphere of community and a sense of emotional safety in which individuals were willing to risk exposing their dreams and vulnerabilities. In addition, because the group was growth-oriented, there was a singular lack of the self-absorption that typically characterizes groups of couples at earlier stages. With the latter type of couples, the nature of their problems and the degree of their stress cause them to be very self-involved and, consequently, they have little energy left over with which to empathize, give support, or generate ideas for other couples who are similarly beleagured by problems.

As an example of the autonomous functioning of this more advanced group, the participants decided to share a potluck meal as a part of their time together. This initiative contrasts with couples at earlier stages who would tend to feel panicked by the time "wasted" on the meal and view it as a disturbing distraction from their therapy time.

Case example: Jenette and Howard

We will describe one example of a discussion that occurred in this group because of its impact on the couple involved and also on other group members. The central issue being addressed by the husband was the vulnerability he felt in loving his wife so deeply. His was not a symbiotic love but a love achieved through years spent sacrificing, fighting, resolving, and building together. Now he was in touch with the enormity of the loss he would face if/when Jenette died. This example demonstrates the difference between individuals who feel frightened of losing their partners because their whole world will fall apart and they will not be able to survive without them, and individuals who are in touch with how much the relationship brings to them on a deep emotional level.

Howard explained that the problem for him was one of communication: he felt a pressing need to tell Jenette how difficult it was for him to express verbally the depth of his caring for her, and how devastated he would be if she died or somehow was taken away from him. Yet at the same time he was terrified of actually putting words to his emotions.

He withheld expressing these powerful feelings to Jenette for fear that she would withdraw from him because of their intensity.

As a starting point, we asked Howard to face Jenette and talk directly to her about the emotional distress he was experiencing. With increasing emotion, he told her how his fear of losing her was much different from the fear he had felt when they were first together.

"At this point in our lives," Howard said, "we have been together for 15 years. We've been through so many good times and bad times that I have really learned to depend on you, and it is difficult to imagine living my life without you in it. So difficult, in fact, that I become terrified at the thought of telling you how much I do depend on you. I'm afraid that you will be frightened by my need for you, and I'm also afraid that by expressing how much I do need you in my life, somehow just talking about it will make you die or go away."

Tears welled in Jenette's eyes as she listened to Howard. She expressed how moved she felt hearing about how important she was to him. She admitted that she would have felt burdened by what he was telling her at previous times in their marriage. Now, however, she warmly acknowledged feeling closer by knowing how important she was to him.

This exchange between Howard and Jenette had a profound effect on all of the group members. Many verbalized fears about losing one another—fears that they had secretly thought but never felt safe saying aloud. Now they were expressing these feelings to one another and sharing the intimacy with six other couples. Another couple described what it had been like for them when the husband almost drowned in a boating accident. This brought to life the very real inevitability of death and loss and served to motivate the couples to expand and deepen their intimacy with one another over the following months.

BEYOND RAPPROCHEMENT: MUTUAL INTERDEPENDENCE

"Ten children and two careers later"

To conclude the chapter, we will describe a couple who progressed through all of the developmental stages to a level of mutual interdependence. In meeting and talking with them about their life experience, we found ourselves inspired by the courage and perseverance they had shown in growing together throughout a 40-year marriage and the raising of 10 children. We feel that they demonstrate what is possible in a couple's relationship when partners are committed to actualizing the bond of love and intimacy that originally brought them together.

We met Cristina and Marcelo while conducting a professional training program in Spain. Cristina attended our workshop and her husband, Marcelo, was introduced to us later in the day, as he was attending other seminars. At the time we met them, Cristina was 55 years old and Marcelo was 64 years old. They had been married for 40 years. During the workshop, Cristina had revealed some fascinating information about herself and her marriage during an exercise we conducted. We were so intrigued by these details about her life that we asked her if she might be willing to be interviewed with her husband so that we could learn more about their life together and their passage through the developmental stages. She asked Marcelo, and they both agreed to share their lives with us. They were indeed an inspiration—far more than we had even anticipated!

Cristina and Marcelo met when she was 13 years old and he was 22. Marcelo, a law school student, was on a Christmas vacation with his family visiting the small village in Spain where Cristina lived with her family. The mothers in both families had been friends for many years, but the children had never met before. On the evening before they met, Marcelo's mother took him to a Christmas event and award ceremony at the elementary school attended by Cristina. Here, he watched Cristina receive an award for her intelligence and high achievement. He was immediately attracted to her. His fantasies began; perhaps his search for an intelligent, sexy girl was over! How could he make her his wife?

The next day the families came together for a meal and Marcelo looked longingly at Cristina. Later in the day they attended a rosary together with the families and continued "making eyes" at one another with "very strong meaning attached to it." Cristina felt excited by the attention he was giving her, and Marcelo was surprised that someone as rational as he could experience such a depth of feeling.

After their initial meeting and attending the rosary, Marcelo received permission to visit Cristina for the next 10 days before he went back to the "big city" to resume his studies. They visited in her home during this time and then wrote letters to one another over the next six months. To this day, the letters remain a precious possession for Cristina because they were written during a time (their symbiotic stage) when Marcelo was very open in expressing tender, loving feelings to her.

After he graduated from law school, Marcelo moved to the small village where Cristina lived. He received permission from her father to visit with her in the home. Hers was a strict Catholic family, and the couple were closely chaperoned. Throughout this time, there was never a doubt in Marcelo's mind that he wanted Cristina to be his wife. Soon, Marcelo asked Cristina's father for her hand in marriage. Her mother was strongly opposed to the marriage because of Cristina's young age, but her father gave his blessing. At that point, Cristina dropped out of high school and worked as her father's secretary until the time of the wedding. She was very close to her father and it meant a great deal to her that he had given permission for her marriage.

Cristina and Marcelo were married just two months before Cristina turned 15 (Marcelo was 23). Ten days after the marriage while they were on their honeymoon, Cristina's father died suddenly of a heart attack. The family was devastated: Cristina and Marcelo hurried home to help with the funeral arrangements and to take care of Cristina's mother, who became quite ill. Both of them described this beginning of their marriage as sad and very traumatic, but also as a time of loving support between the two of them. While Cristina felt devastated by the loss of her father, she also felt fortunate to have a husband who was so understanding and supportive of her emotionally.

They moved into a house that was adjacent to Cristina's mother's property and continued to help her mother. During this time, Cristina and Marcelo talked often about wanting to have a large family with many children. Both experienced their relationship as a rich and happy one and were glad that they had married one another.

Like many couples, their differentiation process started soon after they were married. It was only four months later when the first disillusionment occurred. At that time, Marcelo told Cristina that he would prefer not to go to Mass with her and that, in fact, he did not believe in Catholicism. At first her trust was shattered because she had believed that he had come from a family that was equally as religious as hers. Also, since their first encounter had been at a rosary, she trusted that he, too, was genuinely religious. After much distress over this disillusionment, Cristina reached the following resolution: she told Marcelo that she wanted a husband who would go to church and provide a strong role model for their children; she did not care whether or not he believed the same way that she did, but it was important to her that he attend church with her. He agreed to support her as long as they had a common understanding that when the children were old enough, they would also be told their father's point of view. Although painful, Cristina and Marcelo were able to come to a mutual compromise about how to manage this disillusionment, and the solution they spontaneously created to deal with it provided more strength to the foundation of their relationship.

By the time Cristina was 20, they had two sons and a daughter. She remained very involved with her children at home, while Marcelo pursued his legal career. During this period, their conflicts were pushed underground and were characterized by long silences and cold shoulders. Neither felt comfortable talking directly about their disagreements.

Before their fourth child was born, Marcelo became heavily involved in politics. He was working actively in the resistance movement against the dictatorship. This led to a crucial shift in their differentiation process. Now, it became essential for the two of them to talk about their differences. Cristina was too frightened to remain silent any longer. Each time Marcelo went to jail she was fearful that he would lose his life. She desperately wanted to feel more assured about his physical safety and about the family's future financial security.

At this time Cristina's mother, who had moved to Chicago, invited all of them to come for a visit. Through animated discussion of their different needs, Cristina and Marcelo decided that Cristina would go first. Marcelo would stay behind to tie up his political affairs and then join the family. Cristina left for Chicago with the three children. Soon after their arrival in Chicago she discovered that Marcelo's closest friend and political ally had been shot on the streets in Spain. This trauma intensified Cristina's fear. When Marcelo arrived in Chicago shortly thereafter, they both realized that if they were going to make it as a family, they would have to stop the silent fights of the earlier years and begin communicating and supporting each other again. The combination of fear for Marcelo's physical survival and the complexity of making it as a Spanish-speaking family living in Chicago with small children led them to decide to focus their attention on solving "big

problems" rather than getting so bogged down with upset, unex-
pressed feelings. Cristina, in particular, marks this period as a turning
point, when she decided to solve problems directly rather than silently
blaming Marcelo when things did not work out.

During the year they lived in Chicago, Marcelo got a master's degree
while Cristina remained at home with the children. (They were receiving financial support from family members in Spain.) Meanwhile,
Cristina was experiencing her first inkling that she might want to be
something other than a mother and housewife (the first rumblings of
her individuation process, which was to gradually unfold over many
years). She began to teach herself to speak English by watching television and using a Spanish/English dictionary. Their fourth child was
born during this year in Chicago.

The next year they returned home and Marcelo took a job with a
large corporation. This enabled them to achieve greater economic
stability. They settled in, once again, to a life in Spain in which Cristina
was a housewife and Marcelo had a career that was very satisfying for
him. His job required a great deal of travel, but rather than being
lonely, he found the independent time conducive to creative thinking.
During the next five years another daughter was born, and with five
children and a successful career, life was busy for all of them.

Then, Marcelo's company wanted to send him to the United States
for a year of study, and they preferred that he go without his family.
After much discussion and negotiation, Cristina agreed that he, indeed,
could go alone. However, just prior to this move, Marcelo went to
work alone in a mountain area in Spain for two months. After this
relatively brief separation, he said that although he enjoyed his time
alone, he did not want to miss being with his children and wife, and
would prefer that they go with him. This attitude was a marked
contrast to his earlier position of looking forward to being alone.

So the entire family moved overseas, once again. Their sixth child
was born during this trip, and Cristina continued working on learning
English. Her need for personal individuation continued to intensify
and she recalled vowing to herself, "Some day I will study and learn so
that I can make something of myself."

After the family returned again to Spain two years later, Cristina's
older brother was shot. The trauma of her loss and the turmoil she felt
at seeing her brother's widow left alone without any skills prompted

her to renew her commitment to develop herself and to make something of her life. Soon after her seventh child was born, she vowed to complete her high school degree. She began a correspondence course and worked diligently toward her diploma over the next three years, while two other children were born. Through her studies, she became interested in psychology and decided that as soon as she had an opportunity, she would attend the university for a degree in psychology. After finally completing high school, Cristina did, indeed, attend the university. By the time she was able to complete her bachelor's degree in psychology, all 10 of her children were present for her graduation ceremony!

Soon thereafter, the family moved again for another two-year period. During this time, Cristina attended a graduate therapy training program. Simultaneously, she shouldered the primary responsibility for caring for her five-year-old son, who had developed Hodgkins disease. This was both a painful and growth-promoting time for her because she was forced to cope with her own strong emotions as well as with some distancing she felt from Marcelo. Although never clearly expressed, Marcelo was not able to deal with his son's serious illness and kept himself emotionally insulated throughout this period of time. After her son recovered, she left the family alone for the first time ever to pursue her own interest in family therapy by attending a month-long training program in the Western United States.

At the completion of the training program, Cristina decided to live out one of her childhood fantasies by going on a trip to Mexico. She phoned Marcelo and invited him to go with her. He said that he did not have the money. Her response was, "Well, I do have the money, and I'm going. And I'm not going because I'm angry at you, but because I want to see Mexico. It has always been a dream for me." Off she went and spent some glorious time in Mexico alone. Much to her surprise, Marcelo arrived later and they enjoyed a wonderful vacation together, which they now call their second honeymoon. From then on both of them worked actively in their own careers yet scheduled a time each year to travel somewhere special together. Soon, they returned to Spain where they have lived ever since.

At this time in their lives, Cristina is still working in the field of psychology while Marcelo is retired. He is pursuing his own interests, particularly in spiritual development. They travel frequently, both together and separately. They each pursue their own interests while sharing mutual interest in psychology. They are considering the possibility of writing a book together. In their interactions, they show a deep sense of respect for one another and for the personal and professional directions each has chosen. And, after 40 years of marriage and 10 children, their attraction to one another is visible and expressive.

When asked how they each felt about the relationship at this time, they responded as follows:

Marcelo: I like the trust, security, confidence, and tranquility we have with each other. We count on each other. I know I can count on Cristina and I no longer have any anxiety about maintaining our relationship. I know it will just flow.

Cristina: What's special to me is that I have the freedom to do what I want to do and to develop myself alongside of an equally strong connection with Marcelo.

After this interview had taken place, we asked them to do the Paper Exercise as a demonstration in front of a training group. Much to our surprise, they taught us a great deal about how a couple who had been through so much together could use the exercise as a means of resolving an issue for themselves. Never before had we seen the exercise done in such a way. Their dialogue went as follows:

Marcelo: I'm thinking that the paper is our son—no, it's my *feelings* about our son who was ill.

Cristina: Which feelings are you thinking of? We were all suffering then. It was a very important time, a very difficult time.

Marcelo: I felt guilty, I was depressed. He was only five years old, and I felt like I had been too rigid with him—that maybe his illness was caused by my behavior. I felt so guilty that I gave you all the responsibility to handle his care.

Cristina: Yes, you did. It was a very hard time but it forced us to find new ways. We had to find new ways to be, to live, and to work together as a family, and we did. We all found some new ways.

Marcelo: I want you to know that now I think I could take more of the responsibility. Not only that I *could* but that I *would*. That's what this paper means to me. *It's the responsibility, and knowing that I could really do it.*

Cristina: (lets go of the paper) That makes it meaningful for both of us—that you are holding the paper, that you know that you could be carrying more of the responsibility. *(They look at each other tenderly.)*

Ellyn: (feeling very touched by their interactions) What are you feeling as you complete this exercise?

Marcelo: I feel a relief, a release to some feelings that I didn't even know that I was still carrying.

Cristina: I feel happy that we've had a chance to share this experience together.

At the time that they did this exercise, everyone in the room was moved. It was a deep, tender, private exchange between them and yet they were able to share it with others while keeping it within their own boundaries as they worked together to resolve it.

Cristina and Marcelo are an exception to a common process. I meet my ideal person. All is wonderful. This will last forever. But wait! Something is wrong. Could this be the person I wanted to be with forever and ever? The inevitable disillusionment begins. With more or less grace the relationship ends. The quest for the mythical mate begins anew.

There are many couples who, like Cristina and Marcelo, over time successfully surmount the difficult process of understanding themselves and each other. They learn to respond with respect and sensitivity to their own wants and their partners' unique desires, while maintaining a sense of humor about their foibles. These couples, indeed, discover their mythical mate has always been by their side.

CHAPTER 11

Commonly Asked Questions

Question: How do you deal with the problem of an affair in a couple's relationship?

Answer: This question is the one that we are asked more frequently than any other question. It is not a question to which there is a simple answer. The reason for an affair and the impact of an affair are both idiosyncratic to any couple. Affairs most typically occur for one of the following reasons: 1) one member of the couple is sociopathic or narcissistic and uncaring about the effect of the affair on the partner; 2) the affair is a mechanism for expressing anger or getting revenge; 3) the affair is a statement about a troubled relationship; 4) the affair is designed to create a crisis to open up the relationship; or 5) the affair is designed to enhance the sexual identity of one of the partners. The last situation may occur when one partner has chronic insecurity about individuals of the opposite sex, and as the confidence level of that partner grows, an attempt is made to satisfy curiosity about sexual experiences while enhancing self-esteem.

Affairs are most likely to occur during the differentiation or practicing stage. Typically, if the affair takes place in the practicing stage, it is when practicing is occurring without differentiation. Here the affair usually is a statement of the desire to create a crisis or break out of a suffocating relationship.

The emotional impact of an affair on the couple's relationship runs the gamut from being such a severe betrayal that it is never repairable, to being extremely upsetting and painful, to being mildly hurtful and felt mostly as an expression of a desire for an open marriage. The long-term effect of the affair on the relationship will depend on the extent of the emotional involvement of the partner with the third party, whether or not the affair is still continuing, how the affair was revealed, and the commitment of both partners to resolve the issues underlying the affair.

Helping a couple heal and develop their relationship further after an affair is revealed is often possible when the therapist is able to reframe the motivation for the affair in the context of creating developmental change. This is possible when both members of the couple are interested in rebuilding the relationship. The affair can be framed as a means of opening communication and beginning a more complete differentiation process. Even when all the above variables are favorable, careful time needs to be spent in understanding why the affair occurred, and in resolving the anger and betrayal connected to it. The process used to resolve the feelings that characterize affairs is so complex that to do this topic justice, we have elected to save this aspect of the couples relationship for future publications.

Question: In the recent work of Daniel Stern (1985), he suggests that there may be no autistic and no symbiotic stage in early infant development. How does this affect your use of these concepts as a base in your model?

Answer: Stern shows evidence from research he conducted with neonates that they are far more sophisticated in their perceptual capacities than was earlier believed. He shows evidence that these infants respond selectively to the sound of their mother's voice and the smell of her breast milk. He provides convincing evidence that neonates are more alert and more responsive to external stimuli than had previously been described. This sophistication, he contends, supersedes the stages of autism and symbiosis. However, Fred Pine (1986), who worked on the Mahler research, rebuts the work of Daniel Stern by saying that the phases described by Mahler are periods of time in which specific affective issues are being processed. Pine stresses the distinction between momentary experiences in states of wakened activity versus the affective feeling created in those moments of symbiotic merger (i.e., when the child merges into the mother's body during nursing). Pine also describes how adults in clinical practice show symbiotic phenomena such as panic over loss of boundaries, panic over separateness, delusional merger experiences, and the longing for merger that is experienced by all. Couples therapy even more than adult individual therapy provides an opportunity to see these phenomena.

We tend to agree with Pine. Also, since we use Mahler's model as a rough parallel with the stages of couples development, we do not need to find a literal one-to-one translation between the adult and childhood stages. What is more crucial is the affective developmental experiences that occur in a couple's relationship which, when mastered, serve to enhance the development of each individual and strengthen the capacity for the couple to have an effective ongoing relationship.

Question: How can you use such discrepant theories as transactional analysis and object relations theory?

Answer: These theories are not as far apart as they might appear on the surface. The "redecision" school of transactional analysis was developed by Bob and Mary Goulding. The Gouldings identify 12 primary injunctions in the development of an individual's life script. These are: don't exist; don't be you; don't be important; don't grow up; don't be a child; don't (from phobic parents); don't be well (or sane); don't think; don't belong; don't feel; don't make it; and don't be close (Goulding, 1972). In the ongoing interaction between parent and child, the child receives some of these injunctions based upon unresolved issues from the parents' past. The child then makes a decision about the best way to survive. The decision is based on both the child's feelings and the amount of cognitive capacity available to sort through data and make a decision. The Gouldings work to help the client achieve a redecision, which is an autonomous, deep-level decision based in the child ego state, to no longer respond to the injunction received as a child. Thus, the redecision represents a cognitive and an emotional understanding of one's life script. The results of the redecision process (often carried out within a gestalt dialogue) are strong emotional changes and congruent changes in behavior.

Just as the Gouldings stress the role of the child in the formation of his own script, Mahler describes how "the lion's share of adaptive processes rests with the infant who is at a peak of adaptive capacity.... The child cannot be regarded as a blank slate upon whom experience is etched. Object relations grow out of a reciprocal process in which the child, with his or her unique endowment, plays a dominant role" (cited in Blanck & Blanck, 1986, p. 15). The Blancks go on to explain how self-image and object image refer to specific mental processes that take place at given moments in development. Not only do they contain a concept of mental images rather than real persons, but they also describe a time frame in which an image becomes established when there is an instantaneous affective experience that creates it (the decisional moment described by the Gouldings).

In this area, we see both theories talking about similar phenomena. The "programs of object readiness established in early experience requiring adaptation later in life" described by the Blancks are parallel to the early decision made by the individual in his child ego state. Whether we think of these as child decisions or stable object representations, it is clear that both require adaptation later in life due to the fact that the early situation developed as a survival mechanism but is not successful as a template for current life experience and life interaction.

Both theories provide valuable, yet very different ways to resolve these problems. The object relations theorists describe specific ways to help the client build structure and to resolve transference phenomena. The redecision process uses transactional analysis and gestalt techniques to directly access the feelings connected to the experience when the early decision was made. The redecision method creates a here-and-now experience in which both the cognition and the affect from the early interaction can be reexperienced by the client and can then create a process for changing that decision in the present.

Question: Do couples always evolve at the same rate? Is their progression linear?

Answer: We see each couple as having their own unique developmental pattern. In fact, development is always complex and combines periods of progression and regression. Periods of progression on the part of one partner will create stress in the relationship and frequently serve to mobilize developmental progress in the other partner. Periods of regression can serve to rework parts of earlier phases that were not satisfactorily completed. (One of the most common periods of regression is after the birth of a child.)

For any individual, growth will not be a smooth, even transition from one stage to the next. Growth often involves both the destruction of and building on the past for the creation of the new. The transition from one stage to the next is often an emotional life struggle that spells the doom of part of the past and the emergence of new forms. The drama that unfolds in the therapist's office is a reflection of the struggle to maintain the grip on the past while reaching for the security of a more stable future. As couples move from the present stage, no matter how unsettling it is, there is an accompanying anxiety that the next stage has the potential for being both better and worse than the present circumstances. It takes a considerable effort to evolve from one stage to the next, but there are times when a spectacular or traumatic experience can change our world of values almost overnight. The process of therapy can also create insights that bring us to heights, however passing, that we have never before known.

We also do not see each stage as distinct and contained in time. For example, as a couple are finishing resolving some of the conflicts created during the differentiation stage, they also may be evolving into the practicing stage.

Question: Do second marriages progress through the same stages?

Answer: Yes, we do believe that second marriages will in fact evolve through the same stages. We consider that each stage has tasks that when mastered strengthen the relationship; therefore, we see each stage as necessary and desirable to provide the building blocks for an effective, ongoing relationship. We do see that the stages often are progressed more rapidly in second marriages because one or both people have grown through their experiences in previous relationships and are more able to solve problems and to differentiate themselves.

Second marriages also usually occur later in life, at a time when each individual has had more opportunity to independently establish his or her own identity. This will facilitate an easier practicing stage.

Question: Are there times when you encourage couples to stay together? Are there times when you recommend divorce?

Answer: We like to work with couples in such a way that the decision comes from them. However, there are circumstances in which we might encourage a couple to spend some time in couples therapy before acting on a decision to separate, and there are times when we might not interfere with the couple moving in the direction of divorce. In order to take a stand in either direction, we need a comprehensive history of the relationship to know how long it has lasted, what the beginning of the relationship was like, what have been the characteristics of the bonding between the couple, and whether in the past the relationship has been symptom-free and growth-promoting for each individual, or whether the relationship over time has led to increasing symptomatic behavior and an erosion of self-esteem in each partner.

Some circumstances in which we will recommend couples therapy are: 1) the stress is occurring because one partner for the first time has moved beyond the symbiotic-symbiotic stage; 2) the current problems are a result of the beginnings of one partner practicing and the practicing behavior has precipitated intense clinging in the other partner; 3) there has been a long period of stable bonding prior to the current crisis and the bonding has not led to symptomatic behavior in either partner; and 4) there has been a betrayal, such as an affair, but the affair is short-lived, not part of an ongoing pattern, and it has occurred within a relationship that has had a period of positive previous bonding.

We will not interfere with couples moving toward a divorce when: 1) the developmental stage of the individuals is more than two stages apart; 2) the initial positive bonding never occurred; 3) there has been continual sociopathic behavior on the part of one spouse; 4) there are repeated betrayals; 5) severe substance abuse problems are accompanied by an unwillingness on the part of one partner to do anything specific to resolve the problem; or 6) there have been repeated incidents of physical abuse.

Question: What couples are not candidates for couples therapy?

Answer: Couples therapy will not usually be the primary treatment of choice when one partner is going through a psychotic episode, severe depression, manic episode, or severe substance abuse problem. In these situations, however, couples therapy will often be an important adjunct to the individual therapy necessary for people with these problems.

Couples therapy will not usually be an effective place to begin when one member of the couple is involved in an affair and is uncertain about his or her willingness to put any effort into resolving the problems in the marriage. In this situation, we have found it useful at times to meet with the couple once or twice to establish ground rules for the therapy and to let them know what would be involved in couples therapy if they decide to participate. Our experience has shown that oftentimes the partner having the affair is not ready to commit to the therapy at that particular time but will call back within a few months, if they decide to work on the marriage.

With severely enmeshed symbiotic couples, we usually do not recommend only couples therapy. We generally suggest that each member of the couple be involved in individual therapy concurrently. As mentioned earlier in the book, we find it most effective if a team of cotherapists works with the couple and each of these works individually with one member of this couple.

Question: How do you know when to terminate?

Answer: Usually a decision to terminate is based on the couple resolving the impasse that is preventing developmental movement. Termination will also be based on completion of the initial contract. This could occur when the couple comes to therapy with a contract to decide whether to separate or to stay together. A decision to terminate the marriage could lead to termination of the therapy.

Termination will also be based on the couple reporting satisfaction with resolving their main complaints. Couples do not have to solve all of the problems of their particular stage, as long as they have new tools, mechanisms, and strategies to help them move more easily through the stage. As part of termination, we frequently describe to couples some of the things they might anticipate as they evolve into the next stage. We also explain how differentiation and individuation generally occur throughout life. Once couples are able to look to this journey in a positive way, they will have no desire to remain in therapy with us for the rest of their lives. In general, couples terminate upon completion of the contract they make with us.

Question: How do the power struggles of the practicing-practicing relationship differ from those of the hostile-dependent relationship? As a therapist, how do I distinguish between these two types of relationships when I first see a couple who do a lot of power struggling?

Answer: The major difference lies in how the power struggle is expressed. Hostile-dependent couples focus repeatedly on blaming one another for not adequately meeting their needs. The expectation is that it is up to the partner to be the need gratifier. In the practicing relationship, the focus for each person is "I want what I want and I don't want you to interfere with me pursuing my desires." There may be a great deal of stubbornness in terms of how this position is expressed, but there is not a concomitant investment in getting the other person to change. The interaction in the practicing-practicing relationship is not as primitive as that in the hostile-dependent relationship and displacement and transference occur primarily under charged, emotionally stressful situations. In the hostile-dependent relationship, projection and transference are a part of the ongoing fabric of the relationship.

Question: What is the difference between "acting out" and practicing?

Answer: Acting out occurs most frequently when an individual is unable to act constructively or directly upon his or her own feelings or verbalize them and instead the feelings are expressed behaviorally. Because this would most frequently occur in an undifferentiated individual, acting out will be most common in couples at the symbiotic stage. An individual who moves into the practicing stage without differentiation will also exhibit practicing through acting-out behavior. In these individuals, we often find a parallel between the current form of acting out and the behavior that was used to leave home during adolescence.

If the person who is practicing has gone through a significant amount of differentiation, then the practicing will be very different than acting out. The practicing person will be able to define what it is he desires, why it is important to him, and then find ways to implement the practicing activity. The acting-out person simply bypasses the previous process.

Question: Are there particular kinds of couples for whom you will not emphasize a future focus?

Answer: If one member of the couple uses denial as a primary defense and refuses to acknowledge that there are any significant problems in the relationship, we will not move to a future focus without addressing the discomfort of the distressed partner. The individual who uses denial is basically saying, "We don't have differences between us that need to be addressed and worked out." Examining problems is very uncomfortable for those individuals who use denial. Concentrating primarily on a future focus will reinforce this dysfunctional dynamic in the marriage and lead to feelings of craziness on the part of the distressed partner. In this case we focus more directly on helping the distressed partner be able to talk directly about the problems. We then help the individual using denial to tolerate his or her discomfort, while remaining in the room and listening to the description of the problem. We frame it that as long as one member of the couple is distressed, the couple as a unit has a problem. Therefore, although partners do not have to agree, together they need to develop a mechanism for handling the distress.

Question: Does this model of developmental stages apply equally to homosexual relationships?

Answer: Homosexual relationships seem to evolve through the same developmental stages as heterosexual relationships. However, there seems to be a difference in the symbiotic stage in lesbian relationships. Our observation has been that the intensity of this stage is more pronounced. In *The Mirror Dance* (1983), Susan Krieger describes many reasons for this based on her research of lesbian relationships in a college community. She speculates that the close connections of the women in the entire community and often the need to maintain secrecy serve to intensify the symbiosis. We speculate that another reason for the enmeshment in the symbiotic phase in gay relationships is due to both partners being of the same sex and possibly having more unconscious expectations that the partner will be more like themselves. This can sometimes delay evolution into the differentiation stage.

Question: In this model how does the problem of substance abuse affect the way you work with couples?

Answer: Substance abuse does not affect our ability to diagnose the developmental stage of the couple. However, it does have a direct bearing on treatment. We focus first on the substance abuse itself. We believe that no sustained growth or change is going to occur within the relationship or within the individual until the problem of substance abuse has been handled directly. This usually means referring the client to a specialized substance abuse program. Frequently, this means we interrupt the couple's therapy for a while until the addiction is resolved. We coordinate our work very carefully with substance abuse specialists.

Question: What is the impact of children on the developmental stages of a relationship?

Answer: This is a complex question that could easily involve another book. However, we will highlight a few of the issues that are specific to the couple's developmental evolution.

Children have a major impact on the development of the couple's relationship. This is most true when a child is born before the couple has had an opportunity to resolve the issues of their own earlier stages of couples development.

To begin with, the birth of a child may create an artificial rupture in the symbiotic relationship of the parents. When this occurs, it is common for one of the parents (usually, the mother) to become symbiotically enmeshed with the child and for the other parent to withdraw either into work or into an affair.

If a child enters the couple's relationship early in the differentiation phase, the child will draw energy from the parents for his or her own needs. Typically, it is the mother who immerses herself in responding to the needs of the child. She thereby directs attention away from her own process of differentiation and, for a period of time, away from the interaction with the husband. In this sense, the birth of the child can have a negative impact on the couple who were in the process of differentiating together. Both parents now may put time and effort into providing for the well-being of the baby and find that they have little energy left over to work actively on their own growth issues. Often, there is little remaining energy available for the dialogues with one another that it takes to facilitate increased awareness in the marriage. Instead, interactions may decompensate into fights and arguments in reaction to the many emotional demands being placed on both parents.

When the couple are able to carve out time for themselves as a couple and reestablish a boundary around their relationship, they usually are able to begin differentiating again. However, if they don't reestablish their identity as a couple or if a second child is born, it becomes even more difficult for the parents to resolve their differentiation issues. Often the marriage moves into a period of emotional withdrawal in which there is greatly diminished emotional contact. This shift toward isolation can precipitate premature movement into the practicing stage. Such a couple might present themselves eventually for therapy saying, "We don't know each other anymore and we feel like this marriage is dead." This is because both partners have not gone through the complex, challenging differentiation process. Instead of using the opportunity of the child's birth to facilitate even greater differentiation, the couple has become more distant.

The father who is envious and jealous about the attention the baby is getting from his wife, for example, usually feels left out but has a difficult time discussing these feelings with her. Instead of handling this new challenge to the relationship in a way that promotes growth, the most common pattern is for the father to act out his jealous feelings by saying nothing directly, while making hostile cuts to the wife or by acting in a passive and detached way. The jealous feelings also may be acted out toward the child in subtle, angry ways or by simply ignoring the child. The mother then attempts to compensate for the lack of emotional involvement from the father by engaging in an even more intense symbiotic relationship with the child. As this dysfunctional cycle in the family escalates, it is difficult for the couple to disengage from the problems and enter a healthy differentiation process without the help of a therapist.

Question: What are some non-intrapsychic factors that affect the differentiation process?

Answer: There are multiple factors that may converge and serve to inhibit or facilitate an individual's process of differentiating. The most common factors will be the individual's family (this includes parents, siblings, children, in-laws.) At times, friends and co-workers may also have a vested interest in preventing or aiding the changes that manifest differentiation in an individual.

Religious and educational institutions are powerful forces that affect this complex process. Movies, television, and literature can have a profound affect on a person at particular times in his or her life.

Cultural changes such as the women's movement may also be very impactful. By moving beyond narrowly prescribed sex role stereotypes, the movement was able to proffer the value of differentiation in a culture that was willing to listen. In many other cultures, to the detriment of both sexes, societal prohibitions against women are still too strong to support an equal process of differentiation in its male and female members.

APPENDIX A

Couples Diagnostic Questionnaire

1. What is the problem that led you to decide to come to therapy?

2. How long have you and your partner been together? In what form (i.e., married, dating, living together)?

3. What initially attracted you to each other? How did you decide to get married or live together?

4. What do you find most fulfilling about your relationship?

5. What was the very beginning of your relationship like? How long did this phase last?

6. What was your first disillusionment? What happened and how did you resolve it?

7. When do you feel least fulfilled in your relationship?

8. In what significant ways are the two of you similar? different? What methods have you worked out to accommodate or compromise on your differences?

9. Do you spend time in activities away from your partner? If so, how often? Do you spend time alone with people who are not mutual friends? Does this create conflict in your relationship?

10. How comfortable are you doing activities away from your partner? How comfortable are you with your partner doing things away from you?

11. How safe do you feel expressing your innermost thoughts and feelings to your partner? How do you ask for emotional support from your partner when you are feeling vulnerable? Do you expect to get it?

12. Would your partner say that you are emotionally responsive to his/her vulnerability? Explain.

13. Do you take an active, energetic role in nourishing the relationship? Does your partner do the same? How?

14. Do you support your partner's development as an individual? How (give example)? Do you support his/her growth as an individual even when you don't agree? How (give example)?

15. Do you believe that your partner is giving at least 50% to the relationship?

16. Do the two of you have joint commitments to projects, work activities, or social causes? If so, what?

17. Did you deliberately decide to create something together in one of these areas?

18. Does this project seem to add or detract from the bond between you?

19. If your relationship were a drama, movie, or book, what would it be titled? How would it end?

The Limits Questionnaire

In every couples relationship, it is important to define the limits of what is and what is not acceptable behavior during a fight. Below, please define these limits for yourself in clear, specific terms. Also, define the limits you would like your partner to have. Be sure to cover such areas as physical behavior, voice tone, ending a fight, and what you don't want said. On the back, list what you negotiate as agreeable to both of you.

1. For me, it is acceptable to do the following during a fight:

2. For me, it is not acceptable to do the following:

3. For you, it is acceptable during a fight to do the following:

4. For you, it is not acceptable to do the following:

The Anger Questionnaire

This questionnaire is designed to help you understand what you learned about anger as a child. It will also help you describe how you utilize anger now and then facilitate you to define clearly how you want to express angry feelings.

1. Anger is_____

2. When you were growing up, what did your mother do with her anger? Your anger?

3. When you were growing up, what did your father do with his anger? Your anger?

4. As a child, what did you decide about expressing your angry feelings?

5. In the present, what do you do when you are angry at your partner?

6. Are you satisfied with how you resolve your anger with your partner?

7. What do you want to change so you will feel good about how you resolve anger with your partner?

8. Take a few moments to fantasize an ideal fight between you and your partner. Describe it in detail. Include setting, tone of voice, actual words said.

9. Are you ready and willing to change how you resolve anger?

10. Describe behaviorally the changes you will make.

11. Describe behaviorally the changes you want your partner to make.

APPENDIX D

A Symbiotically Enmeshed Individual

ANSWERS TO DIAGNOSTIC QUESTIONNAIRE—MARILYN
(See Chapter 4)

1. What is the problem that led you to decide to come to therapy?

   My husband doesn't love me anymore.

2. How long have you and your partner been together? In what form (i.e., married, dating, living together)?

   Married 17 years.

3. What initially attracted you to each other? How did you decide to get married or live together?

   Attracted to his kindness. He asked me to marry him after one month.

4. What do you find most fulfilling about your relationship?

   Doing things together.

5. What was the very beginning of your relationship like? How long did this phase last?

   Lots of fun talking and eating.

6. What was your first disillusionment? What happened and how did you resolve it?

My first disillusionment came after 17 years when my husband said he wasn't in love anymore.

7. When do you feel least fulfilled in your relationship?

   When we are separated on a Saturday or when we can't figure out a fun thing to do together.

8. In what significant ways are the two of you similar? different? What methods have you worked out to accommodate or compromise on your differences?

   Similar—lifestyle and beliefs.
   Different—I'm more outgoing. He's quiet. I need people. I hate to be alone.

9. Do you spend time in activities away from your partner? If so, how often? Do you spend time alone with people who are not mutual friends? Does this create conflict in your relationship?

   Not too much time with people who are not mutual friends. I miss entertaining, but he doesn't like it; so I just stopped doing it.

10. How comfortable are you doing activities away from your partner? How comfortable are you with your partner doing things away from you?

    I'm not comfortable doing any fun activities away from him. I miss him if he goes away and desire to be with him after the workday is over. When he wants to go someplace himself, I beg him to go with me instead. (Answering these questions, I see how suffocating I must have been. My ideas of so much togetherness are probably wrong.)

11. How safe do you feel expressing your innermost thoughts and feelings to your partner? How do you ask for emotional support from your partner when you are feeling vulnerable? Do you expect to get it?

    Usually very safe.

12. Would your partner say that you are emotionally responsive to his/her vulnerability? Explain.

    Never thought about it until now.

13. Do you take an active, energetic role in nourishing the relationship? Does your partner do the same? How?

    I thought he was talking to me, but I guess he wasn't really.

14. Do you support your partner's development as an individual? How (give example)? Do you support his/her growth as an individual even when you don't agree? How (give example)?

    If I don't agree, I start fighting. If he really wanted to, I thought he would fight back. Now I think maybe not.

15. Do you believe that your partner is giving at least 50% to the relationship?

    Yes. It might be that if he is always giving in and not fighting, he feels he is giving more than me.

16. Do the two of you have joint commitments to projects, work activities, or social causes? If so, what?

    Church and house.

17. Did you deliberately decide to create something together in one of these areas?

    House redecorating.

18. Does this project seem to add or detract from the bond between you?

    Neither.

19. If your marriage were a drama, movie, or book, what would it be titled? How would it end?

    A marriage made in heaven. They shared everything and lived a happy life as each other's best friend.

APPENDIX E

The Practicing-Rapprochement Couple

ANSWERS TO DIAGNOSTIC QUESTIONNAIRE—MEGAN AND CLAY
(see Chapter 10)

1. What is the problem that led you to decide to come to therapy?

   Megan: We need marriage counseling to stop the buildup of power struggles. There are many incidents recently we're not solving.

   Clay: For self and relationship improvement.

2. How long have you and your partner been together? In what form (i.e., married, dating, living together)?

   Married 20 years. Dating two years before that.

3. What initially attracted you to each other? How did you decide to get married or live together?

   Megan: I was attracted to Clay's forcefulness, his education, and career potential.

   Clay: She was good-looking, intelligent, and wanted to have children and make a happy family.

4. What do you find most fulfilling about your relationship?

   Megan: Not much recently, but for many years I liked the activi-

239

*ties we shared, traveling together, and our openness and willing-
ness to confront issues.*

Clay: She's my best friend.

5. What was the very beginning of your relationship like? How long
    did this phase last?

    Megan: Active, exciting, very social.

    *Clay: Great! It was true love for me, because I knew right from
    the start that ultimately we'd get married. I'd never thought that
    about other girls.*

6. What was your first disillusionment? What happened and how
    did you resolve it?

    *Megan: Finding out how much Clay had to travel for his job (he
    held a marketing position). I was angry at first. I didn't handle it
    well. I'd ignore him when he came home. Finally, we sought
    counseling at that time, about 15 years ago, and learned how to
    address our conflict more openly with each other.*

    *Clay: Finding out how mean Megan could be when she didn't
    like what I was doing. I don't think we could have solved it
    without counseling.*

7. When do you feel least fulfilled in your relationship?

    Megan: When I sacrifice me for the sake of the family or Clay.

    *Clay: When I'm expected to be the strong supporter without any
    needs of my own.*

8. In what significant ways are the two of you similar? different?
    What methods have you worked out to accommodate or com-
    promise on your differences?

    *Megan: Many similarities: age, religion, family background,
    love of family life. Our biggest difference over the years has been
    me being more introverted and Clay being extroverted. Until
    recently we sat down and hashed out our differences.*

Clay: (a) We love to eat! We love family life and simple things like poetry, art and music; (b) We're at different phases in the life cycle. We've worked out differences in the past. This time it seems harder.

9. Do you spend time in activities away from your partner? If so, how often? Do you spend time alone with people who are not mutual friends? Does this create conflict in your relationship?

   Megan: I've spent so much time at home and with the kids that it's only recently that I've begun my own activities. I've waited a long time and I don't want to give these up.

   Clay: I've traveled extensively on business, and have spent lots of time away with friends at conventions. It created conflict in the early years of our marriage, but now my wanting to spend more time at home with Megan is what's creating trouble.

10. How comfortable are you doing activities away from your partner? How comfortable are you with your partner doing things away from you?

    Megan: I want to do even more activities away than I do now. I'm scared I won't fulfill myself.

    Clay: I'm totally comfortable alone and totally comfortable with Megan going alone—I just don't want to be 100% alone. I do desire more of a relationship than we have now.

11. How safe do you feel expressing your innermost thoughts and feelings to your partner? How do you ask for emotional support from your partner when you are feeling vulnerable? Do you expect to get it?

    Megan: Usually fairly safe, although lately I've not felt the need to express my innermost thoughts to anyone.

    Clay: I feel fairly safe, though now it seems like Megan feels that I'm too "emotional."

12. Would your partner say that you are emotionally responsive to his/her vulnerability? Explain.

Megan: Clay has come to me for support over the years and I think I've given caring comfort.

Clay: At times yes, at times no.

13. Do you take an active, energetic role in nourishing the relationship? Does your partner do the same? How?

   Megan: I've done more of this over the years; now I'd like to do less.

   Clay: Megan has been dominant in this area. I responded—I hope the future will be more balanced.

14. Do you support your partner's development as an individual? How (give example)? Do you support his/her growth as an individual even when you don't agree? How (give example)?

   Megan: I've supported his excitement about his career over many years. I'm not sure I can support him now. If I support him, I won't do what I really want to do with my time.

   Clay: I support what she wants in principle, but I feel lonely when she's gone so much of the time. Then I get angry and upset.

15. Do you believe that your partner is giving at least 50% to the relationship?

   Megan: I feel like he's trying hard lately emotionally, but can't quite do it. Over the years he's given a lot financially by providing our means of support.

   Clay: Yes, sometimes more than 50%.

16. Do the two of you have joint commitments to projects, work activities, or social causes? If so, what?

   Megan: No.

   Clay: We enjoy church activities and going on exotic faraway vacations together.

17. Did you deliberately decide to create something together in one of these areas?

    Megan: (No answer)

    Clay: No, except planning trips around some of my business activities.

18. Does this project seem to add or detract from the bond between you?

    Megan: (No answer)

    Clay: We have fun traveling together. It's our time as a couple.

19. If your marriage were a drama, movie, or book, what would it be titled? How would it end?

    Megan: The ending is still too confused for me to answer this question.

    Clay: The best is yet to come.

APPENDIX F

AN OVERVIEW OF OUR DEVELOPMENTAL MODEL

Stage	DESCRIPTION OF STAGE		Diagnosis	Treatment
	Developmental Task	Developmental Stalemate		
Symbiotic-Symbiotic (Enmeshed) "We are one"	Bonding Falling in love Emphasis on similarities Nurturing Establishing "coupleness"	Consuming need to merge; inseparable Dependency Loss of trust Loss of individuality Fear of abandonment Behavior becomes passive and reactive rather than self-initiated Interactions focused on masking differences Ego-syntonic ways of relating	Nonverbal manipulative communication designed to mask or obscure differences Use of *we* and *us* rather than *I* in therapeutic sessions Severely symptomatic child, or severe symptoms in one partner who is the identified patient *Paper Exercise:* Swiftly evokes clear pattern of enmeshed interaction: marked lack of self-definition with excessive efforts to obscure conflict *Diagnostic Questionnaire:* Provides a historical over-view of the emergence of the enmeshment over time	Establish initial treatment contract focused on couple's view of the problem Establish "no-suicide" and "no-divorce" contracts when indicated Build an alliance with couple (family) and then facilitate personal responsi-bility taking in each partner When working with a family, use art or projective technique that elicits each member's perception of the family as a whole When appropriate, begin shifting from the family as a whole to the couple's relationship Use gestalt or TA techniques for working with each partner's family-of-origin Facilitate differentiation between partners

244

| Symbiotic-Symbiotic (Hostile-Dependent)

"I can't live with you, and I can't live without you" | Bonding
Nurturing
Establishing "coupleness" | Conflict and aggression used to maintain distance and emotional contact

Poorly developed sense of self; little differentiation

Emerges when symbiotic fantasy begins to crumble as reality sets in

Common pattern in borderline and narcissistic personalities

Open and ongoing expressions of anger, bitterness, and blame

Competitive, escalating interactions often ending in violence

Unable to negotiate

Unable to perceive impact of their own behavior on partner

Strong projection of feelings and assumptions onto partner

Paradoxical patterns of interaction: Demand nurturance yet reject it when offered

Simultaneous fear of abandonment and engulfment

Pronounced separation anxiety that is adamantly denied

Positive responses of one partner often interpreted as manipulative or rejected outright as given "too late" | In therapeutic sessions, extremely difficult for partners to identify and articulate what each wants, thinks, and feels

Rapid escalation into regressive behavior

Paper Exercise: Competitive, angry, escalating transactions without any negotiation or give-and-take

Question of Attunement: Expect mind reading, so requests are vague, generalized demands for nurturance leading to failed responses; since there is very limited capacity for autonomous interaction, as soon as one errs the other will punish or withhold | Diffuse conflict as quickly as possible

Establish limits and behavioral agreements about fights (see Limits Questionnaire in Appendix B)

Keep both partners thinking when angry and channel their anger through yourself

Teach them to complete transactions

Signal a confrontation

Predict future fights

Provide support and positive reinforcement for partners during session

Help partners learn how to apologize

Facilitate direct, positive interactions

Develop consistent, caring behaviors

Encourage cooperation and joint activities

Encourage partners to develop outside friendships and activities

Use humor

Once conflict is contained: Help partners develop and maintain a vision of a better future that each will work to create

Help couple develop an empathic process |

DESCRIPTION OF STAGE

Stage	Developmental Task	Developmental Stalemate	Diagnosis	Treatment
Symbiotic-Differentiating "Don't betray me"	*Symbiotic* (see above) *Differentiating* Learning to express self clearly and openly Shift toward internally defining sense of self with independent thoughts, feelings, and wants Reestablishment of boundaries Developing the capacity to tolerate differences Learning to risk expressing one's differences Defining clear areas of responsibility and authority	System becomes unbalanced for the first time *Symbiotic Partner:* Feels threatened and betrayed Attempts to tighten the symbiosis via "clinging" behavior May be characterologically passive Little empathy for partner's needs *Differentiating Partner:* Feelings of guilt Anger at denial of differences Increased efforts to define identity	Look for anger, grief, or despair at disillusionment of romantic fantasy *Diagnostic Interview:* Symbiotic partner will focus more on similarities and highlights of initial bonding, while differentiating partner will focus on differences and disillusionment *Personal History Exercise:* Use this exercise to diagnose origin of impasse in the symbiotic partner, such as "I'll never go out alone again" (see Chap. 2) *Paper Exercise:* Symbiotic partner does not define what the paper is and tends to relinquish it rapidly to the differentiating partner, who defines it	Help partners resolve the loss of the symbiotic stage Help partners identify and express thoughts, feelings, and desires Help partners tolerate the anxiety inherent in recognition of differences Encourage *differentiating* partner's movements toward self-expression while interrupting symbiotic partner's dependency patterns Help partners identify their individual contributions to current difficulties Establish clear lines of responsibility taking with regard to issues being discussed Break down issues into manageable homework assignments Generate motivation for change in passive symbiotic partner by stressing personal benefits Help partners learn to tolerate anger

Differentiating-Differentiating "I'll change if you change"	(See above), actively working out how to manage the differences that do exist in personality styles, goals, and desires	Discover how couple has managed conflict thus far in relationship	Pace of therapy is determined by degree of differentiation present in each partner
	Successful fight style not yet developed	Discover if couple has developed a workable fight style	Use of nonstructured involvement to create therapeutic environment that provides autonomy in the unfolding of partners' differentiation
	Use of projection and manipulation to push partner toward change	Discover if partners have begun to reestablish their boundaries via separate activities, friendships, etc.	Use of questions to help partners identify, understand, and articulate feelings
	Ongoing hassling	*Paper Exercise:* Effort spent in examining the *process* of how partners are going to decide who gets the paper	Bring pertinent intrapsychic childhood issues into awareness
		Question of Attunement: The level of differentiation in each individual will determine how clearly the request is made and how accurately they assess their own capacity to respond	Facilitate conflict management via use of the "initiator/responder" format for interaction
			Provide positive role model for partners, as therapist interacts with their demands and outbursts
			Discriminate between problem-solving issues and issues involving more complex developmental factors
			Provide a larger context for viewing of specific problems
			Facilitate differentiation from family-of-origin
			Identify familial, societal, cultural, or work-related factors that may be inhibiting the differentiation process

DESCRIPTION OF STAGE

Stage	Developmental Task	Developmental Stalemate	Diagnosis	Treatment
Symbiotic-Practicing **"Don't leave me"/"Leave me alone"**	*Symbiotic* (see above) *Practicing* Attention directed to external world, independent activities and relationships Rediscovery of self as individual Consolidation of self-esteem and individual power Development of healthy fight style Blossoming of individuation process whereby the individual learns to express him/herself creatively in the world	*Symbiotic Partner:* Feelings of betrayal and abandonment Attempts to intensify enmeshment Fear of loss of relationship escalates into angry and demanding behavior *Practicing Partner:* Stance of stubbornness and self-centeredness Loss of empathy for partner's needs Lack of emotional connection to partner; withdrawal Feels betrayed by partner's engulfment	Previous history of mutually satisfying symbiosis Minimal differentiation between partners; few mechanisms to handle conflicting needs, desires, or emotions An unexpected developmental shift in one partner resulting in increased demands for independence *Diagnostic Interview:* Reveals historical evolution from an intense symbiotic phase, to a phase in which active differentiation did not occur between the partners, to the stage in which one partner shifts to intense individual self-preoccupation *Personal History Exercise:* This exercise often reveals parallels between the current practicing behavior and how the individual separated from the family-of-origin	Help partners learn how to manage differentiation and support one another's independence Therapist must balance opposing therapeutic goals of partners: Symbiotic partner wants the spouse to "be like he/she used to be"; practicing partner wants to continue self-expansion unimpeded Initial establishment of discrepant goals is sometimes necessary Expose common grief that underlies partners' reactive anger Help partners structure time together Help practicing partner set self-selected limits that circumscribe the scope of activities Help symbiotic partner initiate activities that are self-directed and self-focused Use of the "Symbiotic-Practicing Questionnaire" to help partners identify what they want from one another (see Chapter 8) Identify and resolve pertinent intra-psychic conflicts from childhood

Practicing-Practicing "I want to be me!"	(See above)	Energy overinvested in self-development and expression Relationship viewed as secondary Staunch defense of boundaries Fear that greater intimacy will lead to loss of self Power struggles characterized by "I want" demands Use of projection and transference under emotionally charged circumstances Repetition of early script decisions All of the above are greatly intensified when the couple does not have a foundation of positive bonding and active differentiation	Marked lack of emotional connectedness throughout session Defensive presentation of each partner's side, and polarized views Competitive dialogue leading to impasses in problem solving Practicing-practicing couples who have differentiated together will still have power struggles, but with decreased intensity *Paper Exercise:* Both partners are well defined about what the paper represents, but often are unable to give to the other or compromise; often the exercise is not completed in the five minutes allotted *Diagnostic Interview:* Reveals no anxiety for either partner in having separate activities or friendships	Focus on process rather than content Help partners learn ways of protecting separate individualities while resolving conflicts Help partners relax boundaries Help those couples who have not actively differentiated together to learn how to manage differentiation, while continuing their independence Help partners identify and express feelings Use of "The Thirty-Day Plan" Help partners identify and resolve intrapsychic childhood issues Help partners develop a decision-making process that involves giving without anxiety

	DESCRIPTION OF STAGE			
Stage	Developmental Task	Developmental Stalemate	Diagnosis	Treatment
Practicing-Rapprochement **"One foot in, one foot out"**	*Practicing* (see above) *Rapprochement* Return shift toward relationship for intimacy and emotional sustenance Reemergence of vulnerability Greater ease in negotiating Balance between "I" and "us" becomes more firmly established Ongoing utilization of skills learned in previous stages Capacity to respond with consistency Capacity to give to partner even when inconvenient to do so Further resolution of remaining childhood impasses that interfere with successful coupling	*Practicing Partner:* Fearful of "putting myself second" Equating *intimacy with sacrifice* Overcompromising; reduction of options Conflict over empathizing with partner's intimacy needs versus responding to personal needs for growth and individuation *Rapprochement Partner:* Alternates between periods of intimacy and efforts to reestablish independence Conflict over supporting partner's growth and independence versus seeking to gratify personal needs for greater intimacy	*Diagnostic Interview:* Elicits the characteristics described under the developmental stalemate (see Appendix E for how this unfolds)	Identify temporary incompatibility of respective stages Explore each partner's needs with a view toward finding points of intersection and compromise Use a future focus to evoke a mutual image of the relationship that combines both sets of needs Learn to balance one's own wants and desires with partner's
Rapprochement-Rapprochement **"Homeward bound"**	(See above)	At this advanced stage of development, stressors to the relationship usually come from external sources such as a job promotion, a potential move, an ailing relative; intra- and interpersonal processes are generally highly developed and integrated	Diagnosis at this level occurs primarily through the elicitation and observation of what is *right* in the relationship: all the strengths and abilities that are present and operative in the relationship	Therapy at this level is primarily facilitative rather than treatment-oriented Ask partners what most deeply touches them when they are vulnerable Focus them on learning to give when it is not convenient Use a future focus via developing a relationship purpose, setting goals, or using "The Thirty-Day Plan"

250

Bibliography

Bach, G. *The intimate enemy: How to fight fair in love and marriage.* New York: Morrow, 1969.

Beavers, W. R. *Psychotherapy and growth: A family systems perspective.* New York: Brunner/Mazel, 1977.

Blanck, R., & Blanck, G. *Beyond ego psychology: Developmental object relations theory.* New York: Columbia University Press, 1986.

Bowlby, J. *Attachment and loss: Vol. 1, Attachment.* New York: Basic Books, 1969.

Bowlby, J. *Attachment and loss: Vol. 2, Separation, anxiety and anger.* New York: Basic Books, 1973.

Breger, L. *From instinct to identity: The development of the personality.* Englewood Cliffs, NJ: Prentice-Hall, 1974.

Campbell, S. *The couple's journey.* San Luis Obispo, CA: Impact Publishers, 1980.

Goulding, M. M., & Goulding R. L. *Changing lives through redecision therapy.* New York: Brunner/Mazel, 1979.

Goulding, R. L. Decisions in script formation. *Transactional Analysis Journal, 2,* 62–63, 1972.

Goulding, R. L., & Goulding, M. M. *The power is in the patient.* San Francisco: TA Press, 1978.

Greenacre, P. The childhood of the artist: Libidinal phase development and giftedness. *The Psychoanalytic Study of the Child, 12,* 27–72. New York: International Universities Press, 1957.

Hatcher, C., & Himelstein, P. (Eds.) *The handbook of gestalt psychology.* New York: Jason Aronson, 1976.

Johnson, R. A. *We: Understanding the psychology of romantic love.* San Francisco: Harper & Row, 1983.

Kadis, L. B. (Ed.) *Redecision therapy: Expanded perspectives.* Watsonville, CA: Western Institute for Group and Family Therapy, 1985.

Kaplan, L. *Oneness and separateness: From infant to individual.* New York: Simon & Schuster, 1978.

Krieger, S. *The mirror dance: Identity in a women's community.* Philadelphia: Temple University Press, 1983.

Lindenbaum, J. The shattering of an illusion: The problem of competition in lesbian relationships. *Feminist Studies, 11* (1), 85–102, 1985.

251

Loevinger, J. *Ego development*. San Francisco: Jossey-Bass, 1980.

Mahler, M., Pine, F., & Bergman, A. *The psychological birth of the human infant: Symbiosis and individuation*. New York: Basic Books, 1975.

McNeel, J. The early demand. *Transactional Analysis Journal*, 10(1), 47–48, 1980.

Minuchin, S. *Families and family therapy*. Cambridge, MA: Harvard University Press, 1974.

Minuchin, S., Rosman, B., & Baker, L. *Psychosomatic families: Anorexia nervosa in context*. Cambridge, MA: Harvard University Press, 1978.

Piaget, J. *The construction of reality in the child*. New York: Basic Books, 1954.

Piaget, J. *The psychology of the child*. New York: Harper Torch Books, 1969.

Pine, F. *Developmental theory and clinical process*. New Haven: Yale University Press, 1985.

Pine, F. The "symbiotic phase" in light of current infancy research. *Bulletin of the Menninger Clinic*, 50(6), 564–569, 1986.

Polster, E., & Polster, M. *Gestalt therapy integrated: Contours of theory and practice*. New York: Brunner/Mazel, 1973.

Pope, K. *On love and loving*. San Francisco: Jossey-Bass, 1980.

Rajecki, D. W., Lamb, M. E., & Obmascher, P. Toward a general theory of infantile attachment: A comparative review of aspects of the social bond. *The Behavioral and Brain Sciences*, 3, 417–464, 1978.

Rizley, R. Psychological bases of romantic love. In K. S. Pope (Ed.), *On love and loving*. San Francisco: Jossey-Bass, 1980.

Stern, D. *The interpersonal world of the infant: A view from psychoanalysis and developmental psychology*. New York: Basic Books, 1985.

Stuart, R. B. *Helping couples change*. New York: The Guilford Press, 1980.

Index

Bold-faced entries indicate major topical divisions.